HONG KONG: THE CULTURED PEARL

HONG KONG,
THE CULTURED PEARL

NIGEL CAMERON

1478
1978

Hong Kong
Oxford University Press

Oxford University Press

OXFORD LONDON GLASGOW
NEW YORK TORONTO MELBOURNE WELLINGTON
KUALA LUMPUR SINGAPORE JAKARTA HONG KONG TOKYO
DELHI BOMBAY CALCUTTA MADRAS KARACHI
IBADAN NAIROBI DAR ES SALAAM CAPE TOWN
© *Nigel Cameron 1978*

ISBN 0 19 580404 X

Designed by Robert Hookham
Filmset by Asco Trade Typesetting Limited
Printed by Bright Sun Printing Press Co.
Published by Oxford University Press, News Building, North Point, Hong Kong

For
Freda Wadsworth and L.K.P.
with gratitude and affection

CONTENTS

PREFACE

DESPITE its capacity to inspire—if that is the correct word—an avalanche of writing in the world's newspapers and magazines virtually since its birth, Hong Kong is singularly ill-supplied with historical studies in book form. From perusal of this volume, filled as it is with quarrelsome, garrulous, on the whole not particularly erudite persons, glazed over, as it were, with a raffish veneer, perhaps this may not seem surprising. But in fact the place has had its quota of interested persons, scholars, even historians. But most have confined themselves to comment in letters, government reports, and to the pages of learned journals not readily accessible to the public.

Apart from the two histories of Hong Kong (by Eitel and Endacott) there is not much in book form of a general historical kind. What exist in embarrassing prolixity are references in books of travellers of the nineteenth and twentieth centuries, and a galactic cloud of articles in newspapers and magazines. From what one can absorb of all this, the writer on Hong Kong's short and curious life may cull what he can, the exercise fraught with pitfalls inherent in the nature of the material; for writers on Hong Kong in books dealing mainly with other places tended to have a very partial view of the subject. And much that has appeared in the press has tended to be sensational. The learned journals, naturally deal with large needles in the small haystack called Hong Kong, and while details of the needles may be gleaned therefrom, the untidy little place itself does not emerge in very clear focus there.

This volume is intended to interest the general reader—of whom there must be millions round the world who have already read something of Hong Kong, whether of its drug trade, its Suzie Wongs, its commercial export miracle in post-war years, and who would like to learn more about it. It is intended also for those million and a half people who visit Hong Kong every year; and it will interest some of the English-speaking residents whose knowledge of the city and its people and history is not great.

Characteristically, in such an equivocal place as Hong Kong, even its name is still the subject of desultory investigation, forming a topic for some of the less oblique letters to the local newspapers. The reasons are simple, the solution probably impenetrable. The Chinese characters for Hong Kong[1] as written for many a year mean 'Fragrant Harbour', a description that has long ceased to be apt. But the problem about the original name stems from the various ways in which Cantonese and other southern Chinese languages were formerly romanized. Like other tongues spoken by many millions, Cantonese and surrounding languages with which the early Hong Kong settlers had contact had and still have numerous spoken variants—just as English spoken in London, Highland Scotland, Welsh valleys, New York, and New Orleans differs greatly.

'Fragrant Harbour' is pronounced something like *Heung Gong*, the *eu* resembling that syllable in French. This does not take account of the tones (voice inflections) that are essential in differentiating one Cantonese word from another; and it has been argued that the origin of the name was not that at all. The evidence comes from a book published in 1843.

'Hither mariners have been attracted,' the Rev G.N. Wright notes in his book, 'by the facility of procuring a supply of the purest water which is seen falling from the Cliffs of Leong-teong,[2] or two summits, in a series of cascades, the last of which glides in one grand and graceful lapse into a rocky basin on the beach . . . . It is from this fountain, Heang-Keang,[3] the fragrant stream, or Hoong-Keang,[4] the red or bright torrent, that the island is supposed to derive its name.' Red, in Chinese, also means auspicious.

Some support to this is lent by one of the nineteenth century women travellers, Mrs C.F. Gordon Cumming, who, in 1878, remarked with irony when dealing with the theme of Hong Kong sanitation, that 'although this "Island of Fragrant Streams" (which is one of its Chinese names) is really . . . well supplied with such pure sparkling waters' there was never enough for domestic purposes. Unfortunately she does not mention other current names.

It is argued that it was this 'auspicious stream' at what is now Aberdeen that gave the island its name—plausibly, because Captain Elliot at first planned to make the main settlement, Queenstown, there. When Victoria was built on the northern or harbour shores the name was transferred—the sound of 'red' and 'stream' in variant pronunciations being very similar to those of 'fragrant' and 'harbour.'

On page 3, the reader will find the frontispiece of W.D. Bernard's book reproduced. He described 'the high conical mountains' and the fine cascade.

Whatever the origin of its name, Hong Kong is a place very full of people; and I confess to being quite as interested in them as I am in the tapestry of events that they and their predecessors have produced by their interactions. Hence, the reader will find a lot about people in this book, as well as how they formed the Colony and were in turn influenced by the social patterns they made.

There remains for me here the happy duty of saying thank you to many people, especially but not exclusively those in Hong Kong, who have generously assisted me in ways that are too numerous to mention in detail.

The librarian of the University of Hong Kong, H.A. Rydings, and the library staff have been invariably helpful, as has Geoffrey Bonsall, director of the Hong Kong University Press. It is a pleasure to record the friendly help of Lawrence Tam, curator of the Hong Kong Museum of Art, and of several members of his staff; and to acknowledge the cooperation of Ian Diamond, archivist of the Public Records Office, who produced (among other unexpected treasures) the four reportage photographs of the attempt on the life of a Governor in 1912; and of assistant archivist Robin McLean who helped me with baffling but informative microfilms.

I have made use of published material from various sources, old and new. The researches of Henry J. Lethbridge, Carl T. Smith, James W. Hayes, Dafydd M.E. Evans, to name a handful of scholar in various fields of Hong Kong's past and present life, have been of great benefit to me, not only in ascertaining facts but in gauging the temper of times past in the Colony.

Finally, in a more general and also in a personal way, this particular 'foreign devil' is indebted beyond possibility of repayment to Hong Kong Chinese friends and to thousands of other Chinese, from whom he has learned much that a European education does not teach.

If this book has a slight bias toward the Chinese view in historical as in present times, it is because that is the way I have constantly felt in dealing with the story of Hong Kong and its people.

Nigel Cameron, Hong Kong, March 1978

SOURCES OF
ILLUSTRATIONS

Adapted from Freda Wadsworth: 4

Adapted from Tregear: 22 (upper), 23 (upper), 24 (upper), 134, 135

Albert Smith: *To China and Back*: 71

Author's collection: 8, 65, 88, 89, 111

Author's photograph: 174, 182 (upper, lower), 184 (upper), 185 (upper, lower), 188, 199, 192 (upper), 201 (lower), 217, 222, 229 (upper), 231, 232, 234, 241, 246 (lower), 248 (upper), 264

Christopher D'Almada: 78

Collection of Arnold Graham, Hong Kong: 157, 158

Collection of Capt. Garnons-Williams, RN, Hong Kong (sepia drawing by Michael Kirkbride)

Collection of Dr Joan Evans, Hong Kong: 155 (watercolour by Elise Parkin)

Frank Fischbeck, Hong Kong: 81, 177, 192 (lower)

Government Information Service, Hong Kong: 108, 117, 150, 175, 195 (upper, lower), 201 (upper), 202, 211, 221 (upper, lower), 229 (lower), 237, 246 (upper), 247 (upper, lower), 248 (lower), 260

Hong Kong Museum of Art: jacket, 9, 13, 14, 15, 16, 20, 22 (lower), 23 (lower), 24 (lower), 26, 31, 33, 35, 50, 73, 80, 84, 91, 101, 102, 105, 119, 120–21, 122, 125, 126, 133, 143 (lower), 147 (lower), 154 (lower), 171, 216

Hongkong Standard: 198 (upper, lower)

Hong Kong Tramways Ltd.: 149

Illustrated London News: 57 (drawn by M. Baptista), 62, 63, 79, 113, 115, 140

John Pope Hennessy: *A Hong Kong Notebook*: 94

Madame Tussaud's: 7 (left)

Mandarin International Hotels: 180, 184 (lower)

Mansell Collection: 19 (upper) (from a painting by R. Caton Woodville)

Mary Evans Picture Library, London: endpapers, 87, 137

Mass Transit Railway Corp. 244

Myra Roper: 7 (right)

National Portrait Gallery, London: 10 (lower), 30, 51, 52

Popperphoto 154 (upper)

Private collection, Hong Kong: 12

Public Records Office, Hong Kong: 32, 66, 118, 128, 129, 139, 143 (upper), 147 (upper), 151, 152, 153, 159, 172

Sayer Collection: 3

S. Mossman: *General Gordon in China*: 49, 73

INTRODUCTION

F ROM time to time in more romantic days, and even now in the equivocal atmosphere of the twentieth century's final quarter, various places including Hong Kong have been called The Pearl of the Orient. Since it is only one of Britain's older colonies, and was only one of the great travellers' and exuberant merchant-adventurers' ports of call and temporary residence when the East was still a story-book exotic place, Hong Kong might seem to have had rather less claim to such an appellation, even on the wilder shores of imagination, than many another.[1]

It was never without a somewhat dour, Scottish beauty in early colonial times, and in the now contracting 'hinterland' of its New Territories that character may still be observed[2]—bare hills with scrub and outcrops of granitic rock (for the Pearl is a solid lump of granite, like much of the adjacent regions of Kwangtung province of which it was formerly an intergral part). It would seem to have had little to offer in comparison to the fabled Indonesian archipelago—known for much longer to Western men—or to the rampant jungles of mountainous Malaysia; or even to the more restrained oriental charms of Taiwan, or the thousand islands of the cheerful Philippines. Only, perhaps, in recent years has Hong Kong taken on a strange brittle beauty all of its own.

The general idea of Pearl Cities, however, is susceptible of an adroit if wry twist that now makes it fit Hong Kong rather well. For here lies a city of the subtropics, once inelegantly but with a certain geographical panache and physiological accuracy described as 'a pimple on the backside of China', a city entirely the product of artifice as opposed to any local necessity. Into the essentially floral and faunal ecology[3] of an island without the semblance of mineral resource, lying just off the coast of great China, the resort of few Chinese but fishermen and pirates, the British inserted, as do the pearl-culturers of Mr Mikimoto in Japan, the tiny irritant of their alien presence over a century and a quarter ago. The resulting abnormal growth, one that would doubtless otherwise not have taken place at all, gradually attained the appearance and the specious lustre of a great cultured pearl. A cultured pearl, if the words may be used in another sense, virtually without culture other than mercantile until the extremely recent past, a place with only its monstrous monetary shine to serve as recommendation to the outside world.

Yet, like the genesis and growth of a Mikimoto pearl, the seed has matured and is nowadays a great city, a great port, a great centre of sophisticated communication in the world of commerce. Like a cultured pearl, to many an expert eye it is indistinguishable from the real thing without the aid of some intellectual penetration akin to the X-Rays that reveal in cultured pearls the alien object that caused the original growth.

The biography of Hong Kong is worth the telling. Yet, oddly enough for a major city of the orient, a place of four and a half million people, it seems (to date) mostly to have triggered off a kind of automatic-weapon fire of indignant, admiring, often spurious, nonsensical, and generally ill-informed words by the billion, documentary films by the dozen, and magazine stories by the hundred thousand, without much of its essence being captured. Hong Kong has a hundred reputations. It is either a commercial miracle or a saga of drug trafficking and addiction, a haven of bent policemen and at least pliant civil servants. The tales of its super-luxury living for the few, its plush hotels and its sordid sex-parlours mingle with others of life in cloud-cuckoo land where yachts and servants, palaces and jewels,[4] dominate in the manner of the simplified life in a silent movie. It seems, but is not, a sharp black and white contrast of a city.

There are rather few books (as opposed to many a careful and scholarly study on this or that aspect of the place) that deal at length or in reasonable depth with Hong Kong as the urban and social phenomenon it has become over the decades after the initial and dubious miracle of mercantile artificial insemination—one of the world's richest, most densely populous, accomplished, extraordinary, and in some senses most impoverished cities.

The aim of this volume is to try to tell something of the story of Hong Kong; to try to do some justice to it as the home of a very numerous population, most of whom are Chinese, and to the people themselves—

still ruled without a semblance of representative government by a Governor appointed in London, an élite of civil servants who are mostly non-Chinese and, beneath the surface, much as a submarine fleet may be considered to rule the seas above, by the urgent voice of big money, the voice of the great trading companies of West and East.

If there is another factor that enters the Hong Kong picture, it is the presence of the vast People's Republic of China with its more than eight hundred millions of Chinese. There, just over a border that lies only thirty miles from the boardrooms of one of capitalism's last and best outposts, lies the world's most resolutely anti-colonialist and anti-capitalist power. The shifting political and ideological patterns of that great civilization, now unified once more in its long, brilliant history, must be a consideration of the first importance in Hong Kong's existence. Hong Kong plays it cool; and, mostly, so does China: each for its own good reasons.

Such facts and anomalies, human and commercial, social and urban and international, are far easier to understand after a look at the forces of conception, the distinctly irregular birth, the checkered pattern of growth of the uncontrolled colossus of Hong Kong. In the end we may find it emerges as a unique city among cities because of these hereditary and environmental forces. Like many a human being, the surface, the information of the first glance, may be significant; but assuredly it is not all.

1

BEGINNINGS:
CAPTAIN ELLIOT'S FANCY

Hail, little isle! and Hong's fair haven hail!
First fruits of China to the ocean queen
New orient realms, new navies' embryo sail
Glass'd in thy shifting horoscope are seen.
May British virtue shine, in THEE confest;
And IN HER COLONY be Britain blest!

WITH these lines of verse were the early years of Hong Kong celebrated to the edification of the commercially enterprising but
otherwise mostly undistinguished Western community. The Colony
has since inspired, if that be the word, quantities of verse, little enough
of it—even that of Christopher Isherwood in the days before World
War II—much good.

More down to earth on the subject of the new Colony was a reference
in *The Times* in London of 15 March 1859, at a moment when Hong
Kong was scarcely twenty years old. 'Hong Kong is always connected
with some fatal pestilence, some doubtful war, or some discreditable
internal squabble. . . . ' The pronouncement was apt in those early days
and has proved equally apt as a characterization of the life and work of
the Colony down to this day. Those discreditable internal squabbles
continue in the last quarter of the twentieth century in the Colony,
adding spice and libations of vinegar to living and to the substance of
private and public debate.

If we have expunged the fatal pestilences of years gone by, and if
doubtful wars are now no longer fought by Britain as they were on
behalf of the commercial and other activities of that nineteenth century
Colony, the internal squabbles are still with us and the newspapers of
1978 are as bespattered with tales of scandalous behaviour on the part

1

of people in authority, as they were so often in the century past. That they are not as scurrilous and generally not libellous, signals only the firmer application of British law to this if not to all other activities of the community.[1]

Much has been written about the murky beginnings of Hong Kong, about its freebooting community of merchants and traders up to their eyebrows in the illegal import of opium into China, who had, however, voices powerful enough to sway the opinions of governments and foreign secretaries in London. The earliest buildings erected in Hong Kong on its northerly shores were those designed for such commercial purposes, but it was not long before they were joined by another. This was a matshed church to which the business community regularly repaired each Sunday to perform that other important devotion in their lives, whereby the meek are said to inherit the earth.

We are at liberty, doubtless, to judge the present by its own 'best' yardstick. But the past cannot fairly be so judged. It is open to question whether tales of cowboys and Indians, the romance of the American railroads as they were pushed ruthlessly westward, which used to stir the childish imagination, and which later came under more adult and political scrutiny were, in the times when they took place, events and actions as blatantly conscienceless and genocidal as they must now appear. That they were odd policies in the context of a Christian society not long independent from the yoke of British colonialism, is undeniable. But this is hindsight. We live in our present. There were few men in those days little more than a century ago, who had any say in the process, who were capable of seeing the then contemporary scene as it was. Perhaps there seldom are.

Likewise in Hong Kong. Not many people at the beginnings of the Colony or before considered that the wishes and the laws of the Chinese Government in Peking were in any way relevant except insofar as they tended to thwart the most lucrative trade that Western men had ever discovered in the Orient. Compared to the bringing of spices to the West, the illegal importation of opium into the Celestial Kingdom of China was as diamonds are to moonstones.

So there is no special reason to blacken or to whiten the early face of Hong Kong. Smeared with opium as it was, that smear at that time hardly carried the emotional and intellectual charge that now it would. Values change. Today it is not yet too reprehensible for great industrial powers to arm opposing sides in some African state confusedly seeking its identity in the aftermath of colonial status.

The waterfall at what is now Aberdeen, seen by an artist aboard Lord Amherst's ship *Alceste* when she anchored there en route to Peking in 1816

Irony, in the hands of the historian, as in the summation of events themselves over a historical period, is often a tool that cuts nearer the bone of truth than condemnation. There was little about Hong Kong in its early days that did not (then) with entirely 'British virtue shine', as stated in the doggerel verse of the period.

There were two principal protagonists in the establishment of the remote island of Hong Kong as a British colony; Captain Charles Elliot, and the British Foreign Secretary in London, Lord Palmerston. Neither man was an opium pusher, either in fact or by intention. They might, together with an august Chinese official named Lin Tsê-hsü who acted unwittingly as a catalyst, as well be called antagonists as things turned out. Yet it was this trio who, between them, achieved British sovereignty over what Lord Palmerston was to call in high disgust, with comparative accuracy[2] and (as it came to pass) with irrelevance, 'a barren Island with hardly a house upon it'.

Events leading to the acquisition of Hong Kong can be told simply enough, although in detail they were quite complex. The pitfall in the relationship between Britain and China was the opium trade. For decades before the honourable East India Company discovered that the

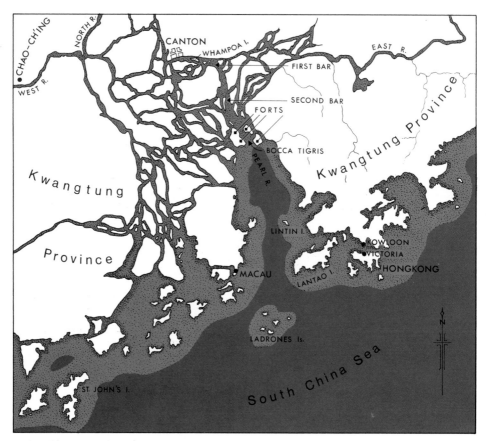

A simplified map of the Canton River delta, with Macau and Hong Kong

drug was a worthwhile export to China, trade between the two nations, although restricted by the Chinese to the winter months in Canton only, had continued more or less peacefully. British ships came up the river from the Bocca Tigris (the Tiger's Mouth, as the channel to the Pearl River leading to Canton was named by the Portuguese, happily settled for a very long time in Macau at its entry), and took on tea and silk and porcelain—even rhubarb with which to relieve the national constipation. Britain was already besotted with tea, so that vast quantities of it had to be brought each year from China. The Indian plantations were not yet in existence. These various ingredients of trade had to be paid for in silver, the national currency of China. The tea clippers, full to the gunwales, departed on their rapid way west (a story all of its own, in which ship outdid and outbid ship for the fastest time to London and consequently the highest price for its tea), not to return until the favourable winds of the following year's season brought them again to Canton.

4

The only problem from the point of view of John Company (as the East India Company was commonly called) was payment. Its ships for the most part arrived at Canton from India in ballast since no commodity of sufficient bulk or value had been discovered that was saleable in China.[3] Long before, the emperor Ch'ien-lung in 1794 had stated clearly in a letter addressed to George III that his realms 'possessed all things' and that the Chinese had no use for the contraptions and products of a society in the West at the beginnings of industrialization.

This Chinese stance was linked with a traditional view that it was the Chinese (and they alone) who dispensed the blessings of civilization (in its developed form, considered to be uniquely theirs) to the world at large. That outer world came in the form of tributary states, receiving the blessings of Chinese superiority in the form of gifts such as tea, jade, silk, porcelain, medicinal substances, and other precious materials. By the very act of sending personnel to Peking, a country was seen by the Chinese to recognize its tributary relationship to the great Chinese empire.[4]

Until some point in the early 18th century this attitude in regard to Western civilization was not unreasonable. The continuously refined, literary, inventive, and artistic aspects of Chinese civilization had no real counterpart in the West. But by the time of John Company at Canton in the late 18th and early 19th centuries, it was no longer an outlook based on fact. The West had begun its next giant stride into the future. All the demonstrable facts of the Western merchants' lowly intellect and barbarian manners could not alter that truth. For the Chinese, however, as insular as ever were the English, the spectacle of of these representatives of Western civilization was hardly encouraging. They were obviously people of coarser texture, product (it seemed) of a way of life that was as crude as that of the nomads of Asia. The Western sea nomads were not taken seriously as representatives of a culture. In the same manner, it would probably be hard for a denizen of some other world to divine and to comprehend the greatness of Western (or of Chinese) civilization from a sojourn in Hong Kong today (or yesterday).

Opium, the cause of it all, had been grown and used medicinally in China for ages past. But when it was imported to China by the British from India (where John Company had put thousands of acres forcibly under cultivation of the poppy, replacing staple food crops with this cash crop to the detriment of millions of Indians) and peddled there via willing Chinese entrepreneurs and to the financial aggrandizement of higher officials too, the demand grew by leaps and bounds.

No one seems ever to have explained satisfactorily why Chinese opium consumption grew so rapidly. One can only suggest something like a parallel in England itself when the increase in importation of cheap Dutch gin led to scenes of drunkenness and debauchery unparalleled in days before, without, apparently, very specific cause. Indeed the scenes in Hog's Lane at Canton, a narrow alley running beside the British 'factory' (offices and warehouses) in the early 19th century, when the 'jolly', 'romantic' Jack Tars of merchant ships patronized the Chinese tavern-brothels and were apparently willing to drink anything of high alcohol content, have verbal chroniclers; just as gin-drinking London had its Rowlandson to record the scenes in lively line.

The figures for opium import to China (the drug judiciously not carried in John Company's own ships, but in those of others) are staggering: at the commencement of the 19th century it stood at 200 chests; by 1821, 5,000 chests; after the abolition of John Company's monopoly of trade with China in 1833, nearly 40,000 chests were imported in the winter season of 1838–9.[5] Instead of silver pouring from the West into China in payment for tea, silver now poured out of China to pay for opium.

Finally the Court at Peking became seriously worried and appointed the Commissioner, Lin Tsê-hsü, to go to Canton and assess the situation, to discover how the opium was smuggled into China up and down the coasts and via Canton itself, and who was responsible for permitting the illegal import; and to stop the trade forthwith. He seemed just the man for the job. Scholar, able administrator, proven opium-supressor elsewhere, an admirable statesman, Lin informed himself of the situation, and addressed letters to Queen Victoria[6] advising her to put a stop to the trade. Finally, after a series of discussions in Canton, on 18 March 1839 he ordered all opium stocks to be surrendered to him, placing the foreign merchants under siege in their 'factories' until this was done.

Captain Elliot managed to reach Canton and the factories, and as Superintendant of Trade took control, eventually handing over the 20,291 chests in stock with a promise to the merchants that the British Government would compensate them. His request to London for military forces, and his offer to defend Macau where the British merchants had withdrawn, were seen by the Portuguese at Macau (where they peacefully traded) as a threat to their established business with the Chinese. So Elliot had to put the British aboard ships and anchor in Hong Kong harbour. Soon after, a Chinese was killed in a brawl ashore with some British sailors, and Commissioner Lin demanded the murderer be handed over to the Chinese. When this was not done, the British ships were attacked by Chinese fire-rafts.

The British were by this time a great and highly aggressive trading nation. Like the Portuguese before them in the East, they saw trade as a right, and failed to understand Chinese reluctance in the matter; failed also to understand the Chinese attitude that counted merchants with soldiers and actors as the lowest forms of human life in and out of China. The British attitude to the opium trade, official and mercantile, was that it was up to China to enforce her laws against opium importation. Sophistry has ever been a potent weapon in the politician's and merchant's armoury.

Events were now beginning to move fast, and the thumb-screws of force which were to play a dominant part in British (and other Western nations') relations with China for a hundred years afterwards were about to be applied. Attempts at 'diplomatic' relations with the Chinese had failed—first because China did not admit the concept of dealings with any other nations on terms of equality, and second, because the aim of British diplomacy was plainly to open up all China to all British trade including, presumably, the sale of opium.

A poster for the contemporary waxwork display of Commissioner Lin and his consort at Madame Tussaud's, London; and a portrait of Lin

Lord Palmerston, British Foreign Secretary, had penned a letter to the 'Minister to the Emperor of China', which in the self-righteousness and hauteur of its terms is the equal of that famous and equally unrealistic epistle from Ch'ien-lung to George III. He demanded 'satisfaction for the past and security for the future'. This meant payment for the cost of the British expedition now arrived in the East in support of its merchant citizens immured on their ships at Hong Kong after the debacle at Canton; and the cession of 'one or more sufficiently large and properly situated islands' where British subjects might not again be exposed to 'violence'.

Elliot, and his cousin Admiral George Elliot in change of the naval force from England, acting as Plenipotentiaries, blockaded the mouths of the Canton River, the Yangtze, and the Peiho (the entry to Peking)

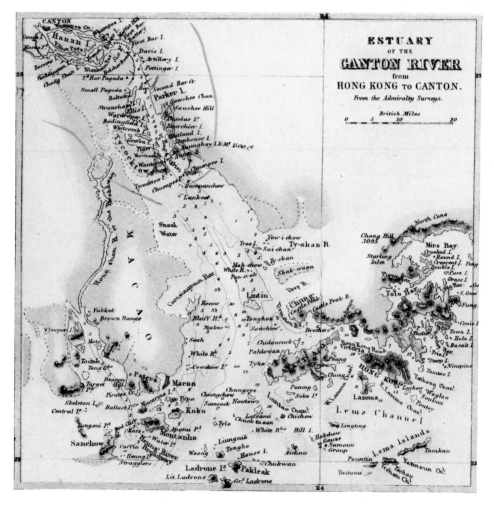

8

'Opium Smuggling—Capsing-Moon Passage (Kap Shui Mun, between Lantao and Ma Wan Islands) in the 1840s. *Opposite:* A miniature map dating from the same time, slightly enlarged

in the north, in 1840. Returning south to Macau in October with a Chinese promise of negotiations, the seafaring Elliot retired sick, and Charles Elliot was left as sole negotiator. He had in general shown himself a conciliatory man. He is on record as having criticized British merchants for showing 'a very heedless spirit' toward the Chinese at Canton, and as having 'a strong persuasion that a conciliatory disposition to respect the usages, and above all to refrain from shocking the prejudices of this government' of China would eventually prove to British advantage. Wise words in a headstrong world. But he was also a realist. 'It is easier in this country [China] to get on than to get in.' His lenient policies were attacked on all sides, arousing particularly strong resentment among the bloodthirsty naval and army personnel of the day. The captain of a naval vessel (Belcher, who has, naturally enough, a couple of Hong Kong streets named after his negligible memory) said that as the city of Canton came under attack, Chinese

The only known picture showing the cession of
Hong Kong in 1841. *Left:* Lord Palmerston,
Secretary of State for the Colonies

appeared on the walls with white flags and yelled: 'Elliot, Elliot, as if he were protecting their joss [god].'

Elliot was against the opium trade, which he thought dangerous. But talks broke down, and by early 1841 Elliot occupied the Chinese forts at the mouth of the river leading to Canton. A settlement was then reached between him and the Chinese Commissioner Keshen (Ch'i-shan) and, prematurely as it turned out, Elliot announced its terms in late January before it was signed. It was by virtue of one clause in this so-called Convention of Chuenpi that Hong Kong was occupied by a British naval force on 25 January 1841. The British flag was raised that day at Possession Point by Captain Belcher and party who 'drank Her Majesty's health with three cheers.'[7] The place is situated on the northern side of what is today Hollywood Road, west by several hundred yards from the old Man Mo temple. The area now consists of a flat paved square with a centrally placed shanty of a Chinese restaurant, sur-rounded on three sides by barbers' and fortune-tellers' booths. Imme-diately flanking the restaurant on either side are two domed octagonal buildings of unknown origin, next to one being the remnants of a cast-iron 'drinking fountain' (for lack of a better term) with the inscription on it 'Keep The Pavement Dry'. From its height it would seem more suited to use by camels (one of which, later, we will find in Hong Kong) than by people, or even horses. There is nothing in this area, except the name Possession Street, a steep alley running up from the water, to mark the historic site.

It was not until more than two years after Elliot's precipitate act of 25 January 1841, that a reluctant home government officially recognized Hong Kong as a colony. Yet such was the immediate effect of British presence and Chinese influx in the first few years that in mid-1845 a 'bungalow' built by a trader two years earlier at West Point (not far from Possession Point, around which Western residential houses were first set up), was advertised for sale in the newspaper *The Friend of China* as follows: 'A substantial house consisting of two sitting rooms, each 30 by 20 feet and in height 17 feet, separated by folding doors, five good size bedrooms, with dressing and bathroom to each; a front and back verandah, closed with venetians, each 100 feet long and 12 feet wide, flat roof convenient for exercise and affording a fine view of the harbour . . . . Commodious outbuildings for servants, store room, and offices: a large compound, garden, etc. . . . surrounded by a good fence. . . .'

The area was to change its character from initial residential to later commercial; and finally, as the Western inhabitants of Hong Kong

William Adolphus Knell's painting showing the crew of the warship *Nemesis* attacking 500 Chinese soldiers on 8 March, 1842. *Opposite:* British ships firing on Chinese war junks in the Bocca Tigris

moved eastward along the coastline, it became a purely Chinese district.

Meanwhile, in effect, the first Opium War had begun. Keshen, the Chinese negotiator at the Chuenpi settlement, was sent to Peking in chains for his part in such an outrageous violation of Chinese sovereignty, and Elliot, though he did not know it at the time, was himself dismissed. In the casual way of that era, British tea ships had been allowed up to Canton to take on the season's shipment, but just as they had left, the Chinese attacked other shipping at Canton. Elliot immediately retaliated by threatening Canton, which was held to ransom for six million dollars. Precisely at this moment news of his dismissal appeared in the Macau newspapers, five days before the official letter arrived from London!

Foreign Secretary Palmerston's letter of dismissal is a minor classic that deserves quotation. Having thundered about the precision of the instructions he had sent to Elliot, he continues: 'You have disobeyed and neglected your Instructions; you have deliberately abstained from employing . . . the Force placed at your disposal; and you have without any sufficient necessity accepted Terms which fall far short of those which you were ordered to obtain . . . . Our forces by Sea and by Land had been everywhere successful. We had taken Chusan without loss . . . we might have kept it as long as we chose. We had shown [at Amoy and the Canton River] the facility with which our irresistible Navy could vanquish every Chinese Force which it could get at . . . . Throughout the whole Course of your proceedings, you seem to have considered that my instructions were waste Paper . . . and that you were at full liberty to deal with the interests of your Country according to your own Fancy.'[8]

Listing hawkishly the matters Elliot had been told to accomplish, and which he had not complied with in full, the Foreign Secretary presents himself as a highhanded exponent of using British force for British ends, regardless of the sovereignty of Chinese in their own country. Elliot emerges as a reasonable man sorely pressed by Palmerston's unreasonable demands, and by the impossibility of dealing with the Chinese in the accepted Western diplomatic manner. It seems likely that, had Elliot been allowed to continue, the baleful events of the future that were deeply to divide the West and China for over a century might not have happened, or might have followed a less acrimonious path. But, in the event, it was Elliot's 'Fancy' that secured the cession, albeit unratified, of Hong Kong. It is gratifying to discover that Captain Elliot, on his

an stick behind the neck

...etacles fastened on by being...
...the ears?

Kellett's Island, a previously unpublished watercolour of c.1850 *Opposite:* A colour sketch sketch signed W.W.L., 1857, part of an album

return to England, was retained in government employment. The Prime Minister, Peel, took an entirely different view of his character and attainments from that of the former Foreign Secretary, Palmerston, and said that he was 'disposed from his intercourse with him [Elliot] since he returned home, to repose the highest confidence in his integrity and ability'. Elliot went on to assignments such as that of Chargé d'Affaires in the Republic of Texas, Governor of Bermuda, and later of Trinidad, dying in England in 1875, knighted by his sovereign.

His successor, Sir Henry Pottinger, arrived with instructions to continue the campaign until satisfaction in full was obtained for insults to the British crown, the cost of the campaign itself, and the loss of all the opium burned by Commissioner Lin (who, poor man, suffering as he did from a hernia treated by the first American medical missionary to China, Dr Peter Parker,[9] was exiled in disgrace to the far frontiers among barbarian tribes). Pottinger was successful, obeying the instructions of Palmerston and of his successor in the post of Foreign Secretary, Lord Aberdeen. And so it is that while Elliot, to whom Hong Kong owes its annexation to the Crown, is unremembered in any tangible manner in the Colony, Pottinger is the name of a short commercial street, and Aberdeen is remembered in the renamed and formerly piratical village of that name. There, long before, in 1816, the vessels of the flotilla

Unpublished watercolours by W.W.L. in 1857: children flying kites against a sketched view of Hong Kong; men poling a boat in shallows

16

conveying the ill-starred ambassador of the British, Lord Amherst, towards Peking, saw the waterfall that cascaded in one 'grand and graceful lapse' towards the shore—as it still did at the time of the events we are recalling now. Not for long, indeed, would it do so, for the growth of the new Colony demanded water supplies and it was diverted to the first of the reservoirs constructed not far away and still in use today.

Lord Aberdeen's intentions were fundamentally to obtain full trading rights for the British at several ports up and down the China coast and thus to open the unlimited market of China to the export acumen of English merchants. On Hong Kong, Aberdeen was at first inclined to the view that 'it was not to be regarded in the light of a permanent conquest'.

Pottinger did not delay in Hong Kong, setting off with his naval force up the China coast less than ten days after his arrival there. By the fourth week of August 1841, he was in Amoy and soon occupied the Chusan Islands. Having likewise taken Ningpo, his somewhat ruthless character suggested to him that it would be a good idea to hold that city to ransom on the threat of its being pillaged, but (for once) the naval and military advisors showed such restraint that he was dissuaded.

The occupation of Tinghai on Chusan has at least the virtue of an amusing incident. The Chinese there requested permission of the British to be allowed to take their dead to burial grounds outside the town, and this was granted. It was not until some time had elapsed that the almost continuous flow of funeral cortèges aroused suspicion. And when coffins were opened they were found to contain not corpses but silks and other property that the nimble-witted Chinese were prudently removing to safer places.

Renewing the campaign in the spring of 1842, forts at the mouth of the Yangtze were taken, and Shanghai was occupied. The British fleet sailed up the river, blockaded the Grand Canal, and reached Nanking in August. It was in order to save the city that the Chinese finally were forced to agree to Pottinger's terms. These were set out in the Treaty of Nanking, signed on 29 August 1842 (p. 18).

The Chinese call this the First Unequal Treaty. With it the first Opium War was concluded, but the fundamental differences between the Western barbarians, to use the Chinese phrase, and the Chinese government remained as deep as ever. What is even more significant, is that the whole affair—illegal opium importation, and Western armed intervention on behalf of Western subjects in and around China who were flagrantly violating Chinese law and encroaching on Chinese sovereignty

17

and territory—was correctly seen by the Chinese as the fundamental and dangerous ingredient in the Western character. The British, on the other hand, contented themselves with the statement that while officially they disapproved of the opium trade they could not stop opium imports to China, and that the action of Commissioner Lin in Canton in laying siege to the factories where the merchants refused to surrender their opium stocks, was the provocation for their armed intervention; further, they wished only to have access to trading posts up and down the coast where British subjects might trade peaceably. The resulting treaty carefully avoided the mention of opium at all, except where it specified the Chinese were to pay six million dollars compensation for confiscated stocks.

Treaty of Nanking

The most important provisions were:

The ports of Canton, Amoy, Foochow, Ningpo, and Shanghai were to be opened to British trade and residence.

The monopoly formerly held by the Chinese government-appointed group of merchants at Canton, through whom all matters had to be transacted, was to be abolished.

An equitable, uniform tariff was to be introduced.

Communication between British and Chinese officials was to be conducted on a basis of equality.

China was to pay an indemnity of 12 million dollars for the cost of the war, 6 million for the opium burned by Commissioner Lin, and 3 million in settlement of Chinese merchants' debts to British merchants.

The later *Supplementary Treaty of the Bogue* provided for a tariff of five per cent on the value of all goods, for extra-territorial rights for British subjects who would be tried by British law, not Chinese; and the so-called 'most favoured nation' treatment—meaning that any privilege granted by China to another foreign nation would automatically be conferred on Britain as well.

The implications of these treaties were so humiliating for China, and of such straightjacket stringency, that it might have been obvious that, signed under duress as they were, the agreements were unlikely to be long respected by the Chinese.

Chinese xenophobia was given a boost, while British merchants now felt they had the home government backing almost anything they cared to do. This, in essentials, was the situation that was to underlie Sino-Western contacts and relations from then onward.

But we are dealing with Hong Kong, and not with the involved and tragic story of Sino-Western relations. It was Palmerston in his letter dismissing Elliot who noted that that unfortunate man had 'obtained the Cession of Hong Kong, a barren Island with hardly a house upon

18

it . . . not to be the Mart of Trade any more than Macau is so.' Further, said he, all that Elliot had in this respect managed to get was an island where the merchants trading at Canton in the winter months as permitted by the Chinese would 'be able to go and build houses to retire to, in the desert Island of Hong Kong, instead of passing the non-trading Months at Macau'. Then he has second thoughts, covers himself in case he errs: 'However, it is possible that I may be mistaken in this Matter; and that Hong Kong may secure to us the same trading advantages which we have hitherto enjoyed at Canton, with the additional benefit of Freedom from molestation of Persons or Property.'

Ironically, for neither Palmerston nor Elliot could have foreseen it, and despite the later rise of Shanghai which they could not have suspected either, it was Elliot's Hong Kong that was to prove the most viable, most lucrative, most long-lived of all Great Britain's myriad colonies—to become not only one of its last but also one of its most extraordinary overseas possessions. The flag was hoisted in Hong Kong first of all to afford the merchant the security he needed to trade. It is still hoisted there for the same reason, and no other.

Pottinger had his way, because that way ran parallel to the merchants' desires, and to the march of events. The treaty provided for the cession of Hong Kong in perpetuity as a place where the British 'may careen and refit their ships'. Pottinger had exceeded his brief but, in his defence, he wrote: '. . . the retention of Hong Kong is the only single point in which I intentionally exceeded my . . . instructions, but every single hour I have passed in this superb country has convinced me of the necessity and desirability of our possessing such a settlement as an emporium for our trade and a place from which Her Majesty's subjects in China may alike be protected and controlled.'

Protected they were. Controlled they were not, as we shall see in following the chaotic events in even the British part of China—Hong Kong island. Ratification of the treaty came on 26 June 1843. Sir Henry Pottinger was declared its first Governor.

Ch'i Ying, Viceroy of Canton, called by the English, who never got Chinese names right, Kiying or Keying, signed the treaty ratification with Pottinger in Hong Kong and was then entertained in most royal style on the same evening at Government House. Despite the scurrilous terms used about him in the weekly *The Friend of China*, which likened him to a 'large boiled turnip', said he was 'considerably obese', and 'dressed just like one of the nodding figures in the tea-shop windows at home'—Pottinger spared no effort to establish good relations. It seems

Sir Henry Pottinger who administered the
Government from August 1841 to June
1843, and was its first Governor, June 1843
to May 1844

20

indeed that for perhaps the first but certainly not the last time, the halls of Government House rang with uncontrolled and bibulous conviviality. It is said that Ch'i Ying went so far (and it was far indeed for a Chinese Viceroy) as to sing some Manchu songs, to which Pottinger replied by singing himself. But it must be remembered that the night before, at another dinner, Ch'i Ying had at his own request been presented with a miniature painting of Mrs Pottinger. He is said then to have placed the picture 'on his head', at one point, and at another to have drunk a glass of wine while holding it in front of him. Finally he sent it home by bearer in his chair of state. Pottinger named his eldest son Fredrick Keying Pottinger—the boy being 'adopted' by Ch'i Ying.

Pottinger's tempestuous nature made him less suited to the administrative post of Governor than he was to the life of action. His popularity was soon reversed when he signed the supplementary Treaty of the Bogue by which, in effect, control of all Chinese shipping entering and leaving Hong Kong was vested in Chinese authorities using a British officer to make the control work.

The outcry from the merchant community was severe. What actually happened we shall probably never know. But Pottinger had published a version of this treaty in which the clauses relating to Chinese shipping were omitted. The British heard of the missing clauses from Chinese who had read them in the Chinese text. The merchants said that Pottinger had been double-crossed by Ch'i Ying who had inserted the clauses without the Governor's knowledge. To which Pottinger replied that the English version was not intended to be a complete and definitive text. It all sounds as if he feared the traders' reactions and wished somehow to soften the blow. If so, he proved himself a ham-handed administrator. For the result was that the clauses were never brought into force and the idea of using a British officer to enforce them did not become a reality as none was ever appointed. Pottinger therefore achieved precisely what was not intended, a situation of uncertainty and lack of principle in relations with China.

Hong Kong itself had grown by this time. A proclamation back in 1841 had declared the island a dominion of the Queen 'by clear public agreement between the high officers of the Celestial and British Courts'. Everyone was assured of freedom of religion, ceremonies, and social custom, and Chinese would be governed according to the laws and usages of the Chinese, 'every description of torture excepted'.

The invitation to Chinese business was implicit, and the Chinese were not slow in the uptake. Despite the events between the Elliot era and

HONG KONG: THE CULTURED PEARL

VICTORIA IN 1845

KELLET'S ISLAND

EAST POINT

CAUSEWAY BAY

THE ROYAL BATTERY

WELLINGTON BATTERY

MORRISON HILL

POLICE STATION

HAPPY VALLEY

GRAVE YARD

BEGINNINGS

Below, opposite: A European sketch of Victoria
in 1846. *Below:* a painting by an unknown
Chinese artist of the city a little later. *Overleaf:*
An engraving of the officers' quarters in
Murray Barracks with the harbour and town
at the left—about 1850

VICTORIA IN 1848

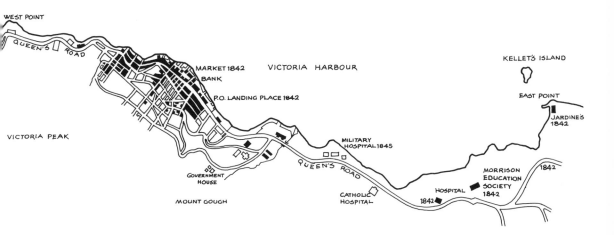

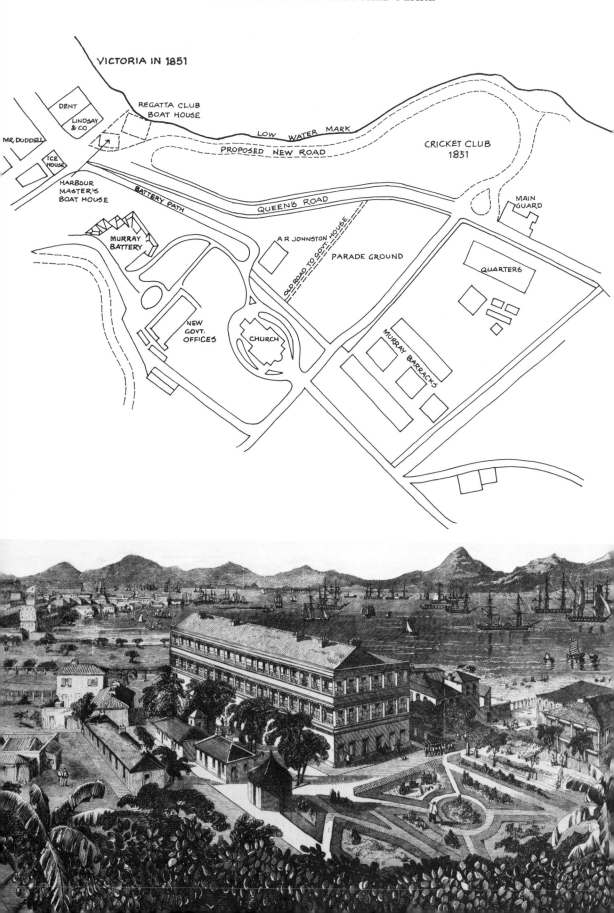

VICTORIA IN 1851

DENT

LINDSAY & CO

MR. DUDDELL

ICE HOUSE

REGATTA CLUB BOAT HOUSE

LOW WATER MARK

PROPOSED NEW ROAD

CRICKET CLUB 1851

HARBOUR MASTER'S BOAT HOUSE

BATTERY PATH

QUEEN'S ROAD

MAIN GUARD

MURRAY BATTERY

A R JOHNSTON HOUSE

OLD ROAD TO GOVT. HOUSE

PARADE GROUND

QUARTERS

NEW GOVT. OFFICES

CHURCH

MURRAY BARRACKS

the signature of treaties, and the acceptance of Hong Kong as a colony by the British government, building began, and soon Elliot had had to decide on some system of allotting land. At that time there was a track running by the northern shores of the island. This soon became a road, Queen's Road, and the main thoroughfare of the growing settlement. Land was being expropriated or sold without regard to any plan, and buildings were springing up in a manner reminiscent of the building boom of the 1960s, more than a century later. Among the earliest were those of Jardine and Dent, the two principal trading companies from Canton days. Soon the whole waterfront was a patchwork of lots varying in depth with the distance of Queen's Road from the shoreline. Everyone joined as best he could in the land-grabbing spree. Hong Kong has always been an artificial place where opportunities of one kind and another are presented, and taken up so fully and quickly that the results are squabbles, restrictive legislation, backbiting, and general unpleasantness.

The first magistrate, Captain William Caine (commemorated by a long twisting road running with the contours of the hills halfway up the Peak) was appointed, and a jail built. A public works department was set up, a harbour-master named Pedder was appointed (his memorial is the most congested short length of street in central Hong Kong); and the army established itself near Possession Point as well as in central Victoria where the Commander-in-Chief's house, Headquarters House, was soon to be built, and where it still stands today. At that time it crowned a small bluff above the new Queen's Road, itself skirting the shoreline. Today the house is all but three hundred yards from the harbour, land having been extensively reclaimed. The house, a fine example of colonial British architecture of the time, was designed by a Mr M. Bruce, a Scots Inspector of Buildings in the fledgling administration, and who (it is recorded) also played the bagpipes well and was a good watercolourist. The structure was completed in 1846 having taken about three years to build, and was first occupied by Major General D'Aguilar, of whom we shall hear more later. The house, renamed long afterwards Flagstaff House, is possibly the oldest residence in the Colony still in use and in fine condition.

The reason for its construction in the first place was the massive typhoon of 21 July 1841, which flattened all the matshed buildings in the vicinity in which the military and others were accommodated.

At that point, and following the most rough and ready regulations, defining 'marine lots' with a maximum distance of 200 feet from the

An early photograph of Dent & Company's premises, about 1858

shoreline, 'town lots' at specified parts of Hong Kong, Stanley, and Aberdeen, and suburban lots anywhere else, the skeletal structure of the town began to firm up. Other areas were set aside for what the British all over the East had always called 'bazaars'; that is, areas in which the local population might live and trade.

By December 1841 there were 12,000 Chinese in Hong Kong, mostly labourers and shopkeepers. By the time Pottinger took office, he was governor of quite a sizeable place in terms of real estate, population, and trade. He stabilized the currency, making two and a half East India Company rupees equal to one dollar. Defending himself against Lord Aberdeen in the Foreign Office at home for having without authorization removed the Superintendancy of Trade office from Macau to Hong Kong, he wrote: '. . . that was forced on me by the extraordinary and unparalleled progress which this settlement has made. . . . This settlement has already advanced too far to admit of its ever being restored to the authority of the Emperor.'

26

Willy-nilly, the Colony was founded. Queen Victoria, far away in London, wrote to her favourite uncle, Leopold, King of the Belgians: 'Albert is so much amused at my having got the island of Hong Kong, and we think Victoria [their eldest daughter] should be called Princess of Hong Kong in addition to Princess Royal.'

With these uncertain, muddled, aggressive, and thoroughly ill-organized beginnings, the Colony was born, yelling lustily in its first few minutes of life. A reluctant British government took over a barren island, and the Royal Family treated the matter as a huge joke.

It was, in fact, neither. Fumbled into the Empire it may have been, but the facts of the matter were that British mercantile considerations of the time required the annexation of Hong Kong as the base for safer and more profitable operations. The stakes were too high in the East India Company's vast tracts of India that had been forcibly turned over to the cultivation of opium, to allow anyone or anything, either British or Chinese governments, to interfere with the opium trade with China. Legal it certainly was not under the laws of China: at some times it was considered of doubtful propriety by the British parliament, and at others viewed with less reprehension, dependant on which faction had the upper hand: but one thing was certain, that the miserable process by which a mere handful of British had overturned the traditional rural economy of very large tracts of northeastern India in Bengal and Bihar, and the livelihood of millions of Indians, and substituted the growing and manufacture of opium in various stages of purification for export, could not be stopped now without the Company's virtual bankruptcy ensuing in a year or so. The stakes as seen from the offices of the most powerful trading company in all England were too high for anything but ruthless pursuance of the illegal export of opium to the main market—China.

The stage, in fact, was set for more than a century of tragic events involving the prolonged clash of Western nations with the ancient and faltering government of the Chinese empire.

2

THE ILL-CONDUCTED ISLAND

THERE was trouble enough in Pottinger's brief spell as Governor of Hong Kong, the majority of it caused by the unruly merchant community of English who objected to submitting to any reasonable law or regulation, yet invoked the protection of British and colonial law whenever it suited them. Pottinger, his object of having the Colony recognized as such by the British government achieved, and finding action had given way to the necessity of administration, complained bitterly of overwork. Indeed one historian has upheld his statement that he 'stood alone', remarking that Pottinger's 'secretary was an assistant surgeon in the Bombay army; his financial secretary, the mate of a ship; his judge an Indian soldier; his assistant judge, the second mate of a country ship....' Another contemporary, the Rev. James Legge, observed of him: 'Sir Henry Pottinger ... was governor of the Colony when I came to it, and I was surprised to find that he was not by any means popular. He was a good man, people said, to conquer China, and a bad man to rule Hong Kong. The impression which I received from my intercourse with him was of a man condensed, reticent, powerful, who would have his own way, and was able to force it.'

Despite these qualities and handicaps, it must be said of the first Governor that during his time the embryo of future Hong Kong administration appeared—in the shape of Legislative and Executive Councils set up to advise him. In expanded form, these exist today and the Governor is bound to seek if not necessarily to accept their advice. There was opposition on all sides, not only from swashbuckling merchants such as Matheson (of the powerful Jardine, Matheson and Company, the major opium dealers of the time) but from the army and navy as well. While the government in London opined that British opium smugglers must not have protection or support, it went on to remark that 'HM Government ... have not the power to stop this trade ... but they may perhaps impede it in some degree by preventing the Island of Hong Kong or its ... waters from being used as the point from whence British smugglers shall depart on their illegal adventures.'

Pottinger issued a degree supporting this statement, and for a while the merchants believed that he intended to do something about its contents. Matheson took to sailing his ships under a Danish flag of convenience, but by April 1843, a few months before Pottinger resigned, Matheson wrote: 'The Plenipotentiary has published a most fiery proclamation against smuggling, but I believe it is like the Chinese edicts, meaning nothing, and only meant for the saints in England. Sir Henry never means to act upon it and no doubt privately considers it a good joke. At any rate he allows the drug to be landed and stored at Hong Kong.'

Matheson's cynical amusement was justified in the case of both Chinese and English local authorities. His company prospered, cautiously anchoring a huge opium-receiving ship in the harbour, along with ten others elsewhere, all supplied from India by five fast clippers. Smuggling up and down the China coast was carried out by six other ships. By 1850, the estimated number of chests of opium smuggled into China had risen to 52,000 per year, and the Government of India derived five and a half million of its total revenue of twenty-seven and a half million pounds from opium sales.

Jardine, who had retired in 1839, became a member of parliament and died in 1843, smartly replaced in his parliamentary seat by Matheson. Maurice Collis, whose entertaining book on the opium trade, *Foreign Mud*, covers the subject in very readable fashion, remarks of Matheson that he spent 'the sum of £574,000, only a small part of his great fortune, we may suppose, on purchasing and improving a house and estate at Lewes [it was in fact the Hebridean island of Lewis that he bought, building Stornoway Castle and being made a baronet for famine relief on the island] where he lived till his death at eighty-two.'

With the army and navy, Pottinger had other headaches. Both services insisted on claiming great tracts of land on the shore and extending inland, right in the middle of the newly-named town of Victoria, thus precluding any sensible planning involving a praya or waterfront road. Until reclamations within the last twenty years, Hong Kong suffered from their insistence, and the waterfront road circled the back of the naval dockyard for more than a hundred years.

If Sir Henry Pottinger felt, as he appeared to do before he finally

Sir John Francis Davis, Governor from
May 1844 to March 1848, a fine
contemporary drawing

left the Colony in 1844, that he was plodding through an ever-thickening
jungle of thorny local problems, his successor was to find Hong Kong
even more inimical. Sir John Francis Davis was a scholar, specialist in
Chinese matters, translator of Chinese prose and poetry, an able official
who had reached the highest position in the East India Company's
service in the Far East (presidency of the Select Committee in Canton)
when only thirty-seven). In 1834 he took over there from the ill-fated
Lord Napier who had died of fever (doubtless aggravated by his total
lack of success at Canton whither the British government had sent him
to deal *directly* with its Governor—an impossibility) as Chief Superintendent of Trade. This post Davis disliked so much, especially after
the ending of the East India Company monopoly, when all the ruffians
of the high seas took to trading at Canton, that he relinquished it and
went home. He had already served 22 years in the East. He was one of

30

what must have been at that time no more than a handful of non-Chinese in the whole world who understood spoken and written Chinese.

Back in England he busied himself with his studies, adding to a list of translations already published a volume that was to be for many years a standard work: *The Chinese. A general description of the Empire of China, and its Inhabitants*. By the time he was chosen to return East, his *Sketches of China* with its account of the abortive mission of Lord Amherst to Peking, and several articles in learned periodicals, had appeared. He was an obvious choice to succeed Pottinger as Governor of Hong Kong and Superintendent of Trade—the two offices now held by one man.

What was the Colony like, that he had come to govern? We are fortunate in having at least a physical description of the town of Victoria from an articulate contemporary source. The Rev. James Legge, whose opinion of Pottinger was an accurate one, was one of the nineteenth century's best known sinologues. For close on thirty years he was resident in Hong Kong and, as the historian G.B. Endacott writes of him, 'closely identified himself with its daily life and its social problems'. Minister of the Union Church, he was respected by many Chinese. He was a Scotsman, born in Huntley, Aberdeenshire, and came East to the London Missionary Society's Theological College in Malacca in 1840. In 1843 he moved with the Society's college to Hong Kong as a more suitable place from which to spread Christian religion throughout China. Pottinger refused a grant of land for the college because he had his own pet institution, the Morrison Education Society. But on appeal to the Secretary of State in London and with the help of Sir John Davis when he took over from Pottinger, Legge was given land. He was first

A large European house named Glenealy at the head of a ravine directly above central Victoria. Signed W.W.L. and dated June 13, 1851

and foremost an evangelist, but he also believed that without an education based on Christian values the Chinese could never be converted. Besides these pious matters, he was also a Chinese scholar, and was instrumental in the secularization of government schools in Hong Kong. Some further insight into the character of the man can be had from his stipulation when he finally went into Kwangtung province that if he were murdered (a quite likely event in these very anti-foreigner times) no gunboat should be sent to avenge his death.

Another aspect of Legge's character, related to his Christian and educative purposes, was the translation of the Chinese classics—the publication of the first volume, the *Analects of Confucius*, expedited by Joseph Jardine who had been bowled over by hearing a Chinese boatman declare that Legge's Chinese was better than his own. Such irrelevant events occasionally have a positive effect.

By 1852, the year in which his wife died, Legge himself had already suffered from bouts of fever, and four of his six children were also dead,

Hong Kong seen from east of Causeway Bay, with East Point (*centre*), and the light-coloured Cathedral tower prominent in the distance

Victoria in 1845, with what was probably the temporary Government House with its flagstaff (*left*). Drawing by E. Ashworth. *Below:* a view from further east by M. Bruce, dated November 29, 1846, showing Murray's Battery

such was the mortality rate in the Colony in the early days. Legge spoke (at a lecture in the City Hall in November 1872, the year before he finally left Hong Kong) of the worst year for health as being 1843. 'And nothing can be more delightful than the change in the Colony in this respect. I do not think there is now a healthier residence on this side of Africa. This has been gradually arrived at by the increase in good houses, effectual drainage, the better supply of water, and the growth of trees and vegetation in general.' He was inclined to think that 'for young people coming out here, who will live regularly, and somewhat abstemiously rather than the contrary, the chances of their living out, and being uninjured by, the years of their sojourn, are quite as good as they would be in London.' A brief inspection of the Old Colonial Cemetery hardly confirms this—but Legge left before the plague years, and before the population burgeoned greatly.

One way and another, Legge made a lasting impression on the life of Hong Kong and was one of the most worthy of its nineteenth-century citizens—a fact that, in the light of later events in the Colony, is all the more remarkable. He was to become the first professor of Chinese at Oxford, in 1875, and with the help of another Chinese specialist, Max Muller, he managed to complete his monumental translation of the Chinese classics, the first in a Western language.

In the course of his lecture at the City Hall before he left Hong Kong, Legge gave a description of the place as it was when he first saw it, one which fits neatly in time with the period when Pottinger was replaced by Davis as Governor.

Coming from Macau, 'I have not forgotten the sensations of delight with which . . . I contemplated the ranges of hills on the north and the south, embosoming between them the tranquil waters of the bay. I seemed to feel . . . I had found at last the home for which I had left Scotland.'[1]

'The hillsides now occupied [in 1872] by the graceful terraces of our city then presented a very different appearance.'

From the original approximate area of Possession Point and a little to the west where, from Hollywood Road 'the streets running down from it to the Queen's Road, were . . . indicated in a rudimentary fashion' proceding eastward there was little but a naval stores and 'tents and huts peopled by the 55th Regiment.' And from that point eastward 'all was blank to the bluff where the Civil Hospital rises, and on which was a bungalow [which we have already noted] occupied by Mr Edger. . . . On the other side of the road were some godowns. . . .'[2]

The next European buildings were Gibb, Livingstone & Co.'s premises, enclosed within a ring fence ... where partners and employees all managed to reside.'

Running up the sides of the Peak were 'thread-like paths, with a Chinese house here and there, but the ground was mainly boulder and sandy gravel. Turning to the west where Wellington Street runs into Queen's Road [where it still does] you could see a few Chinese houses, and Jervois Street [now Jarvois] was in the course of formation, the houses on the north' of it 'having the waters of the bay [harbour] washing about among them.'

A glance at a modern map demonstrates the extent of the land reclamation that has taken place in stages since those first years of Hong Kong.

From there eastward, Legge continues, 'on to Pottinger Street, Queen's Road was pretty well lined with Chinese houses; the Central Market was formed; and on the other side were some foreign stores and a tavern or two.' Much later in Hong Kong's history, we will take a look at this whole stretch with its taverns and other establishments.

Spring Gardens by M. Bruce, dated 20 August, 1846

'Looking up Pottinger Street you could see the Magistracy and the Gaol of the day [where later buildings of similar function now stand] where the dreaded Major Caine [of whom more later] presided.' Eastward a little 'a few English merchants had established themselves, and ... the Commercial Inn was a place of great resort. On the West of D'Aguilar Street, not then so named, ... and just opposite it, was a small house called the Bird Cage, out of which was hatched the Hong-kong Dispensary. All the space between Wyndham Street and Wellington Street was garden ground' with a house belonging to Mr Brain of Dent and Co. 'That great firm [whose fortunes proved less firmly founded later on] had its quarters where the Hongkong Hotel now is.'

'On the Parade Ground [site of the present day Hilton Hotel] was a small mat building, which was the first Colonial Church: about where the Cathedral and Government Offices now stand [and still do], were the unpretending Government Offices of that early time and Post Office. Far up ... might be seen a range of barracks, out of which have been fashioned the present Albany residences [a building of that name still occupies the location], and beyond the site of the present Government House was a small bungalow where Sir Henry Pottinger and Sir John Davis after him held court. ... On the right was the General's House, looking much as it does now.'

'Following the bend of the road ... we came to Spring Gardens [around where Spring Garden Lane now runs up the hill].' Then eastward there was little until Morrison Hill where the Morrison Education Society 'was in vigorous action'.

'Arrived at Happy Valley, there were to be seen only fields of rice and sweet potatoes ... and on the heights above it were rising two or three foreign houses built by Mr Mercer of Jardine, Matheson & Co. All these proved homes of fever and death, and were soon abandoned.'

'Beyond the Valley ... was a range of buildings, which had already become tabooed as unhealthy, and then came the offices of the great Firm [Jardine, Matheson & Co.] with the workmen still busy about them.'

Legge was of the opinion at the time of his address in 1872 that there were few of the foreign houses he first saw still standing. He goes on in a lyrical passage: 'When I contrast the single street, imperfectly lined with hastily raised houses, and a few sporadic buildings on the barren hillside, with the city into which they have grown, with its praya, its imposing terraces, and many magnificent residences, I think one must travel far to find another spot where human energy and skill have

36

triumphed to such an extent over difficulties of natural position.' And he concludes with a fine rhetorical flourish: 'I sometimes fancy Britannia standing on the Peak, and looking down with an emotion of pride on the great Babylon which her sons have built.'

It was into this 'great Babylon', this entirely artificial society, that poor Governor Davis was injected. A scholar by nature and achievement, he hardly stood much chance from the outset. He was confronted by a colony of philistines to whom his achievements in Chinese language were distasteful and, worse, probably indicated his sympathies might lie with the Chinese. He was almost from the first arraigned at the bar of public opinion much in the way that an Urban Councillor of Hong Kong[3] in the late 1960s was handed down just such a 'sentence' by a committee of investigation. But the ironies of history are many, and in fact both Davis and the Urban Councillor vindicated themselves by their actions, proving the opinions and prejudices of their accusers to be grotesquely wide of the mark.

Davis arrived in May 1844. By November in the same year he was to say: 'It is a much easier task to govern the twenty thousand Chinese inhabitants of this Colony, than the few hundreds of English.' It must have seemed to him that Hong Kong was little different from the factories of Canton, only its population more numerous.

The trouble was that he had to raise revenue, on the instructions of the British government. The port had been declared a free port, so there was no hope of imposing customs duties. He fell back on a decision taken by Pottinger that land leases were to be 75 years and no more, and that a rent would be charged. He also required those who dealt in salt, hard liquor, and tobacco, and all auctioneers and billiard-saloon keepers, to pay for a licence. Monopolies in quarrying stone and the retail sale of opium were also sold to the highest bidder. His tax on property met with such a storm of protest that he was forced to lower it by sixty per cent in the face of furious merchant opposition.

Worst of all, in merchant eyes, was a measure Pottinger had proposed and Davis introduced—a seemingly innocuous registration of persons in the effort to keep some sort of law and order and have the documentation to back it up. This measure was to apply to Chinese and British alike, in order not to offend the Chinese community. It succeeded in offending both. The Chinese closed their shops, stopped work, and threatened to leave the Colony in a body rather than be registered and pay the one dollar fee. The Europeans sent Davis a 'memorial' in such insulting terms that he sent it back to them. Mildly enough, Davis termed this 'ill-conducted opposition', but it was impossible to go through with the measure. In the end, and somewhat later, only Chinese were registered—Hong Kong Westerners' opinion was ill-prepared to accept anything that looked like equality with the Chinese, although it was just this equality that successive Foreign Secretaries in London had been calling on the Chinese in China itself to recognize.

Whatever may be thought of some of Davis's more sweeping ideas on governing the Colony, he was nothing if not a realist. Before leaving England for Hong Kong he applauded the British Government's intention that the Colony should not be used as a focus for dissemination of contraband. Yet, after a short time in office, he had seen how totally impossible it was to carry out such a directive, given the two factors germane to the problem. European merchants could easily circumvent any such proposal since there was insufficient means to stop and search— the police force being in its infancy. And the Chinese, as Davis said, 'now tacitly tolerated' opium.

The Colony had to pay its way, apart from defence, said the British government. Davis managed to collect £22,242 in revenue in 1845. The budgetary deficit was £49,000, made up by London. But by 1848 expenditure had been reduced and the deficit was only £25,000. An English Colonial Secretary remarked, however, 'this promises to be a very expensive colony'. For a few more years it was indeed.

It is hard to recreate, nowadays, the atmosphere of buccaneering, administrative improvization, contempt for law and order, and absence of a sufficient force to keep what law and little order there was in Hong Kong at that time. It is surprising that there was not more serious crime and more profound disorder. A desperate call from Davis produced, in the spring of 1845, *one* police officer from London, Charles May (commemorated, of course, by May Road, a lane of expensive residences to this day, in the mid-levels), as Superintendant of Police; and two others. This brought the pathetic little force up to a round fifty—half of the formerly recruited Europeans having died of fever. With the addition of 30 men from the army, 46 Indians, and 51 Chinese the police force was then stronger than ever before. Doubtless its function was deterrent in various ways, but the lawlessness of the Colony continued unabated in the main with merchants sending petitions to the government in London about being taxed and squeezed by the Governor's monopolies and levies, and the London authorities replying that 'the mercantile body have altogether mistaken the object of Great Britain in the occupation of Hong Kong ... [a place that] except for the security of commerce is unnecessary.'

Alas, poor Davis! There were at least two other thorns in his flesh, one being his Colonial Treasurer named Robert Montgomery Martin, the other the Chief Justice of the Supreme Court, John Walter Hulme.

Martin was one of those Victorians with a passion for writing long and windy reports on almost any subject even remotely connected with his work. And he was also the author of numerous long books, many of which were much respected in his day. His *History of the British Colonies* (in ten volumes), *History of Taxation within the British Empire*, and *Statistics of the Colonies*, to name only a few, doubtless allowed him to feel free to pontificate on anything and everything in the colony of Hong Kong. Within two months of his arrival (most of which, Governor Davis was to complain, he had spent ill in bed) Martin had compiled two lengthy reports, one dealing with finances (very properly, since he was Treasurer), and the other, improperly, raising the whole question of the utility of Hong Kong as a colony. In the first he called the place a 'small barren unhealthy valueless island'. In the second he dealt with everything else from climate to religion. The climate was unhealthy, the nature of the terrain would prevent the growth of a sizeable town, the decomposing granite of the island gave out fetid odours productive of disease, the mandarins prevented respectable Chinese from coming to Hong Kong and only the worthless with no sense of morality arrived, the conditions for commercial prosperity were absent; and in any case the harbour was filling up with silt. 'I have in vain sought for one valuable quality ...' but 'I can see no justification for the British government spending one shilling on Hong Kong.' The British Government, from time to time, was half-inclined to agree.

Davis, not unnaturally, did not take this report too seriously and left it lying on his desk for a month before sending it without comment to London. But Martin was personally acquainted with the recipient, the Secretary of State, and with profound disregard for the ethics of the service wrote to him privately giving his views on Davis and Hong Kong and the whole (in his eyes) unpleasant situation, and requesting permission to resign.

London wrote back to Davis saying that if Martin resigned, his resignation was to be accepted, but that if there was substance to his statements, Davis must comment. And so it went on. Davis, goaded continually as he was by this and other obstructions to almost any administrative act he took, at one point wrote about Martin to London: 'Whether from want of method or from attending to other matters as bookmaking [he meant authorship], he is a most inefficient and trouble-some person, and I should be very glad to get rid of him.' Replying to queries from London on Martin's strictures on the climate, Davis enlisted the aid of the General Officer Commanding (Major-General D'Aguilar, the first occupant of the new Flagstaff House), who said: 'Mr Martin must be mad or something worse. . . . His assertion meets only my contempt.' For an officer who had lost so many soldiers from fever this was a bit strong. In the state of medical knowledge at that time, the burden of truth lay with Martin.

In the end, Martin's resignation was accepted, and although he was listened to politely on arrival in London, he was not again offered public office. One may suspect that his frequent references to Chusan as a better island than Hong Kong were intended to have the centre of British trade on the China Coast placed there, doubtless with himself as governor. He failed, and went back to writing.

Perhaps the real flavour of these early times in Hong Kong emerges from the personality of the Chief Justice, Hulme, and the highly charged emotional duel fought between him and Davis. These two, diametrically opposed in temperament and in attitude to life, were almost fated to come to blows, and their story adds a spicey if not entirely savoury note quite in keeping with Hong Kong's 'ill-conducted' life and 'dis-creditable internal squabbles'.

Hulme came to Hong Kong to recoup his fortunes, having married the daughter of one of London's leading lawyers, fathered a large family, and spent more lavishly than prudence and his income permitted. It seems he was a convivial man, bibulous, sensuous, very fair in his administration of the law, but a bit of a bulldozer and therefore very much to the taste of Hong Kong merchant society. He arrived in Hong Kong in the same ship as Davis—the latter having decided at Bombay that the numerous Hulme family and Mrs Hulme had better disembark there and take the *next* boat to Hong Kong, because of shortage of accommodation on HMS *Spiteful*. Hulme was annoyed, particularly as this change of plan was to cost him money. He had in fact only taken the job at Hong Kong because of the then princely salary of £3,000 a year (a salary raised to that level on account of the Colony's reputation as a cemetery for Europeans, who were said to die there like flies, of fever). So there was probably not much love lost between Governor and Chief Justice even before they reached Hong Kong.

Unfortunately, in the casual way of the times, when Hulme arrived the Attorney-General had not, so he could not function since the

Supreme Court was not yet open. 'He could not stir,' remarked a local wit, 'but like a comet, he was wondered at', suggesting at the same time that the high officers of the Supreme Court were arriving in dribs and drabs because the British Government was afraid, were they all to have arrived together, that 'neighbour would have assaulted neighbour from sheer desire of being tried by his peers, and favoured with a bumper of English justice'.

Wit aside, it was not long after their arrival in the Colony that Davis and Hulme quarrelled seriously over the six-month vacation the latter awarded himself from trying criminal cases, and over other matters that gave ample opportunity for the local populace to make its caustic comments and take sides. But the beginning of what was to become one of the most celebrated of British colonial confrontations really came with the aggressive act of an anti-Chinese British merchant at Canton. This unpleasant man, named Compton, caused a riot there by kicking over a Chinese hawker's stall and beating the Chinese with his cane. Compton was very properly fined (rather lightly, it would seem, $200 for an estimated $46,000 damage done in the riot) by the British Consul at Canton. Appealing to the Hong Kong Supreme Court, Compton succeeded in having Hulme reverse the verdict, remit the fine, and speak out against the 'irregularities' of the Canton Consul's hearing of the case.

The Governor was indignant. Writing to London that 'it will never do to have two plenipotentiaries in China, one doing justice to our ally, and the other immediately undoing it.' Since the Hulme verdict, he wrote, and as long as Hulme was in his post, the English in Canton would feel 'they can shoot the Chinese with impunity'. There was a fundamental divide between the opinion of Davis that all British subjects in China were under the control of the British administration, and Hulme's opinion that the courts should act to correct and curb the power of the administration.

For Davis there was no turning back. He determined to get rid of the Chief Justice. A letter to the Secretary of State in London put his point of view officially. Another, to Lord Palmerston, privately alleged that Hulme was a habitual drunkard. Palmerston sent this second missive to Grey at the Colonial Office, who insisted to Davis that the charges were much too serious to pass without public notice, and ordered the Governor to afford Hulme the chance of refuting them. Davis's feelings may be imagined. He had had no intention of bringing Hulme's addiction to the bottle into the open, merely of using the fact privately to bolster up his case for getting rid of a man with whom he could not work. He resigned.

Three specific charges were preferred against Hulme. One stated that at a public entertainment on 22 November 1845, aboard the flagship HMS *Agincourt* in Hong Kong harbour, he was in such a state of intoxication as to attract public attention. Another alleged that on 23 July 1846, in the house of Major-General D'Aguilar, the Commander in Chief, he was desperately intoxicated and unable to look after himself. And the third accused him of habitual drunkenness.

D'Aguilar himself was an eccentric autocrat whose twists of behaviour for the most part seem to have caused more amusement than dismay, although not on all occasions. When out one day on Gap Road, he saw a man galloping his horse. The man was soon under arrest, later to be fined by the courts for 'furious riding'. And one evening when a neighour called Welch was giving a party and burst into song, D'Aguilar sent a policeman from his residence, Headquarters House, to tell him to stop. In fine colonial style Welch threatened to horse-whip the policeman, but he soon afterward found himself before the courts at D'Aguilar's instigation, and was fined twenty dollars.

The accusations levelled at Hulme in regard to the bibulous party in D'Aguilar's own house, however, raised all the Englishman's instincts on the subject of his home being his castle. He sprang to the defence of Hulme. The Executive Council, before whom the hearing took place, contained two members called to give evidence against him, who were thus both his accusers and his judges. Other witnesses were no longer in Hong Kong. Hulme explained his unsteady gait as the consequence of varicose veins—which seems rather lame. Davis, presiding, summed up after each member had given his opinion. Hulme was judged guilty of the first and not of the other two charges, and suspended from his office. He left the following month, December 1847, in a blaze of glory with testimonials from citizens, firecrackers and, predictably, libations of champagne.

It might be supposed that that was the last of Hulme. But in fact he returned, his character rendered spotless by decision of the Secretary of State, the following year. The satisfaction of the colonials knew no bounds.

Alas, poor Davis, who had (justifiably) such a low estimate of the merchant community's opinions that he disregarded them, had done so to his peril. Despite the fact that he was probably one of the most able and intelligent governors the Colony has had, he was detested by its populace. Once, when he presented a cup for a race at the immensely popular Happy Valley racecourse, not a single horse was entered for that race. For a man who knew more of the Chinese, and was a better administrator, and infinitely more intelligent than most people then and for some time afterward in positions of power in Hong Kong, his was a sad fate. He left Hong Kong 'studiously ignored' as the historian Endacott aptly puts the matter, without a speech or a banquet. That scurrilous sheet, *The Friend of China*, remarked with laboured sarcasm: 'Never surely, in the Heavens above, or in the earth beneath, or in the waters under the earth did there ever exist, embodied or disembodied, such a pleasant little gentleman as Sir John Davis.' The message is clear enough, if confused. That of another paper was even clearer. It alleged that the Governor preferred to walk out rather than wait to be kicked out.

But it appears that Davis was not greatly perturbed. He retired to Oxford and funded a scholarship for the study of Chinese, was given the signal honor of Knight Commander of the Bath by Queen Victoria in 1854, a Doctorate of Civil Law by Oxford University in 1876, and lived on to the great age of ninety-five, dying in 1890.

3

LIBEL AND ARSENIC

A good case could be made for the idea that it was in very large part during those early years of Elliot, Pottinger, and Davis—different as these men and their administrations were—that the curious unsavoury, resourceful, and flashy character of the Colony of Hong Kong was formed. Some of the events of those days, and of the following decade under the two succeeding governors, together with some of the persons involved in those events, remind one forcibly of reports in Hong Kong's daily newspapers of the past few years when bribery and corruption in high places, absconding police chiefs and bank clerks, forgers of share certificates, arson, gang and triad society depredations, large-scale drug-peddling, and other occidental and oriental delights have been all but daily front-page news. The Colony, like the leopard, has not changed its spots.

Looking back on the early years, it is quite hard to put a finger on one man, apart from the Rev. James Legge and Governor Davis, who might be termed both influential and upright, moderate, well-informed, just, and at the same time a conscientious servant of the struggling and ill-favoured Colony. Perhaps William Caine, first appointed a magistrate by Elliot, and destined to live and work through the rule of the first four governors, is one of the few who fills the bill; yet even in his case there is room for doubt. We will hear more of him shortly, under Governors Bonham and Bowring.

If poor Davis proved forthright in his administrative methods, and too much of an egghead for the boneheads, money-grubbers, and opium-peddlers he had to govern, Sir Samuel George Bonham was almost exactly the reverse. His exercise of the governor's office was no doubt much constrained by a British government policy of financial retrenchment, which he carried out to the letter, displaying some nicety of judgement in the process. But nothing positive that he did commends him as a man willing to perform more than the absolutely necessary and safe acts required of him. He was a man who would not attempt anything that might lead to his own unpopularity. A Frenchman of the times described him as a *bon vivant* who performed his function *tranquillement*.

There have been several like Bonham since then, but few of his successors had the luck to govern in such untroubled times. Davis had taken the brunt of unpopularity in introducing new measures: Bonham reaped the moderate harvest. For in his time Hong Kong prospered modestly, actually becoming self-supporting in all but defence in the year after he left. But, looking at the Colony of those and later years, it is hard to escape the feeling summed up by Tennyson in his 'better fifty years of Europe than a cycle of Cathay.' The first sixty years of Hong Kong (the Chinese cycle is six decades) were strange times in which decay of Imperial rule in China became rampant, and in which the internal situation in the country was one of revolts and rebellions that all but toppled the Ch'ing dynasty several times in the nineteenth century. The part played in the demise of a two-thousand year old system of government in China by Hong Kong and the other treaty ports, and by the activities of their Western inhabitants, is not a pretty one, and even in the light of the times when these events took place was often, to use a mild word, unjustifiable.

During the term of Bonham, in the wake of the recommendations of what was called the Select Committee, in London in 1847, not only were stringent savings effected in running the Colony, but for the first time two citizens who were not government officials were asked to join the legislature as unofficial members—a system that endures to this day in expanded form. Needless to say, a Jardine of the leading merchant house was one. Government House was begun on much the same site as that of the present one, just up the hill from the Anglican Cathedral, which was also completed at this time, 1849, and the first reclamation of land from the sea was begun in the eastern part of the island's north shore—to be called Bonham Strand, as it still is.

Something of the flavour of the government offices of Bonham's time in Hong Kong can be had from part of the 'Auditor General's Memorandum of Stationery and Small Stores required for the use of the Government of Hongkong, for the year 1854'. For the Colonial Secretary's office the request included a compendious list of materials required for its scribes, the atmosphere of whose offices is implicit in its terms:

5 Reams 1st. Class Foolscap—20 lbs.
5 Do.   2nd Do.   —18 lbs.
$\frac{1}{4}$ Do.   Thin Post
$\frac{1}{2}$ Do.   Blotting Paper—(white)

About 4,500 envelopes of various types were requested, and then:

4 Pieces Narrow Silk ribbon. Green
4 Skeins Green Silk cord for despatches

And then a little further down the list:

2,000 Quill pens
1 Glass Bottle with stopper and brush, for Gum

Hard to imagine that in a land of porcelain, and indeed Chinese glass, such a container could not have been discovered locally. And the item:

3 Japanned Tin 'Date Boxes', with 3 sizes of shifting cards—to exhibit the month and the day of the week and month

strikes one now as a piece of bureaucratic madness, since any Chinese tinsmith and a supplier of thick card or even painted metal slats could have made these. However, continuing:

6 Quart Bottles Black Ink—'H. Morrell's'
6 lb Hyde's extra hard India Sealing Wax
12 $2\frac{1}{2}$ inch Brass padlocks

It must be supposed that those two thousand quills would not flow on a diet of the ubiquitous Chinese ink that could be ground fresh each day as it was and is for every Chinese calligrapher of worth, instead of being imported from London. At least there is no mention of any Gum to place in that expensively procured Glass Bottle. Certainly excellent Chinese gum was available and used by various trades such as scroll-mounters; perhaps the Auditor General found they had enough of the British variety from the year before, and he didn't have to order it again.

In the same year, 1853, in which this order was placed, the detailed constructional drawings for additions to the jail that lies (still) in the angle between Hollywood Road and Old Bailey Street, were forwarded to the Colonial Secretary in London for approval. The sole remarkable feature (viewed from the standpoint of today) was the proposed Tread-Wheel—an elaborate machine with complicated gearing so that it could be trodden by one or several prisoners with the same expenditure of effort. This punitive machine was in wide use in English jails at the time, occasionally harnessed to a mill for grinding grain or some such purpose, but often, as was the one proposed for Hong Kong, apparently harnessed to nothing more than the curious concept that the prisoners' labour at it would be corrective of criminal tendencies. Nicely adapted, it could have ground all the ink for the whole of the bureaucracy each day in five minutes or so.

But the seeds of dire events were germinating. British requests on matters affecting trade with Canton and other ports encountered the stonewalling of a Chinese Imperial Commissioner and a new Governor of Kwangtung province, both anti-foreign. Bonham simply temporized, pleading that the death of the Emperor in 1849 and other matters made it not the proper time to pursue expansion of British opportunity in China. He was quite right. But on his return from leave in 1852, internal revolt in China was aflame and the T'aip'ing rebels were established in Nanking.

Much to the surprise and little to the edification of London, but to the acclaim of British merchants up and down the Treaty Ports, Bonham went to Nanking and met T'ien Wang—the Heavenly King, as the T'aip'ing rebels' leader styled himself. Unlike many Christian missionaries of that time, who deluded themselves into thinking that the allegedly Christian base of the T'aip'ing movement would open China to their own ministrations, Bonham was not deceived and returned with a most unfavourable impression. He then retired.

One of the first historians of Hong Kong, E.J. Eitel, calls him 'the first model governor of Hong Kong'. If Bonham is to be seen as a model, it is fortunate that most of his successors diverged from it. A later historian, G.B. Endacott, characterizes his approach as 'a nice sense of what was better left alone'. He was a model of prudence, a good example of how to do nothing while appearing to be busy. He had some very retrogressive ideas such as that a study of Chinese language warped the mind and was detrimental to good judgement—in pursuance of which manic opinion he refused to promote men who knew the language.

By 1854 when Bonham retired, there was already emerging what has been called a 'Chinese élite' in the Colony.[1] Back in 1845 an official survey noted that 'both in numbers and respectability the Chinese are improving, being accompanied in a greater number of instances by their families.' But, not unnaturally, the confidence placed in Hong Kong by Chinese waxed and waned with its commercial and political fortunes. By 1848 the same source states: 'There exists no local attachment, which may be ascribed to the absence of respectable families born on the island, with which the adventurers could contract marriages.' The use of the word 'adventurers' is significant. In 1845 there was an almost equal number of brothels and of families, 25 families and 26 brothels, counted in an annual census of buildings and shops, most inhabitants being un-

47

accompanied by relatives. But within five years the total of families had increased to 141 and only 32 brothels were noted. It was not until the fifties and sixties of the century, in part due to the terrible years of suppression of the T'aip'ing revolt in which tens of millions of Chinese died, that the Colony seems to have acquired its more influential Chinese population.

Carl T. Smith, in a paper read in 1971 before the Hong Kong branch of the Royal Asiatic Society (founded, incidentally, in 1855 with Sir John Bowring, the Governor, as its first president), divides the élite into groups: contractors, merchants, compradores (the term for Chinese agents used by foreign companies to buy and sell for them), government servants, and Christian employees of missionary groups.

Among contractors, few survived the hazards of business. Unused to building in Western style, they hopelessly underestimated costs. An official comment of 1844 tells the sad story. 'Almost all contracts... entered into with Chinamen have been ... finished by Government, for the works were taken at far too low an estimate, and when the parties found they would become losers, both contractor and security decamped.' One, Tam Achoy, did succeed in mastering the intricacies of Western construction—or apparently so—for, after an initial spell in prison for debt, he emerged as one of the early élite. And in the manner of the newly rich built, with another Chinese, Loo Aqui, the Man Mo Temple which still stands on Hollywood Road. He rebuilt the 'bazaar' whose destruction by fire had resulted in the first reclamation and the construction of Bonham Strand, and he was a leading charterer of emigrant ships. On his death in 1871 he left a large fortune. Predictably, *The Friend of China*, described him ambiguously as 'no doubt the most creditable Chinese in the Colony'.

By 1865, merchants were well established. One company of Chinese, Wo Hang by name, took American partners and formed the American Trading Company of Borneo. Although this failed, one of the Wo Hang families, called Li, survived to become a broker in coolie labour, an emigrant ship charterer, and bought the gambling monopoly in the Colony. With the coming of the second Opium War, they 'gave contributions to foreigners ... of over a lakh [one hundred thousand] of ready money and recruited native braves who went to the front at Tientsin', (prior to the Allied attack and capture of Peking in 1860). When peace came, the Li family 'shared in the War Indemnity as well as in the effects and curios of the Yuen-ming-yuen [Summer Palaces looted and burned by the British and French.]'

48

An engraving of *c.* 1860 showing what is possibly the Western Anchorage

The compradores of Jardine, Matheson and Company, and of the other leading foreign firm, Dent, were both quite soon in property business, and the various sections of the town where Chinese resided were soon in their and other, Chinese, hands to some large extent. The compradore of the P & O Steamship Company, Kwok Acheong, died in 1880, the third biggest rate-payer in the Colony and worth nearly half a million dollars—a tidy sum in those days.

As to Government servants, the group found in early times as some of its members find today, and have been found to find, that opportunities for amassing riches are available in this employment.

But, whatever the methods by which the new Chinese élite may have gained its gold, it has to be recorded that a very large number of the early and enduring charitable institutions in the Colony such as schools and hospitals were instigated and financed by them—the most significant being perhaps the Tung Wah Hospital opened in 1872. The list of the founders and committee of this hospital is virtually a check-list of the Chinese élite at that time. With the oppointment of a Chinese to the Legislative Council in 1880, the élite may be said to have 'arrived'.

Under the indecisive rule of Sir John Bowring, 1854 to 1859, the process was of course not complete. Bowring started with a handicap unique in the annals of Hong Kong governors, the mad and maddening

49

The committee of the Tung Wah Hospital, 1873

result of the 1847 Select Committee's total lack of political and even commonsense appreciation of the colonial situation. Bowring was to be Plenipotentiory and Superintendant of Trade up and down the China coast, and Governor only in name. Caine, the Colonial Secretary, was to administer the Colony. The position was intolerable, as even Westminster might have foreseen, and was ended in a year by Palmerston. But he kept Bowring's salary at half the normal amount.

Bowring was something of an egotist, a fact that did not escape the cruel wit of his contemporaries. It was said, one historian notes, that 'he had come back big with the fate of China and himself'. And Bowring wrote of himself at that time: 'To China I went ... accredited not to Peking alone but to Japan, Siam, China, and Corea, I believe to a greater number of human beings (indeed no less than one-third of the human race) than any individual had been accredited before.' This was surely bombast or facetiousness, for in fact apart from accreditation as Superintendant of Trade in the Treaty Ports, it is highly doubtful if the inclusion of other countries meant very much. He was nothing if not

50

self-confident. Oddly enough, he seems to have become friendly with Mongut, King of Siam, when in 1855 he went to Bangkok to negotiate a treaty on behalf of the British government. Mongkut was learning Western culture from several sources—Latin, mathematics, and astronomy from the French scholar-missionary Bishop Pallegoix, and from American missionaries he was attempting to absorb English, becoming in the process most enthusiastic about this language. In time it became his second tongue and he signed all state papers in roman characters.

'My gracious friend,' he wrote to Bowring, 'It give me today most rejoyful pleasure to learn your Excellency's arrival here . . . . Please allow our respects according to Siamese manners. Your Excellency's residence here was already prepared. We are longly already for acceptance of your Excellency.' Bowring reproduces a facsimile of this letter with its fluently charming deformations of grammar in his book *The Kingdom and People of Siam*, published in London in 1857.[2]

Bowring himself was a competent linguist, quickly learning Chinese and using his knowledge to enjoy Chinese theatre and to make many Chinese friends. His policies toward Chinese were far-reaching in their implications but, ironically, this friend of the Chinese failed exactly where he had thought most easily to succeed. In 1856, a Chinese boat called the *Arrow*, technically registered in Hong Kong, was siezed by the Chinese at Canton. Despite doubts whether the technical details of the situation were correct or not, Bowring protested and demanded apology from the authorities. Receiving no satisfaction, he at once called for forces from England and began hostilities.

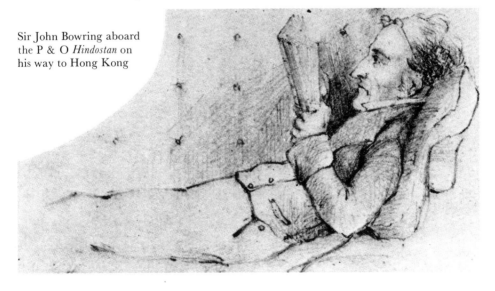

Sir John Bowring aboard the P & O *Hindostan* on his way to Hong Kong

Sir John Bowring, Governor of Hong Kong from April 1854 to May 1859. An oil painting by J. King

Bowring's private war with the Chinese led to condemnation in London, and it was decided to appoint Lord Elgin to negotiate. A bitter blow for Bowring, for this meant that he was no longer British diplomatic representative to China, merely Governor of Hong Kong. 'He had succumbed,' as the historian Endcacott writes, 'to the temptation to make events serve his sense of self-importance'. Arriving in Hong Kong, Lord Elgin simply ignored Bowring.

Elgin's private secretary, a somewhat pompous man named Laurence Oliphant, whose two-volume official history of Elgin's peregrinations in the East between 1857 and 1859 are among the dullest nineteenth

52

century reading of the type, gives a pathetic picture of Elgin's party aboard their ship, anchored for two months in Hong Kong harbour awaiting the arrival of the French plenipotentiary, Baron Gros, to complete the force destined to capture Canton, and after that to proceed north towards Peking.

'In the meantime,' Oliphant writes, 'the interval of inaction at Hong Kong ... involved an existence under circumstances of a somewhat trying character. A steamer of the Peninsular and Oriental Company, however comfortable its accommodation ... is not exactly the residence one would select in which to pass two summer months in one of the worst tropical climates in the world. Nor, even if the attractions of Hong Kong were less than they are, which is scarcely possible, is it a pleasant thing to be anchored a mile at least from the shore. During typhoons this distance doubled. We then sought shelter under the Kowloon promontary; and a dinner ashore was a serious undertaking, when it involved a midnight voyage in an open Tanka boat, possibly in a gale of wind or a pitiless storm of rain.' Getting well into his stride on the subject of the malevolence of Hong Kong and its weather, he continues: 'Sometimes we were detained on shore from stress of weather; and on the occasion of a typhoon ... the *Ava* [their ship] was obliged to keep under steam all night.

'When it was not blowing or raining, the heat was intolerable. . . . Often for days we remained sweltering on board. . . . The charms of the Club or the excitement of a game of billiards failed to tempt us. Hong Kong boasts of only two walks for the conscientious valetudinarian—one along the seashore to the right, and the other to the left of the settlement; then there is a scramble to the top of the Peak; but this achievement involves an early start, and a probable attack of fever. The monotony of life is varied by this malady alternating with boils or dysentery, so that the proverbial hospitality of the merchants at Hong Kong can only be exercised under very adverse circumstances. . . .

'It was provoking [Oliphant seems easily dismayed by most physical exertion] that a place possessing so many scenic attractions should have been so entirely devoid of other charms. Like a beautiful woman with a bad temper, Hong Kong claimed our admiration while it repelled our advances.' So indeed, one might feel of the author from time to time.

Yet, at this very same time, the Rev. R.J.L. M'Ghee, chaplain to Lord Elgin's expeditionary force, was of a somewhat different opinion. This fairly typical product of nineteenth-century Christian evangelism, went on to Peking where he witnessed (with a few crocodile tears) the sack and destruction of the Imperial Summer Palaces outside the city, and could then write: ' . . . a good work has been done. Yes, a good work, I repeat it though I write it with regret, with sorrow. . . . ' Arriving by Lei Yue Mun,[3] the narrow channel that forms the eastern entry to Hong Kong harbour, 'the town of Victoria came into view, stretching along the foot of a mountain for a distance of more than four miles [from] the Chinese town . . . to Jardine's at East Point; then there are terraces rising over each other up the steep hillside, and villa residences large and small . . . in well laid-out compounds, and built in the best English style.'

He comments that the barracks, and even the Commander-in-Chief's house, are in a 'hot and unhealthy position'. The intrepid parson then took a horse and rode along the coast to Chai Wan in the east, and back by Happy Valley ('beauteous but deceptive')—a reference to its reputation as a fever spot. The house and warehouses of Jardine and Company 'lie to the left of the road. . . . These gentlemen have their own pier and village for their workmen, and their own guard of Indian troops.' He observes that 'if there is anything of a northern breeze . . . you will meet the rank, beauty, and fashion of Victoria taking their evening drive in carriages of all sorts, from the London britscha [sic] of the governor down to the buggy or wagon of the storekeeper. But if the wind is in the other direction the haunt of fashionable society is towards Pokfulam, in the opposite direction, out of town to the west.' There is little hint of that desolation of spirit that afflicted the doleful Oliphant.

Ignored by Elgin, Bowring had his hands very full in Hong Kong. *The Times* in London summed it all up: 'Every official man's hand in Hong Kong was against his neighbour,' and went on: 'any attempt to deal in London judicially with these congeries of intrigues, accusations and animosities' must fail. And with a nicety of wit that long distinguished the House of Commons, the Colonial Secretary, Bulwer Lytton, when asked to lay the papers dealing with accusation and counter-accusation in the Colony on the table, replied that he 'shrank from the responsibility. . . . He would rather lay the table on them.' They revealed, he said, 'hatred, malice, and uncharitableness in every possible variety and aspect' of Hong Kong life. The papers had been sent to him by the Governor and dealt with the extraordinary state of disarray in which he found his colleagues and the administration of the Colony.

The protagonists in the series of resounding rows and libellous statements that ripped through Hong Kong in the five years of Bowring's governorship were of varied background and dubious intention. One source was the new Attorney-General, T. Chisholm Anstey, a man whose mission in life appears to have been a rabid and puritanical desire to root out evil wherever he saw it or even imagined it. And a chronic inability not only to mind his own business but a pathological impulsion to mind everybody else's for them. *The Times*, with restraint, called him 'a man of imperfectly-regulated energies' and it was said in London that the government had done well in sending him to one of the remote colonies—so little had he been liked in the House of Commons.

Anstey's first target was a barrister, Dr W.T. Bridges, who was accused indirectly of extortion and malpractice. Bridges was indeed a colourful character. A barrister, he had no compunction about advertising his services by means of two brightly coloured signboards in Chinese and English outside his office in Queen's Road. He was also a money-lender at exorbitant rates, and his legal offices were often incongruously stacked with goods left there as security. Accusations were levelled that Bridges had financial dealings with a man who obtained the opium monopoly while Bridges was acting Colonial Secretary. A committee of enquiry found that while he accepted a 'retaining fee' from the monopolist, this could not be regarded as *cumshaw*, the local word for 'bribe'.

But having escaped from Anstey's purgative zeal once, he was soon implicated in another enquiry, this time into the affairs of Daniel R. Caldwell, the Registrar General and Protector of the Chinese. Anstey accused Caldwell of malpractices in the licensing of brothels, and also of consorting with Ma Chow Wong, a notorious 'informer' on pirate activities who eventually turned out to be a pirate himself. This time a scandal of first class dimensions blew up. The commission of enquiry pronounced Caldwell guilty of four of Anstey's nineteen charges, but also averred that his guilt was not such as to require his dismissal or to stop him being a Justice of the Peace.[4] Anstey was suspended by Bowring but remained as a lawyer in the Colony.

During this enquiry it transpired that documents found at the house of Ma Chow Wong implicated Caldwell, and that these had been burned by Bridges when they were taken to him. The editor of the newspaper *The Friend of China*, another colourful character named William Tarrant, declared that Caldwell had been cleared by deception, by a 'contemptible and damnable trick on the part of Government'.

For this he was charged with libel. At the ensuing trial Bridges admitted to burning the papers in question as well as to being a close friend of Caldwell. Tarrant was therefore acquitted and even managed to obtain damages from the government.

In these squalid years of vituperation and corruption it is hardly surprising that a man such as Tarrant should feel impelled to act as the conscience of the Colony. His own personal history was an unfortunate one, his service with the government in Hong Kong having been terminated in 1847 in circumstances which he regarded as unfair. This made him a man with a sizeable chip on his shoulder, but quite often also with right on his side.

In July 1847, Tarrant, an assessment and valuation officer in the government, reported to his superior that the compradore of Major William Caine, who was Lieutenant Governor at the time, was taking 'squeeze money' from stall-holders in the Central Market on the grounds that he held such authority from Caine that he could put them out of business. At an enquiry the acting Attorney-General found the charges completely baseless and committed Tarrant for conspiring to bring Caine's reputation into evil repute. The Executive Council extracted from Tarrant that his information was eight or nine months old and, and was 'hearsay'. Brought later before a Justice of the Peace, he was sent to the Supreme Court for trial on a charge of conspiracy laid against him by Caine. The Governor, Davis, suspended him from his office, and wrote to the Secretary of State in London that Tarrant's original charge against the compradore was without foundation, and that Caine was blameless. Alas for Tarrant, it also came to light that he was in debt to one of the stall holders and might conceivably have had a reason for bringing the charges.

In the outcome, the case never came before the courts because of insufficient evidence to proceed. Tarrant appealed to be reinstated in his job, but it had by then been combined with another office and he was refused on this account.

With the help of friends he purchased *The Friend of China and Hong Kong Gazette* in 1850, taking the position of editor. Tarrant's zeal for the public good was doubtless genuine but his lack of political sense or tact brought him into many a dubious position. Governor Bonham wrote that the paper 'has levelled all sorts of abuse and scurrility against the local officers', and opined that its days were numbered anyway. In this he proved wrong. The paper continued sporadically to attack Caine, the latter holding his peace for the time being.

In the year 1857, Tarrant found what seemed a fine target to attack in the public interest. This concerned the Ah Lum affair. The Europeans in the Colony were in the habit of obtaining fresh bread each morning from the E Sing Bakery belonging to a Chinese named Cheong Ah Lum, and situated in Wanchai. On 15 January, large numbers of the community became ill, some seriously, and the cause was soon traced to large quantities of arsenic which had been added to the morning loaves.

Ah Lum the baker of the poisoned bread (*full-face, standing*) at the police office in Victoria in January 1857

Fortunately for the bread-eaters, the quantities were so large that the majority of those poisoned vomited at once and thus assimilated rather little arsenic. But Lady Bowring, the Governor's wife was seriously ill, and so were others. Ah Lum himself had left that morning for Macau with his wife and children, so it was assumed that it was at least with his complicity that the arsenic got into the bread. When he was brought back and tried, he alleged that he too suffered from poisoning. He was eventually acquitted, but 52 of his workmen and bakers were thrown into jail. The real jail happened to be full at the time so their place of incarceration was a police station where they were kept for four days in a room fifteen feet square. Ten were then tried, but the remaining 32 suffered in the same room for another 15 days before they were released from this Hong Kong equivalent of the Black Hole of Calcutta, and put in the proper jail. It says much for Bowring, and also for some European and Chinese citizens who protested, that their release was secured, although on the proviso that they left the Colony.

The situation was tense. Just before the poisoning, the Chinese Commissioner at Canton had instigated measures against the British, and posters all over Victoria town had appeared urging all Chinese to join the campaign against the colonizers. It was eventually decided, therefore, that the poisoning must have been ordered from Canton, but no proof was ever found. Mass arrests followed and hundreds of Chinese were deported. In that year over 26,000 Chinese left as immigrants from the Colony to the Pacific coast of America and to Australia —over 6,000 more than in the previous year. The supplying of bread was taken over by a man named George Duddell whose bakery then came into its own. But shortly afterward it was burned down, and it seems that for a time Europeans went without their fresh bread.

Tarrant, the editor, then took upon himself the indignation of the English community, sued Ah Lum for damages, and was awarded $1,010. The wily Ah Lum, set free quite suddenly, prudently and expeditiously left the Colony before Tarrant could collect his money. But the dogged editor accused Dr Bridges, acting Colonial Secretary at the time, of letting the culprit go. Bridges then brought a suit against Tarrant for libel and Tarrant was forced to pay one hundred pounds sterling in compensation—a sum that was subscribed by sympathizers who were later cited by name in the newspaper.

Ever since the 1847 affair involving Caine, Tarrant had publicly in print, and privately in conversation, attacked the unfortunate Major's 'compradoric methods' as nothing more than extracting bribes or 'squeeze'. Finally, as Caine was about to leave Hong Kong for good, he decided the time had come to clear his name once for all, and began proceedings for libel against the indomitable Tarrant after a 'particularly sharp' comment printed in *The Friend of China* in August 1859.

The shrewd Caine retained every single barrister in the Colony, thus forcing Tarrant to conduct his own defence. Caine had the last laugh, and the satisfaction of seeing his old enemy found guilty, fined fifty pounds, and sentenced to one year in prison. Publication of the newspaper ceased on 21 September 1859, and was not begun again until 13 October of the following year (and then from Canton whence Tarrant had gone on his release after only half his sentence had been served). Public indignation, even on the part of some of the jurors at his trial, and also in the British press which took up Tarrant's case, had been considerable, and questions were asked in Parliament. His release was ordered from London, but he was immediately jailed again for debt to Bridges. Public subscription again saved him, although he could have saved himself if he had left the Colony, at Bridges' suggestion, in lieu of paying the debt.

There was no doubt where public sympathy lay—with Tarrant. But for him life in Hong Kong was no longer bearable. In Canton his paper failed, and he moved to Shanghai where he published once more. He finally left for England in poor health, and on his death it was found—no doubt the irony of the action was intentional—that Tarrant had left a complete file of *The Friend of China* to the Hong Kong City Hall Library.

Tarrant's story is matched in its vituperative aspects by that of Yorick Jones Murrow, a Welshman who took charge of the *Hong Kong Daily Press* which had come into being in 1857 as the fortunes of *The Friend* dwindled. He edited the paper until 1867, involving himself in a stream of abusive, public-spirited, but libellous assertions for which he was once sentenced to six months in jail. At the Governor's suggestion (Bowring, in 1858) he was permitted to go on publishing his paper from jail, but on release, far from being grateful for this lenience, he brought an action against the Governor for false imprisonment. He lost.

It would be tedious to recount the scandals of that back-biting era in Hong Kong public and private life. Not until the 1970s was Hong Kong to see the beginnings of the process of cleansing the Augean stables of official life and business practice, a process to which the local press has responded with mixed public-spirited enthusiasm and doom-laden predictions of the inherent possibilities of the denial of British justice—a form of justice as administered in the Colony that had patently not always managed to live up to its good name elsewhere.

It is obvious that no governor could remain for long in office sur-rounded by a series of public scandals such as these, his cabinet (as it were) totally at odds with one another and with him. Once the affairs of Britain and China were taken from Bowring on the arrival of Lord Elgin, his position, even in his own eyes, became untenable, and he resigned. The curious contradictions in his character doomed almost everything he tried to do to failure. He was in favour of peace with China, yet he brought war between Britain and China, his unsuitable reforms in Hong Kong threw his government into near total disarray. When he left in 1859, the Europeans ignored his departure although the Chinese community presented him with gifts in token of what he had tried to do for them.

Curiously enough, his daughter became a Roman Catholic while in Hong Kong, took the veil, and lived on in the Colony for eleven years, after her father and mother departed for England, as one of the Daughters of Charity in the Italian Convent.

And Bowring, the man who had come with high hopes of using his liberal outlook, his languages, his love of peace, and his undoubted talent in the service of Britain and China, and of Hong Kong, must have reflected as he left for home, stripped of his diplomatic office, disliked by almost every European in the Colony, and without having succeeded in much but establishing a small museum and the Botanical Gardens—that life and fate are sometimes both cruel and unjust. He survived shipwreck in the Red Sea on the way to England, and lived on to the ripe old age of eighty.

It is tempting to speculate about the causes of this social behaviour in Hong Kong that began virtually at the Colony's inception and continued unabated, even increasing in bitterness, at least until the last of the original settlers, merchants, and other Western inhabitants had gone or died. The whole period invites detailed research in the very numerous surviving documents—official, press, private correspondence, and the published comments of visitors and others. Until such research is done we cannot know the reasons. Doubtless in a society artificially constituted chiefly for reasons of personal financial gain, a society largely released by residence in the faraway Colony from the taboos, the inhibitions, the bonds, and the boons of its origins, yet attempting at the same time to replicate that society from which it sprung (even in such matters as wearing Western clothing and eating and drinking in the manner of the day, in defiance of the six or seven months of the Hong Kong year which, in those days when the heat could not be abated, were inimical to such attempts)—doubtless in this avaricious society, the phenomena of the Colony's early decades are not sociologically surprising. The subject is one of considerable fascination and there are parallels, although doubtless partial ones, to be discovered in the social history of Shanghai, and doubtless of early Calcutta, among other settlements of the 18th and 19th centuries.

4

LAPRAIK AND DUDDELL

Shipping Tycoon, Jack of All Trades

THE early and middle years of the Victorian era not surprisingly
bred Englishmen who, for one or other reason, found it either
expedient or attractive to sail away to the new colonies in search of
fields to conquer that might prove less prosaic than those their own
land offered. The black sheep of the family, unfitted for the army, the
diplomatic service, or the ministry, either went to sea or to some long-
suffering colonial society where he was conveniently out of sight and
out of mind from the point of view of his conformist relatives in Victorian Britain. Splendid stories of patrician decay in the form of drunken
planters, Maugham-esque, gone-native sons of gospelling clergy cavort-
ing in the stinking heat of Southeast Asian places, rollicking ditties of
adulterous middle-class males in mad-dogs-and-Englishmen's land,
commemorate the pitiful, doomed attempts of numberless characters
of pure white stock to find release from the plush and pusillanimity
of high Victorian times.

Hong Kong had its share. The Colony was one of the most remote
from England, and had the reputation in early days of a place whose
mortality rate from fever was accommodatingly high—so that uncomfortable blood relations might possibly either make good (that is
money) or die off, conveniently out of touch.

There is no evidence as to the origins of Douglas Lapraik or George
Duddell. But both seem to have arrived in Hong Kong without either
work or much of that essential prop to social status, cash. The first made
a fortune, and the second made do. The stories of both still have a
familiar ring in Hong Kong where fortune-makers and those who make
out one way and another re-enact them from year to year. From
shipping to ice-making, the tycoons and the entrepreneurs are still
hard at work along the same lines in contemporary Hong Kong. So

61

The junk *Keying* berthed at Gravesend, London, on 27 March, 1848. *Opposite:* the interior of the *Keying* when she moved to Blackwall and opened to the public

Lapraik and Duddell are in a sense archetypal characters.

Douglas Lapraik arrived in Hong Kong in the early forties, and by 1845 was listed as an assistant to L. Lust, one of the first watchmakers of the Colony. By the following year he had set up his own business. 'Watchmaker' doubtless covered the more lucrative activity of chronometer repairer to the ships that frequented Hong Kong in increasing numbers. And in this way Lapraik could have become more and more deeply involved in the shipping business as a whole. His first venture in this line seems to have been as one of a group of merchants who bought a Chinese junk. There are stories, perhaps without much foundation, of how the young Lapraik went to Canton in disguise (*what* disguise would have deceived the Chinese is a matter for speculation) in order to secure this ship, their only justification perhaps being the Chinese ban on the sale of shipping to foreigners.

The junk was named *Keying*, after Ch'i-ying, the Chinese Commissioner who had been sent to Canton to deal with the problems arising from the first Opium War. His bonhomie, his apparent liking for the foreigners, who had entertained him royally, hardly met with approval from higher authorities, and he was later demoted in the Chinese government service. Sir John Davis had a high opinion of

Ch'i-ying who was 'by far the most elevated in rank, as well as the most estimable in character, of any person with whom the representatives of European states in China had ever come in contact'. But in fact his 'bonhomie' is historically open to question; for in a memorial discovered in Canton, written by him about the end of 1850, he explained his relations with the foreigners were 'to keep the barbarians in hand', and thus to hold them at a safe distance. Confronted with this document by British representatives of Lord Elgin much later (in 1858) he retired crestfallen.

The British-owned junk *Keying* that was named after him sailed from Hong Kong on 4 December 1846, carrying a complement of twelve British officers under the command of Captain Kellett, and a crew of thirty Chinese. Rounding the Cape, she encountered a violent storm and had to change course for the United States for this reason, and because of currents and the growing indiscipline of the crew. At New York it is said that up to 8,000 people visited her every day—a statement that must be doubted if only because of the vessel's size (which was 160 feet long and just over 25 feet in the beam).

From there she crossed the Atlantic in fine time, disproving the

opinion widely held at the time that all junks were river and coastal vessels (the fact that it had been disproved centuries before by the epic voyages of Cheng-ho from China to the east coast of Africa, was little known then). In the Thames she tied up at Blackwall and opened her hatches with an exhibition of Chinoiserie. The *Illustrated London News* of 1 April 1848 gives a sketch of the vessel and a graphic description of her and her voyage.

A writer on Hong Kong history, Dafydd Evans, has revealed[1] the comments of no less a writer than Charles Dickens on the subject in the *Examiner* of 24 June of that year.

'The shortest road to the Celestial Empire is by the Blackwall railway,' he begins sarcastically. The squalour of this trip through some of the poorest areas of Victorian London served only to transport the passenger 'in half a score of minutes' into China. Dickens used the chance of visiting the vessel to air his astonishingly primitive and ill-informed opinions on the subject of China. It is a literary performance of some gusto and considerable foolishness, lacking in either humour or wit, but perhaps in line with the spirit of much of Dickens the man—a zenophobe if ever there was one, parochial in the extreme.[2]

The *Keying* was a great success, however, with the crowds in London. She was eventually broken up on the Mersey and her timbers used in the construction of ferry boats. Not, however, before the somewhat bizarre spectacle was witnessed, at the London anchorage, of the ageing Metternich, now fallen from the heights of power, being shown round the ship by none other than the Duke of Wellington.

But we have come far from our starting point in Douglas Lapraik. Years later he was to aver that he never made a penny out of the venture. In other matters he did. By whatever means he obtained the capital, only a little over thirteen years after his arrival in Hong Kong he owned docks and his own shipping company that was later to be named The Douglas Shipping Company Limited. 'Of all the public enterprises,' wrote the *Hongkong Telegraph* on 28 July 1883, 'commenced in Hong Kong of late years, not one has had a more genuine ring or shown more favourable prospects than that which was circulated the other day.

'The object of this important undertaking is to acquire and carry on a long established and lucrative business founded in 1860 by the late Douglas Lapraik and since ... associated with the popular local firm of Messrs Douglas Lapraik & Co. There was a time when the whole of the coasting trade between Hong Kong and the ports of Swatow, Amoy, and Foochow ... was practically monopolised by the admirably ap-

pointed fleet of steamers bearing the Maltese Cross flags of this ...
Hong Kong firm.'

The fleet at this time had seven vessels varying in size from 406 to
1,999 tons. At the time when the company converted itself into one of
limited liability in 1883, its founder had long left Hong Kong. But the
legacy of this early shipping magnate continues with us to the present
day.

In the early 1930s there was a clock on the second floor of the old
Post Office, now demolished in favour of a more modern building, that
bore the name 'D. Lapraik & Co.' on its face. The original plans of
the old Post Office called for a clock tower, but for one reason or another
this was not built, and it is possible that the Lapraik clock installed in
the building had another origin.

Pedder Street about 1880. *Overleaf:* the clocktower seen in the previous photograph

65

In 1863 a clocktower of imposing proportions which, in those days, constituted no special obstruction to traffic, was built at the junction Pedder Street and Queen's Road, the clock donated by Lapraik. It appears in many an old photograph. By a couple of decades later it was an increasing hazard to traffic and the protracted and comical agitation to have it demolished, began.

In a letter dated 26 March 1884, written from 2, Club Chambers, Hong Kong,[3] Mr M.J.D. Stephens addressed the Colonial Secretary: 'Sir, I have the honor of forwarding for presentation to His Excellency the Governor a Memorial by the Inhabitants of Hong Kong for the removal of the Clock Tower.' The Memorial (a curious word to use, one usually applied to missives sent to the Emperor of China by his officials) suggests alternative sites for the tower, since it was obstructing traffic, 'the line of foot passenger traffic on that side of the Queen's Road . . . is forced into the carriage road and passenger traffic thereby becomes greatly impeded and oftentimes dangerous by passing chairs and vehicular traffic.' The reply was that the matter would be investigated and, later, that it must wait for more urgent public work to be done.

A year later, Mr Stephens was writing again, but to no effect. In December, 1888, just before Christmas, he returned to the attack. 'The traffic in Queen's Road having in the meantime greatly increased the Tower impedes traffic considerably, and it is often dangerous crossing the road, when chairs and vehicles come from the other side of the Tower unobserved.' And also, because of building and the growth of trees, the clock could be seen from very few points. The government curtly refused to remove it.

Ten years later, the presevering Mr Stephens 'ventured' to write again, this time to the Director of Public Works. He sums up the previous correspondence, notes the Tower still impedes traffic and is a danger to pedestrian and 'ricksha', remarking that it was only since the 1884 letter that the ricksha came into use in Hong Kong in numbers (it was invented in Japan by a Western missionary after 1870). 'Besides since this time . . . the streets are more used by Europeans on foot. . . . It is practically impossible for the pedestrian to pass by a carriage when between the Clock Tower and the Hong Kong Hotel.'

Only the clock was the gift of Lapraik, while the tower was built by public subscription, and Mr Stephens suggests that since a memorial stained-glass window was placed in the Cathedral in memory of Lapraik, that his memory will be perpetuated anyway, even when the Tower is removed. 'When the time arrives . . . the wonder will be how was it that it was not removed before.'

But nothing happened, and it is to be presumed that the indefatigable Mr Stephens gave up in disgust and took another road past the Hong Kong Hotel. Not until 1913, twenty-nine years after his first letter, was the Clock Tower finally removed. We may wonder if Mr Stephens was still alive, and also speculate why no one saw fit to dedicate a memorial to that unusually earnest citizen.

At about the same time that he was donating the clock, Douglas Lapraik was building himself a miniature castle in the nearby country-side at Pokfulam. Douglas Castle, as it came to be known, was small but splendid. Much of the floor space was taken up by the foundations of towers with machicolated battlements and other fripperies, functionless but indubitably prestigious. Two generations of his family lived there after him, administering the thriving shipping line. Among them was the mother of the English cartoonist and author, Osbert Lancaster. She was born there and recalls the earthquake of 1878 when furniture began to dance around the bedroom floor. The machicolations, however, survived earthquake and much else, and the part of the original castle still extant (and now incorporated in later buildings) gives some idea of its anachronistic splendour. The place is now a student hall of resi-dence for the University. In their magazine, the students roundly declare that they 'defend their hall with something akin to chivalry'. And, predictably, they go on to quote Shakespeare's 'This castle hath a pleasant seat; the air nimbly and sweetly recommends itself to our gentle senses.' Doubtless these were the sentiments of Douglas Lapraik too, before he left it for retirement in England.

But history has its little continuations. In the 1970s there still exists a company named George Falconer whose founder was the senior assistant to the man to whom Lapraik sold his watchmaking business in D'Aguilar Street in the early 1860s.

The apparent rapidity and ease with which Lapraik made his Hong Kong fortune, is not paralleled by the story of his contemporary, George Duddell. Where he came from seems not to be known, but he first appears in the Colony's records in March 1845, when he secured the opium monopoly for $8,520 for one year. He did rather well out of this for he was paid by a Chinese syndicate a monthly sum of $1,710 for the privilege of operating it. The institution was abolished in 1847 since no one could enforce the monopoly, and its value had declined.

Duddell's principal occupation was as an auctioneer. With several others, he successfully petitioned the Governor, in 1848, to abolish the two-and-a-half per cent levy on all sales by auction, and to increase the annual auctioneer's licence from $50 to $100 instead. At this time he was friendly with a man named Holdforth who was assistant Magistrate and Sheriff, from whom (by illegal and unethical purchase, it was said at the time) he acquired the right to hold 'Sheriff's Sales', and with whom he worked closely, knocking down cheap lots to himself. The shady side of the business raised its head in 1850 when Duddell was empowered to sell a ship at auction, and knocked it down to himself. At the re-auction ordered by the Chief Justice, the ship was sold for $400 more and the wayward auctioneer came short of his profit. But, luckily for him, Duddell's peculations only rarely came to light, and when the Government Auctioneer was murdered in 1857, Duddell got his job.

Diversifying, Duddell established a bakery, as we noted already. He signed a contract with the government to supply the armed forces with bread and biscuit for one year from 1 April 1857. In mid-January, however, due to the Ah Lum poisoning affair, when 'this diabolical proceeding placed the British authorities in great difficulty and exposed the whole British community to great peril,' Duddell agreed to begin his contract two months earlier. He himself believed that this made him a marked man because of the state of Chinese opinion at the time about Europeans, and that rewards had been offered by the Canton authorities for his death. He may well have been right, but instead of his head falling, his bakery and stocks of flour and biscuits were burned to the ground on 6 March 1857. He sought but failed to get government compensation.

The proposal of 1846 to build an ice house by public subscription prompted the Governor (Davis) to send a sketch of the site to the Colonial Secretary in London. The sketch shows a proposed road, later called Ice House Street, as it still is today, running parallel to a street named Duddell Street. It would seem from this that Duddell at least had a fair amount of property there by then. When the Ice House Company was dissolved in 1851, Duddell bought the building. He already had much other property, as a lease of 1849 shows.

His fortunes had waned in the land value slump of the late forties, and since he was at that time the third largest landholder in the Colony he was for a time badly hit. But in the fifties when the economy of Hong Kong took an upward turn he was once more a man of substance.

69

Doubtless in the smallish European business community of those times, he and Lapraik must have known each other well enough, but there is only one recorded instance of their contact. This was in 1845 when parities were established between various British and Indian coins, and the silver dollar. The dollar went up in value because the Chinese (their own tradition behind them) preferred it. Duddell rented property from Lapraik and wanted to pay in British money. Lapraik took him to court and got an order for payment in silver dollars.

Almost the final news we have of Duddell dates from 1870 when the government bought from him some land above the Botanical Gardens for a new hospital building. Duddell wanted much more money than that offered, and made a great song and dance about the matter, whereupon the government withdrew its offer altogether. Duddell then insisted that the government's original undertaking to purchase be carried through. The land was purchased and added to the area of the Botanical Gardens. Thus—an 'inadvertant benefactor of the Colony' as the historian Endacott calls him—he passes out of Hong Kong history. But if one is to believe the *Hongkong Times* which extracted from the *Brighton Times* in England for 21 March 1873, a note saying that Duddell could not be indemnified from the unallotted balance of a certain fund (in relation to the loss of his bakery), he had by that time left and settled in the fashionable south coast resort.

But the short stretch of Duddell Street, running up the hill parallel to Ice House Street is still there, ending as it always did in a steep flight of steps to meet Ice House Street as the latter curves round. The Ice House itself from which ice was delivered each day between five and seven in the morning and two and four in the afternoon, has long since disappeared and the site is now occupied by government offices.

Those days of Lapraik and Duddell are the subject of a section in an interesting book called *To China and Back*, by a man named Albert Smith—an entertainer who visited Hong Kong in 1858.

'... From the majority [of gentlemen he met] it was difficult to get any practical hints respecting the native habits of the people themselves,' he complained; just as such a person arriving in the Colony in the seventh decade of the 20th century still finds most Westerners almost entirely ignorant of Chinese language and custom. 'The young men in the ... large Houses [companies] have a sad, mind-mouldering time of it. Tea-tasting, considered as an occupation, does not call for any

Opposite: Albert Smith, and his programme at the Hong Kong Club

VICTORIA, HONGKONG.

Programme

OF

Mr. Albert Smith's

ENTERTAINMENT,

CHIEFLY RELATING TO

THE TRAVELLING ENGLISH,

AND

THEIR AUTUMNAL PECULIARITIES

ON THE CONTINENT,

AS REPRESENTED FOR THE BENEFIT OF THE LOCAL CHARITIES,

IN THE DRAWING ROOM OF THE CLUB HOUSE, HONGKONG,

SATURDA

THE 25th

The Lecture will commence at Half   *ut two hours.*

Price of Admis

NOTICE. The Audience are res   e in their
places by the time fixed for the   will be
kept very punctually.

OFF TO

With a few words about the Ol   uth-Eastern
Railway, *via* Dover, Calais, Lille,   . Of BROWNE
and his peculiarities abroad, especi   ration.

SONG, " THE Y   ER."

Of the four Miss SIMMONDS's   so ; FLORENCE, the
fast ; JANE, the neither   the unpleasantly
candid. Also   raveller ; and of
Mr. MUFF, a

The F   erl (the
German

Betw   nen

great employment of the intellect, and I never saw one of the young clerks with a book in his hand. They loaf about the balconies of their houses, or lie in long bamboo chairs, smoke a great deal, play billiards at the Club, where the click of the ball never ceased from earliest morning, and glance over the local papers. These journals are mostly filled with the most uninterestingly incomprehensible, and infinitesimally unimportant local squabbles, in which the names of Mr Anstey, Mr Bridges, Ma-chow-wang (a convict pirate), Sir John Bowring (Governor) and Mr Caldwell are pitched about here and there.

'To breakfast with Sir John Bowring, walking up pretty winding paths with wild convolvulus and bamboo blooming all the way. Found him in the garden, with a native, cutting flowers for the table ... At 7.30 p.m. to dine with Mr John Dent, whose French cook sent up one of the best dinners I ever sat down to, in London or Paris. A claret cup was also a thing to recollect.

'And we drove along the Happy Valley, and passed Mr Jardine's at East Point. . . . Granite rocks coming nearly down to the sea—water rills falling—Chinese graves and fishing stations all the way. Many people out in carriages, and some Yankees in light iron four-wheeled trotting gigs; and also a string of Mr Jardine's horses, led out for airing by black grooms. . . . It is terribly hot tonight. I am finishing my diary in my room in the costume of an ancient statue—the crickets wearing themselves out with creaking, and the click of billiard balls, and perpetual cries of 'Boy!' sounding all over the Club. This night, mosquitoes, cockroaches, small red ants, prickly heat and a rat, keep me very lively.'

Albert Smith captured the fancy of the local populace—both English and Chinese. People, it seems, could hardly do enough for him. Even the great Mr Lapraik helped him with shopping; and the Club was agog.

When he left, the *Hongkong Daily Press* said: 'Mr Albert Smith must leave China a happy man.' He had afforded the community 'the felicity of witnessing his powers of entertaining ... and for the benefit of Charity, evinced noble feeling. . . . . The Chinese were greatly puzzled what to make of [him]. He mixed with them as much as he possibly could, and tickled them immensely with his drollery. They saw he was a celebrity among his countrymen, and ... came to the conclusion he was something between a sage and a funny devil. . . . They paid him a compliment that was never before accorded to any white mortal man.[4]

'At the time appointed for Mr Smith to leave the Club, a very handsome sedan chair awaited him, with all the paraphernalia of a celestial procession—music to drive away demons ... flags with devices setting forth his virtues and talents. . . . Thus conveyed, he was carried through the town down to the wharf of the P & O Company, where he embarked amidst a display of firecrackers.'

So it was not impossible for a European with nothing to give but, apparently, his entertaining self, and that freely, to become a popular hero with the Chinese. In the history of Hong Kong, this has been a rare event, and it is hard to escape the impression that the chasm between the two races was one largely of Western making.

A Chinese family group in the latter part of the nineteenth century

5

A TRIO OF IRISHMEN

A̲FTER the departure of Sir John Bowring things slowly settled down in Hong Kong. The first of a succession of five Irish governors, the bravely named Sir Hercules Robinson, took office. Sir Hercules and his two immediate successors were of widely divergent character, a fact reflected vividly in the history and society of the Colony. But broadly speaking the period during which they governed, from 1859 to 1877, was one of growth and the gradual putting in order of the Hong Kong house. A measure of order, at least.

We have already heard much and will hear more of the expatriate society of Hong Kong. But most of it concerns the segment of society composed of the dominant class. Most of the English and other Westerners who formed the early and later society of the Colony came from the middle classes (even though some of them swiftly jumped up several rungs of the social ladder and assumed the status of pseudo-upper class, at least in their own and in the colonial community's opinion). It was they who headed departments of government and staffed its upper echelons, or were officers in the army and navy; it was they who ran big businesses (the *taipans* of popular speech) employing a work-force that was mostly Chinese.

But there was another category of Westerners called *pong-paan*, those in or out of uniform working in the capacity of overseers, engineers, men with some special Western skill not to be found among the Chinese; and also police, and others. Added to this were the passing hordes of sailors from the merchant and naval vessels, and the longer-staying soldiery. The lowest on the social scale were termed beachcombers (although they were not strictly speaking that), and outcasts, men who had arrived in Hong Kong by one means or another, many having jumped ship, and who drifted from one menial job to another, despised alike by Westerners and Chinese.

74

All those below the rank of *taipan* and their families and visiting friends and relatives were lumped together, much in the manner of the middle class in England in those Victorian days, as the lower classes, or the lower orders. There were also numerous brothels mostly populated by Chinese prostitutes, but others had Western women from as far afield as San Francisco, Portugal, and a few British women also. Periodic purges of these brothels were carried out and the inmates subjected to all the rigours of a smug middle-class society whose self-righteousness perpetuated the hypocrisy accepted as the norm of their class. Doubtless the services of the prostitutes were largely used by Chinese and by the so-called lower class men, but not exclusively, by any means.

Little enough is known of this whole stratum of life. A start has been made—manfully, indeed, for the subject is not an easy one to research—by H.J. Lethbridge, on discovering more about this segment of society. Without such knowledge our picture of society in the Colony must necessarily remain unbalanced—as lopsided as was that of a *taipan*'s wife who would know little of the lower classes since she seldom came into contact with them.

The artificiality of the whole social structure of a colony such as Hong Kong is apparent. It was a society formed not as the result of interaction and evolution of a long-settled human community, but as the result of commercial enterprise by a small segment of such a society in a foreign place, with an unskilled work-force of another race. It not only attempted in its upper segment to replicate middle class life at home in Britain, but took exaggerated attitudes that were in some instances caricatures of middle class values of the period. And of course, to all but a few members of this Western society, the Chinese were regarded as a worker class that had to be segregated as far as possible from the ruling class. No Westerner who lived with or married a Chinese was acceptable in polite society. But there is some evidence that a sizeable number of lower class Westerners lived in Chinese residential communities, that some even spoke a little Cantonese, and that if not exactly accepted by the Chinese (who were quite as zenophobic as Westerners), at least managed to rub along with their neighbours, being outcasts from their own race.

Such, briefly and inadequately, is the picture of Hong Kong society into which Sir Hercules Robinson at thirty-five years of age, together with his wife and infant daughter, was injected in September 1859. He was the Colony's youngest Governor.

Young though he was, his was no haphazard appointment, but the result of careful selection to ensure that a man of firm character would replace Bowring and—hopefully—restore order to the scandalous situation in Hong Kong, put a stop to its petty wars, and still the vituperation of those libellous and defamatory citizens whose suits and sallies had made the place notorious. The new Governor was lucky. Most of the old lags had already left or were soon to leave. So he started with a nearly clean slate, at least as far as his top aides were concerned. The faithful Caine had gone, the rather sadistic Anstey had been dismissed from office, and the bibulous Hulme left in 1860. Charles May of the police, and the Registrar-General, Caldwell, remained and were suspected of doubtful behaviour—Caldwell to be suspended as the result of an enquiry, and May to be exonerated. The old rogue Bridges left before the Caldwell enquiry. That left only Mercer, Sir John Davis's nephew, who had arrived with his uncle in 1844 and did not finally leave until 1867.

Mercer, a man denied what he had quite rightly expected to get, the governorship of Hong Kong, after administering its affairs for a total of something like three years, finally left on sick leave, and was permitted to retire on pension while in England at the early age of forty-five. Governor Bonham had reported of him that he had a 'capacity far above the office he holds', that of treasurer of the Legislative Council, and that he was an elegible candidate for Colonial Secretary. Since Mercer was at the time only twenty-six, this was praise indeed. At the age of thirty-two he was appointed Chief Magistrate, a position that was at once altered on the recommendation of Caine who pointed out to London that Bowring and Bonham had both agreed that Mercer should be Colonial Secretary and Auditor-General. Bowring, in fact, was in two minds about Mercer and wrote to Sir George Grey, Secretary of State, that he was 'one of the most accomplished men in the Colony but an unwilling reformer'.

Unfortunate as Mercer was in his colonial service, he left without the usual campaign of smears, justified or unjustified, having appeared in Hong Kong's unbridled press. But his pique was evident, for, soon after arriving in London he published a volume of *Addresses presented to W.T.M. ... recently Acting Governor of Hong Kong*. And, having got the publishing bug under his skin, two years later he produced *Under the Peak; or, Jottings in Verse written during a lengthened residence in the Colony of Hong Kong*—a volume of over 300 pages published by the disreputable John Camden Hotten. As a writer on the subject, H.J. Lethbridge, remarks:[1] 'That Mercer should have entrusted his precious verses to such a man

76

is . . . startling.' Hotten published what were in those days thought to be 'fleshy' poetry by none other than the comparatively innocuous Swinburne, but also published such titillating items as *A Discourse on the Worship of Priapus*. Doubtless Mercer paid his own costs for publishing, but one may speculate why he chose this among the variety of minor and fly-by-night 'publishers' of the time. Hotten was to succumb, four years after Mercer's *Under the Peak*, from indulging in a 'surfeit of pork chops'. Five of the poems in his book deal with Hong Kong subjects, the most confidently banal of which is entitled 'The Chinaman's Grave'.

> *Oh Chow, or Wong! or by whatever name*
> *Men call'd thee, or the Gods may call thee now,*
> *Why so extravagantly vast thy claim*
> *To mortuary earth upon the brow*
> *Of yon fair hill? If all men spread as thou*
> *No room for things created would be found*
> *Throughout the Seric land, but all the ground*
> *Would teem with graves, and well might it be said*
> *That living ones were pushed from off their stools*
> *By men all useless, now that they are dead*
> *And vanished. Did Confucius leave no rules*
> *To bind a soul's ambition by the tomb?*
> *Then let survivors show themselves no fools*
> *But dig thy bones up to make elbow-room.*

Line three refers to the omega-shaped shape of the South Chinese tomb, cut into a propitious hillside and forming a spreading cusp, faced with stone or plaster, to which relatives each Spring Festival repair to sacrifice. Lethbridge calls his article on this aspect of Mercer: 'Hong Kong's Poet Laureate?' Which, with extreme economy of means, puts the matter in its place.

Mercer and others departed, we may pause to wonder what the young Irishman and his wife thought of Hong Kong, coming straight from the West Indies island of St Kitts, a much older colony, where life must have been simpler, more open, and less troubled with internal backbiting.

A contemporary report by an English naval officer, Henry T. Ellis, in a book published in 1859, tells something of the upper crust of the English community. 'The English residents at Hong Kong . . . were divided by exclusive feelings, which rendered society far less agreeable than it might have been had a better understanding existed between them. As each little coterie was headed by its own peculiar lady patroness, it was a difficult matter to find any half-dozen who would meet any other half-dozen, without evincing mutual marks of contempt or dislike. Naval officers ... mixed little with them, and caring as little who sank or who swam in these turbid waters, had the best opportunity of judging of the game, which was often more amusing than edifying. The most absurd part of this purse-proud stuck-up-ism, was that with the exception of a few Government employees, they were all more or less rowing in the same boat, i.e. striving to amass as many dollars as opportunity would admit of: and though some were called merchants, and other shopkeepers, such was the undercurrent of retail speculation, that it was hard to define where one batch ended and the other began.'

So much for Hong Kong expatriate society in those days. In essence it had little altered a century later when the same class of merchants, shopkeepers, and their wives were even more prosperous and often just as stuck up. Fortunately, the new Governor, Sir Hercules, had a great deal more to do than bother with the society of the day. But his wife must have suffered. Robinson described his new charge, Hong Kong, as 'publicly and socially ill at ease with itself'. His opinion in his first annual report was that it was 'so totally unlike any other British dependency ... in many respects so grotesquely anomalous'.

Eitel, the historian, who must have known Robinson, describes him as 'affable and possessed of pleasing social manners'. A part of his success, he continues was due to the 'extensive and beneficial social influence of Lady Robinson'.

The new Governor was not an innovator in the real sense of that word, but many reforms undertaken in his time had the effect of renewing the strength of the Colony, and refurbishing its image. His reform of the shady civil service whereby officers in public positions were to be chosen for their suitability and not just because they happened to be men on hand in Hong Kong, was backed up by the institution of a cadet system in which young men from England underwent a two-year training before being appointed to governmental positions.

Hong Kong stamps from 1862 to 1962 when the design was changed

The British warship *Chesapeake* at gunnery practice in Hong Kong harbour, 1860

Kowloon peninsula was ceded in 1860 after the events in Peking.[2] The Government *Gazette* began to be published in Chinese as well as English. A Post Office under Hong Kong control was opened in the same year and the first Hong Kong 'stamp labels', as they were then quaintly known, were issued in 1862, the design remaining much the same until the reign of Edward VII in the twentieth century. In fact the original Hong Kong Post Office was established in August 1841, when mail from the Expeditionary Forces was placed under the control of Mr T.G. Fitzgibbon. After a short term he expired and was replaced by Mr D. Mullaby who set up shop in a wooden hut somewhat above the site of the present St John's Cathedral. In the following year the office of Postmaster General was instituted, the oldest government title in Hong Kong, and filled by Mr Robert Edwards at the munificent salary of $50 per month with an extra amount of $50 to pay his assistants and buy stationery and the like. The first letters marked as originating in Hong Kong seem to have arrived in England, at Falmonth, in 1843, and in July of that year prepayment of letters to England was begun.

The British government sent out a postmaster, Thomas J. Scales, in the spring of 1844, his job entailing the handling of about 7,000 letters a month. There are amusing stories of ships' captains handing over to him great wads of mail all impacted into lumps by the sealing wax that had melted and adhered to every surface during the voyage out. Scales was even accused of swindling on postal charges—indeed it would have been surprising if he had *not* been accused of something in the climate of the times—and having submitted his complaint at this accusation he soon afterward passed away.

Reclamation of the foreshore went on apace, and the Post Office found itself further and further from the harbour. In 1846, it was moved from Garden Road to a handsome neo-classical building on the corner of Wyndham Street and Queen's Road. The man in charge at the time—a Mr Hyland—lived on the waterfront and noted that much

A tennis party on Christmas Eve, 1879. *Opposite:* a five dollar note issued by The Chartered Bank in 1871

mail was collected by avid citizens directly from the vessels as they tied up in the harbour. He sent off a dispatch to London to the effect that the Post Office ought to have its own pick-up boat, and this duty was eventually given to the Harbour Master, Lieutenant Pedder.

From May 1860, the Hong Kong government took charge of mail, making its own separate arrangements with other countries in this regard.

Once more, as years passed, the Post Office found itself inland, and it was announced in 1903 that a new building would soon be begun to house it on the reclaimed land in Connaught Road. 'Lin Woo Hop Yik are . . . opening up foundations for a building which, when finished, will reveal the most imposing of Hongkong's structures.'

We have already noted that the result was not quite what was planned, the clock tower being missing; and the opening did not take place until 1911. It proved a popular building, many government departments moving into its various floors. Its subsequent history is not particularly notable except for efficiency. But on the special issue of a limited number of two-cent Queen's Head stamps overprinted in black, in January 1891 (to commemorate the half century of Hong Kong), such a stampede occurred that two Portuguese were crushed to death and a Dutchman appears to have been *beaten* to death.

Banking facilities expanded—the old Oriental Bank that had opened its branch in Hong Kong in 1845, acquired its first competitor in the Chartered Mercantile Bank of India, London and China. These were joined by two more, one of which was the Chartered Bank of India, Australia and China, in 1859 (only six years after its first Charter in

England), and still one of the city's leading banks. Then in 1864 the Hongkong and Shanghai Banking Corporation was set up with local merchant capital. This great bank, too, has lasted through the years. All the banknotes of the Colony today are issued by the Chartered Bank, the Hongkong and Shanghai Bank, and the Mercantile Bank.

Robinson was at pains to reform both police and judiciary, attempting to raise the former from its state of near total corruption at lower levels, and to professionalize the latter. Laudable ambitions.

The one field in which he was unsuccessful was the knotty problem of health and sanitation. The report of the Colonial Surgeon in 1860 stated that drainage and sewage disposal 'had never yet received adequate attention'. He condemned the inadequacy of the hospital which had no wards for infectious diseases and no provision at all for treatment of Chinese. Besides, it possessed no baths which, he remarked sarcastically, were 'often most useful aids to medical treatment'. The picture of Hong Kong in those days is a squalid one in many ways. The prison stank overpoweringly, and was overcrowded with prisoners often fettered in such a way as to leave permanent deformities. In the streets the refuse bins were used by the Chinese as lavatories, and the collection of that euphemistically termed but rich material known in the East as 'night soil'—human excreta—left a lot to be desired. On these matters little that was concrete was done in Robinson's time. But he did manage to improve the water supply, although the increase in demand for water soon caught up with the improvements—a story to be repeated over and over again down to the present.

One of the problems in Hong Kong was the almost complete separation of the residential areas for Chinese and Europeans. Conditions in the former were not really known in detail. While Bowring had the right idea that the physical and social gulf should be closed, Robinson wanted to retain it. 'My constant thought,' he wrote to the Colonial Secretary in London, 'has been . . . how best to keep them [the Chinese] to themselves and preserve the European and American community from the injury and inconvenience of intermixture with them.' This sentiment reflected then and for a long time to come the general Western attitude in the Colony.

The Chinese population at the beginning of Robinson's time numbered about 86,000, while the non-Chinese were only 1,611. By the time he left Hong Kong the total population was 125,000, of which only just over 2,000 were non-Chinese. The convulsions of the T'aip'ing rebellion in China were the principal cause of the huge influx of Chinese. With increasing population came bigger revenue. During Robinson's time government revenues increased three hundred per cent.

The impression that Sir Hercules Robinson's rule in Hong Kong gives in broad terms is of sensible modernization in many ways, and of a Colony taking its first major step into adulthood. When he left, it was a safer, somewhat less corrupt place to live in—at least for the minority, the Westerners. But the Chinese population also benefited to some extent. There was a general expansion of trade, and by 1865 local industries were developing fast. In that year there were 427 ships' chandlers, 93 boat builders, 20 rope-making factories, and a dry dock.

Education made some strides, both official and in the form of missionary and other charitable schools. One of these, set up by Miss Jane Baxter who came to the Colony in 1860, was named the Diocesan Native Female School, and its young Chinese girls were taught in English instead of in their own language. The result was as amusing as it was unexpected—most of them promptly became the mistresses of Europeans! The horrified Miss Baxter—a spinster of unimpeachable integrity—realizing her mistake hurriedly switched to boys and Eurasian children.

There are other interesting sidelights on life in Hong Kong at about this time. Even within two years of Captain Elliot's annexation of the island there were said to be 'hotels . . . quite up to date and comfortable', some of them equipped with billiard tables. By 1860, an old directory of Hong Kong lists the 'hotels and taverns', nearly all of them on Queen's Road. Any Englishman of those days with the intention of doing that very English thing, a pub-crawl, would have found he had twenty-seven possible ports of call on that road, ranging from The Bombay Tavern, kept by Joze Fernandez, and the British Queen, to the Old House At Home, kept by J.F. Borges, and the White Swan, 'Prop. Joachim Caldeira' in Queen's Road West. But, even back in 1847, there had been twelve taverns in Queen's Road. One of these, which—alas—did not survive to 1860, was called The Beehive, and its sign outside the door 'flaunted a piece of verse'.

> *Within this hive, we're all alive, and pleasant is our honey:*
> *If you are dry, step in and try, we sell for ready money.*

On the first of January 1865, just a month or two before Sir Hercules left, all those taverns of Queen's Road were lit up at night by the new gas street lighting. It must have felt that the Colony was becoming very sophisticated indeed.

Precisely a year after the Governor's departure his successor, Sir Richard Graves Macdonnell, arrived. The disillusioned Mercer, still in Hong Kong, having administered the government for a year since Robinson left, and having been turned down in his request for a governorship, vented his spleen on the new Governor by permitting him to arrive at Government House and find it completely unprovided with even the commonest household necessities. A year later he left the Colony an embittered man, unable to get on with Macdonnell. The Governor was kind. He called Mercer a 'gentlemanly, scholarly person', and said he seemed 'discontented and used up'. Thus the last of the old brigade of administrators vanished from an increasingly professional scene.

Macdonnell started as a new broom and went on trying hard to sweep clean for his whole tour of duty. In a few months he had outlined a series of reforms dealing with taxation, house and servant registration, local shipping, deportation of criminals, and the prevention of piracy. Finally, convinced that in the somewhat depressed economy of the times, the Colony was heading for bankruptcy, he borrowed $80,000 from the Hongkong and Shanghai Banking Corporation. In fact the recession that had set in forced the closure of the famous rival of Jardine's, Messrs Dent & Co., in 1867, and brought about the failure of one bank. The Mint that had been set up was closed since it lost money in making it. Its equipment was sold to Japan.

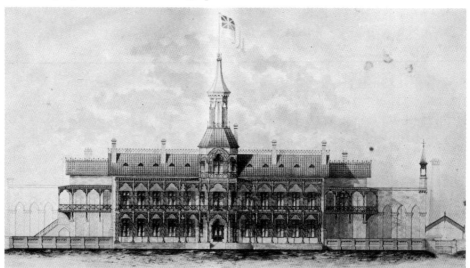

The architect's drawing for the Mint in Hong Kong, dated 1864

Among the more pressing matters were the suppression of rampant piracy—a nut that Macdonnell tried hard but failed completely to crack—and gambling. In a long exchange with two Secretaries of State for the Colonies, he argued and argued until he had wrung from London permission to license certain gambling places in order to control the affair, and to use the money for specific ends such as further control of gambling and to help build a Chinese hospital. But he became bogged down in the controversy and defended his views with too much zeal.

The Tung Wah hospital which received gambling license money came into being in a roundabout way. Soon after Macdonnell arrived, it was discovered that a temple named I Ts'z was being used as a death-house where the aged and ailing were sent to spend their last days (the Chinese have always disliked a death in the house), and was also being used to store the coffined dead until the most appropriate, geomantically decided, day for burial. The Registrar-General (who was also Protector of the Chinese) commented on 'dead and dying huddled together indiscriminately in small filthy rooms.' The local press took it upon itself to castigate the Chinese for their inhumane attitude, and some of the more wealthy Chinese appear to have been shamed into action. A site for the hospital was described officially as a 'gift from the Queen', and the Chinese subscribed the bulk of the money to build it. The Governor opened the Tung Wah hospital in 1872. Today, over a hundred years later, it flourishes and, vastly extended in its scope, does great work for the sick.

Macdonnell, from 1870, was the first governor to find himself in the (by turns) useful and frustrating position of being at the end of a tele-graph line to London. A submarine cable was laid to Shanghai, and from there messages went by the Danish Trans-Siberian land-line. He was also the first to be visited by a member of the British Royal family when the Duke of Edinburgh came to open the new City Hall in 1869. This was the crowning glory of the day, a building in what was thought to be the most elegant and refined style containing a museum, library, ballroom, supper room, a theatre, and a hall. Two years earlier, Sir Richard had laid the foundation stone and made a very long speech. In its midst he had permitted himself a small passage of humour which doubtless lightened the prosy quality of the rest. Referring to the Chairman, Mr Rennie (a mill-owner who was later to go bankrupt and drown himself by jumping from a ferry with a weighted dispatch case tied to him), he remarked that 'all were so grateful for his exertions that it must add to their regret that he had not been more fortunate during the last week at the races. (Laughter). Like Hong Kong residents in general, Mr Rennie had to endure the spectacle of all the good prizes going north to Shanghai.' This was an allusion to the horses brought down by their Shanghai owners who that year apparently captured all the prizes at the race course.

The theatre in the City Hall was named Theatre Royal perhaps because Queen Victoria's son opened the building, but perhaps also because there had been a Theatre Royal in Hong Kong every year for a long time. This was a matshed building erected for performances and then demolished. In fact the first Amateur Dramatic Crops (as it was called) came into being in 1844 and appears to have had an intermittent existence most of the time after that. Some moments of high comedy have been recorded of the activities and personalities of the ADC, as it was commonly known.

A gentleman named Vincent H. Jarrett, writing under the pseudonym 'Colonial' to the local press in the mid-1930s describes some of the more hilarious incidents in his own inimitable style. Of the performance in the last of the matshed Theatres Royal, he remarks: 'The president of the ADC in the early sixties was a certain Colonel of whom it was said that he never spoiled a good story by a too rigid adherence to fact.... He had got together a company that rose to the height of Grand Opera. The leading tenor was a gunner in the battery quartered in the town.... He had however one unfortunate failing. His life was a spirited protest against the errors and extravagances of total abstinence. [He was] fairly sober during the early rehearsals, but the excitement of the coming performances generally ... delivered him into the hands of convivial friends with results that might have been expected. Having the commendable spirit of the real actor he knew the need for keeping faith with the public, so on his own urgent application he was put under arrest and kept a close prisoner in the guardroom for three days before the opening performance. On the last night, after he had made his bow to an enthusiastic audience, he was formally released from arrest, carried shoulder-high to the canteen, and given carte blanche to all the hell-brew the barman could supply.'

Hong Kong was prejudiced against actors. 'In the sixties, and ... for long after, those who acted in plays were darkly suspected of a raffishness properly disapproved of a polite society.... This unctuously rectitudinous feeling ... is illustrated with ... unconscious humour in the following newspaper criticism of one of the best known amateurs of the time.'

'"He is one of the very few amateur actors that have been brought up and educated as a gentleman. How far he has availed himself of this peculiar advantage it is not our purpose to enquire."'

'It is therefore ... not surprising that for more than thirty years all the actors adopted stage names. The *taipans* [owners or top executives] of the big *hongs* [commercial companies] objected to the names of young

The arrival of the Duke of Connaught in 1870. A triumphal arch was erected in his honour

gentlemen employed in their merchant houses appearing on theatre programmes! There was, however, no objection to the names of the same young gentlemen appearing as owners on racing programmes.

'Until 1880 all female parts were played by men . . . . Eliminating, therefore, Miss Fitzblushington, Miss Siwell, Miss Gay, Miss Dolly Varden and other obvious impersonators prior to 1880, we have little difficulty in identifying [the first actual woman on the Hong Kong stage] as Mrs Philip Bernard. Appropriately enough she faced the uplifted eyebrows of mildly shocked society in *The School For Scandal*.' Later she appeared with a Mrs Hockey who turned out to be yet another female impersonator by the name of Coxon. His friend Mr Beart also appears to have had a penchant for transvestite roles, such as his burlesque impression of a sampan woman, named The Faded Flower of Shauki-wan. But his most famous impersonation was of a later governor, Sir John Pope Hennessy who happened at the time to be unpopular with the British community. 'We learn from newspaper reports that it was only with difficulty that the production could proceed for the audience was convulsed with laughter.' The sole exception was the Lieutenant-Governor who sat rigid, his facial expression superbly controlled, from a misplaced sense of his duty. 'His Excellency was not in the theatre . . . but he was obviously not without a sense of humour for he asked Beart to lunch at Government House the following day and laughed heartily over the photographs [of Beart as himself].'

Thus did the upper crust of mid-Victorian Hong Kong amuse itself.

Macdonnell, who, a year after he arrived, called the Colony 'a mere depot' had, by the time of his departure in April 1872, probably changed his mind. Partly the alteration in Hong Kong was his own doing and

Queen's Road West in about 1870. Right, shops selling shoes and socks, fireworks, stationery; on the left, cloth shops and others. *Opposite:* in another part of the road, See Fay, photographer, is at No. 26

partly it was due to the efforts of a growing Chinese population which, through the Governor's actions in some respects, was being integrated if not socially, then financially with the ruling class of the Colony.

The third Irish Governor in succession was Sir Arthur Kennedy, a man with a strong Irish accent, a large sense of humour, and a genial personality. Under his firm, kindly rule the Colony was quiet, and little of great moment took place. But Hong Kong was far from being the law-abiding place it ought to have been, as a certain visiting naturalist discovered. Dr Cuthbert Collingwood recounts in his book *Rambles of a Naturalist* how he had been warned by friends before he came to Hong Kong of the activities of footpads, but that other friends had said they had never been attacked, even in China itself.

'Feeling no sense of insecurity while surrounded by busy crowds of people, I naturally . . . went into the streets . . . . I had walked down

89

Queen's Road . . . and turned into a street leading up the hill. It was just mid-day, and the streets . . . were thronged with people, all, without exception, Chinese. I found myself suddenly in the midst of a knot of some eight or ten Chinese . . . and I was just passing on, when they made a simultaneous rush upon me and pushed me down, one of them striking me on the face. . . . While several pinned me to the ground . . . one detached my gold watch and chain, upon which they made off, leaving me to gather myself up as I best could.' And he concludes: 'The Governor, the Admiral, and many other leading people . . . were well acquainted with [the attack on him] but nothing was done which could have the slightest influence in abating the evil.'

The past echoes in the present. In Hong Kong there are seldom any witnesses to accidents or robberies. No one wants to be implicated with the police in any way at all.

A journalist writing in the *Illustrated London News* of the period gives this picture of Hong Kong at night: 'At eight at night the streets are deserted, save now and then a solitary Chinese with his paper lantern, or an Englishman returning home. The dusky-looking policeman, armed with a loaded musket, is seen in every part of the town. Not a sound is heard; it is like a town of the dead.'

The most alarming event in Hong Kong during the five years of Kennedy's governorship was the great typhoon of 1874. No one who has experienced a tropical cyclone (as the old-fashioned typhoon is now wordily called) ever forgets the experience, and some of the most vivid records of Hong Kong deal with the devastation these storms cause. Many years have come and gone in the Colony without any typhoon, but each year from May onward, coinciding with the hot weather, there is the knowledge that it is 'typhoon season' once more. Nowadays, with satellite photography, an early warning system, and the prevalence of transistor radios, the public is always suitably warned. But such is the force of those circular winds in whose vortex—the eye, as it is called— lies a treacherous calm, that tremendous damage can still occur. When the eye of the storm passes directly over the Colony, the devastation is generally most severe.

1874 saw the biggest typhoon disaster since the founding of Hong Kong, one not equalled until 1906. Gale-force winds struck without warning at dusk on the warm summer evening of 22 September, and raged throughout the night, accompanied not only by torrential rain but by an earthquake. The scene on the morning of 23 September was tragic. The city looked as though it had suffered a major military

90

Mountain Lodge, the Governor's summer house on the Peak, *c.* 1870. Only the podium remains, the area now a public park

bombardment. Not only was every matshed structure demolished, but hundreds of Chinese and European houses were in ruins, their roofs ripped off, their walls collapsed. The streets were impassable, choked with mounds of debris and fallen trees that had in some cases been uprooted by the winds and carried considerable distances. All the drains were either burst or choked. It was soon estimated that between two and three thousand people were dead or missing.

In the harbour the toll was heavy. Seven vessels were never seen again, although pieces of them were picked up. The sole ship in harbour whose anchors held was a hospital ship. Later, when her anchors were hoisted, they were found to be a mere twisted mass of iron. One British schooner (ironically named the *Seabird*) went ashore, but was later refloated. Two Spanish schooners collided, and both sank. A gunboat was thrown on to the bathhouse of a club and had later to be sold for scrap. Another boat sank after wrecking a large wharf, and a mail steamer was left high and dry at Aberdeen. Yet another three vessels sank like stones, while dozens of other craft were badly damaged.

The waterfront was in ruins, the sea wall of huge granite blocks tossed into formless heaps, and the buildings unroofed, standing in three feet of water from a combination of the rain and the tidal wave that came with the winds. On the Peak damage was also great. The Governor and his family and several guests who were at their summer retreat, Moun-

91

tain Lodge, spent a night of terror in which the whole building except for one room lost its roof. With furniture and fittings all but completely wrecked around them, they huddled together in that room until the bleary light of morning and falling winds released them.

Contemporary reports tell of the terrible screams from the Chinese quarters that could be heard even above the roaring of the wind. The wreckage of sampans and other small craft littering the waterfront road and the waters of the harbour told a tale of many hundreds of boats lost with all their occupants. Bodies by the score were washed up.

In those days the general commanding the troops was normally commissioned as Lieutenant-Governor, and in the absence of the Governor, deputized for him. But under Macdonnell, a Lieutenant-Governor named Whitfield had made blunders. As General he used also to address letters to himself in the role of Acting Governor—a 'whimsical proceeding', as someone charitably described it. So the custom was discontinued and the Colonial Secretary took over in the Governor's absence. When Sir Arthur Kennedy left for England where his wife was seriously ill in 1874, and General Colborne was informed that the Colonial Secretary and not he would administer the government, Kennedy wrote that this 'nearly caused General Colborne a fit. He fairly exploded, and judging from the effect... he must have had an enormous stock of explosive matter stored up.'

Lady Kennedy died, the news reaching the Governor as he arrived in Singapore; so he soon returned. Colborne, greatly put out, refused to attend meetings of the Executive Council, such was his rage. But, remarked Kennedy coolly, 'this was not attended by any ill effects to the Colony'. Nonetheless relations between the worlds of civil and military power were difficult. A colonial offical commented dryly: 'There is always a row between the Government and the General at Hong Kong ... and I conclude it is one of the local occupations.'

But despite typhoons, not to mention buffoons in the shape of choleric generals, Kennedy's administration was a calm enough time, its main failure being the complete inattention paid to reports of the scandalous state of the drainage and the insanitary state of the Colony at large. When Kennedy was later drowned in the Red Sea, the citizens of Hong Kong made a decision still unique—they put up a statue to him in the Botanical Gardens. The statue was removed by the Japanese during World War II. The historian Eitel remarked that Kennedy was 'one of those few men who deserve a statue because they do not need one'. Trite, but true.

6

MR HENNESSY'S PROCEEDINGS
AND LATER MATTERS

No one, as we all know—and the reading of any book of history
heavily supports the truism—is perfect. In 1877 Mr John Pope
Hennessy came to the Colony from various other governorships in
darkest Africa and dullest Labuan (in Borneo), the Bahamas and the
Windward Islands. His opinions on how to deal with the Chinese, and
on various other affairs, were well to windward of the social and political
backwaters of European opinion in Hong Kong.

The problem for a man of Hennessy's brilliance within the deadening
disciplines of the civil service, and especially in the colonies at his time,
was that his impatience to see the fruits of his ideas was altogether at
loggerheads with the ponderous bureaucratic backwardness of the mech-
anism established for bringing them to fruition. Rather than consult the
government in London—or indeed anyone else—Hennessy went ahead,
on the resignation of one member of the Legislative Council, and appointed the first Chinese to that body. The fact that Ng Choy was a good
choice, and that a Chinese voice on the Council was obviously needed,
did not mollify those in England and Hong Kong who by rights should
have been consulted and should duly have acceded to the request.

Ng Choy did not in fact serve out his full three-year term on the
Legislative Council. This was not primarily on account of any embar-
rassment he may have felt at the climate of British opinion in Hong Kong
about his appointment, but because at that time in China any Western-
educated Chinese was welcome in a country attempting the first tentative
movements toward modernization in order to counter the depredations
of the foreigners. Ng Choy was an ideal man for that cause—the first
Chinese ever to qualify as a barrister-at-law in London (at Lincoln's
Inn). That was in January 1877, and in May of the same year he was
admitted to practice as a barrister in the Supreme Court of Hong Kong.

Sir John Pope Hennessy, Governor from April 1877 to March 1882

The day of his taking his seat in the Legislative Council in the Colony (18 February 1880) 'was a great occasion of rejoicings among the Chinese community and a deputation of leading Chinese . . . called at Government House to congratulate the Governor and themselves on the appointment. This appointment was unfortunately interpreted by some members of the British community as an attempt to create an anti-English party feeling in Hong Kong.' Thus, according to T.C. Cheng,[1] did the foreign community in the Colony react to what they saw as an invasion of their preserves.

Ng Choy left for China and took a post as Secretary and Legal Adviser to the Viceroy Li Hung-chang, a man infinitely more powerful than the Governor of Hong Kong, and one whose influence on China's destiny in the latter half of the 19th century was at times crucial. Choy, now known as Wu Ting-fang, was later to be ambassador of China to the United States. He lived until 1922, having occupied a large number of onerous positions under the Republic, his last being Governor of Kwangtung province. He was described by one responsible Westerner (John Stuart Thomson in his book *The Chinese*) as 'the Chesterfield of China in all the graces of speech and manners'.

Thus Hong Kong lost a potentially valuable citizen.

It was partly Governor Hennessy's fault. Diplomacy, of which Hennessy had little, has nothing much to do with the *speedy* realization of ideas, and everything to do with the personalities involved; and has an ingrained penchant for putting off action so that natural pressures and causes will have time to show the way. Sometimes this works well (because time allows men to think again): mostly it succeeds in braking the pace of change prompted by intelligent ideas.

So Sir John Pope Hennessy (as he was to become after reaching Hong Kong), pre-eminently a man of what we would nowadays call left-wing ideas, found himself either stopped by the bureaucracy, or tearing his way through it regardless either of the consequences of the deflated egos falling like hay to the scythe all around him, or the difficulty of administering measures that have no common assent to them. He was one of the most intelligent and sensitive governors the Colony ever had. But not one of the most successful.

Naturally the merchant and Western community loathed him most of the time—even going so far as to refuse his invitations to Government House. Hennessy's statement of policy had few if any European takers. ' . . . the duty of a Governor in dealing with a community such as I find here, is to avoid the encouragement of any body or of any class, but to

95

simply hold the balance evenly between all men.' A perfectionist view which proved impossible for him to achieve. Democratic ideas were unpopular with the administration, the memsahibs, the mercantile men, the Anglican fraternity, and everyone else except the Roman Catholic Church led by Bishop Raimondi, and the Chinese community who on the whole benefited. Despite the fact that his opponents were in a numerical minority, they formed a vocal majority, and not only Hennessy's ideas but his polemical defence of them under fire, coupled with his administrative weakness, made him fair game for colonial snipers. All of this was a pity, for if he had been able somewhat to integrate the educated Chinese class, as he attempted to do by inviting them to Government House and by consulting them frequently, with even the few forward-looking and liberal elements in his administration, he might have done great things.

One of the community in the Colony who had no time for its Governor was the commander of the Hong Kong garrison. Traditionally, the Queen's Birthday was celebrated at Government House by a dinner, during which it was equally traditional for a military band to play. By the year 1880, the commander was so incensed by Hennessy's encouragement of Chinese to take up residence within 'European' areas, and in particular those near the military barracks, that he refused the formal request for the band. The two men were not on speaking terms, and the problem was solved by reference to the Colonial Office in London which naturally overruled the commander; and the guests at the dinner were entertained in the usual manner.

But Hennessy's headstrong ways soon brought him into conflict with the *taipan* of Jardine Matheson, Mr Keswick. Like many of the colonial squabbles before and after Hennessy's time, it concerned a matter that must now seem incredibly trivial, but was not thus viewed at the time— the right of entry of Chinese to the Hong Kong Museum. Keswick was chairman of the Museum which was mostly funded by business houses such as his, but was also subvented by a small grant of public money, some of which of course came from Chinese ratepayers. When the Governor found out that Chinese were not permitted access to the museum and its library except in the morning, and that the museum was then closed over the lunch period in order to be cleaned (presumably to expunge any trace of their bodily presence) before opening for Westerners only, in the afternoon, he stopped its government grant.

Once more it was the Colonial Office in London that had to take the decision which Hennessy had wished to take himself to open the museum at all times to both races. But the Secretary of State, the Earl of Kimberley, remarked in his reply that 'a little tact might usefully have replaced these impassioned harangues', and that 'garlic-eating ratepayers must be endured by those who use their money'. Thus with that special brand of British hypocrisy, the noble lord upheld the principle of British colonial justice while permitting himself a disparaging aside. What the Chinese thought of the English is little recorded in the story of Hong Kong.

Kennedy had largely ignored the reports of shocking sanitary conditions in the Colony, from preoccupation with other matters. But Hennessy largely ignored them because he thought that to impose Western sanitation on the Chinese was unjustified: and that they had their own means of coping with such matters; and that contrivances such as flush toilets were a waste of money. He set aside reports, writing: 'The Chinese inhabitants maintain that attempts made ... by successive [British administrators] to force what is called "Western sanitary science" upon them, are not based on sound principles.' The Surgeon-General of the army accused Hennessy in 1880 of a complete reversal of the policy of his predecessors in these matters. Lord Carnarvon, Secretary of State, was perhaps correct in his suggestion: 'I am afraid that a watchful eye is necessary over Mr Hennessy's proceedings.'

A couple of years before that, on Christmas night 1878, the 'Great Fire' broke out, destroying large sections of property on Queen's Road and eighteen other streets. The fire brigade discovered, when steam had been raised in the engine, that their main hose-pipe was cut in two places, by whom it was never discovered. But the old volunteer fire brigade worked manfully, and all their engines were in use for a total of 181 hours pumping sea water on the blaze.

The hazards of these days may be imagined—the naval dockyard pump didn't work at all, the soldiers sent to blow up buildings in order to limit the spread of the flames before a strong breeze, soon ran out of powder and their fuses refused to burn. Three hundred and sixty-eight houses were destroyed before the blaze was put out on the evening of Boxing Day. At the height of it, the Governor himself arrived on the scene and lent a hand with the hoses. The Peak was bathed in light, and every ship in the harbour could be seen clearly in the glare.

At least some of the slums were cleared by this great fire. And, by strange coincidence, a certain Miss Isabella Bird arrived in Hong Kong by ship as it was raging, in time to give dramatic first-hand impression of what it was like.

The Palace, Victoria, 27 December 1878. ' "It's no use going ashore, the town's half burned," said a man who came aboard from the city.' But she took a ride on a boat, and went all the same. 'Escaping from an indescribable hubbub, I got into a bamboo chair, with two lean coolies, who carried me . . . at a swinging pace through streets as steep as those of Varenna. Streets choked with household goods and the costly contents of shops, treasured books, and nicknacks lying on the dusty pavements. . . . Chinamen dragging their possessions to the hills; Chinawomen . . . carrying their children on their backs and under their arms; officers, black with smoke, working at the hose like firemen . . . . Mr Pope Hennessy, the Governor, ubiquitous in a chair with four scarlet bearers; men belonging to the insurance companies running about with drawn swords; the miscellaneous population running hither and thither . . . heavy crashes as of tottering walls, and, above all, the loud bell of the Romish cathedral tolling rapidly . . . made a scene of intense excitement.'

When, eventually, she reached the Anglican Bishop's Palace, she saw the 'wreck of the city and the homeless people . . . among the things they had saved . . . Hoses were playing on the mountains of smouldering timber, whole streets were blocked with masses of fallen brick and stone.

'The flames burst out again. It was luridly grand in the twilight, the tongues of flame lapping up house after house, the jets of flame loaded with blazing fragments, the explosions, each one succeeded by a burst of flame, carrying high into the air all sorts of projectiles, beams and rafters paraffin soaked, strewing them over the doomed city, the leaping flames coming nearer and nearer, the great volumes of smoke . . . rolling towards us, all mingling with a din indescribable.'

A 'blockade' of Hong Kong trade had begun before Hennessy arrived, and still continued. The Chinese grievance was that they lost revenue because of smuggling from Hong Kong. Nine land and sea customs stations were set up by them round the Colony, and all local small vessels were stopped and searched. But despite these measures Hong Kong's revenue and trade figures continued to rise. Hennessy remarked tartly, in justification of his policy toward the Chinese in Hong Kong, that the increase in revenues seemed 'not uninfluenced by the policy of treating all HM's Chinese subjects . . . on terms of perfect equality with the other residents in the Colony'.

However that may have been, there were other factors in the improvement of the Colony's trade and finances. As even the British Minister at Peking wrote in 1868, Hong Kong was 'little more than an immense smuggling depot'. The usual defence that it was also a free port and that it was up to the Chinese to suppress illicit trade was advanced. Not that opium was now illicit. By the Treaty of Tientsin ratified after the capture of Peking and sack of the Summer Palace in 1860, it could legally be carried in non-Chinese vessels trading to the treaty ports. But the Chinese in Hong Kong, being under British jurisdiction, were exempt from this proviso and used their opportunities to the full. The real squabble was between Canton and Hong Kong for control of the coastal and entrepôt trade.

The Chinese were the Colony's biggest ratepayers by now, and were beginning to operate steamships instead of junks. And doubtless Sir John Pope Hennessy took heart from their improved postition *vis-à-vis* the Western mercantile community. When he left Hong Kong, he was virtually ignored by the European community but well thought of by the Chinese. It is a measure of the man that in his next governorship, Mauritius, he aroused such hostility from the Western population that Sir Hercules Robinson, formerly of Hong Kong, was sent there on a mission to 'restore tranquility'. Hennessy did not alter his aim of making some sort of reality out of his opinion that the 'subject peoples', as they were called, should be treated with fairness, and an attempt at equality made.

One of Hennessy's many guests at Government House, whose stay in Hong Kong is seldom remarked, was the King of the Sandwich Islands (now the Hawaiian Islands). The royal sojourn in the Colony in 1881 is recounted in a book named *Around the World with a King* by William N. Armstrong. Due the fact that large numbers of Chinese lived in his Pacific Ocean kingdom, and also to the fact that there was a 'considerable commerce' between Hong Kong and the Hawaiian kingdom, its King was represented in the city of Victoria by a consul-general, 'a British merchant of high standing' whose name is not disclosed. This gentleman came aboard at once when the ship carring the King anchored and 'proposed to take the King to his fine residence . . . . But the twelve-oared barge of Sir John Pope Hennessy . . . suddenly appeared at the gangway, and Dr Eitel, his private secretary, brought an invitation from the Governor . . . in the name of the Queen, to be his guest.' A nice quandary arose as the King had to break his promise to his own consul on the ground that a Queen's wishes take precedence. 'At the landing we entered sedan chairs, borne by coolies, also in the Queen's livery, in which we were taken to Government House, which has a superb situation on a hill overlooking the city. Here the Governor received the King at the door, and led him to his audience-room, where he, with the suite, was presented to Lady Hennessy . . . .

'While we were taking coffee the next morning, the forts, with seven warships, fired the usual salute of twenty-one guns. From the balcony of Government House . . . we looked down on a dense mass of smoke . . . pierced with the flashing of the guns; the Hawaiian flag at the mainmast of every warship; the merchantmen also . . . hoisting the King's colours. It was a pretty sight, very noisy and warlike.

'The Government paper [the *Gazette*] contained an announcement . . . with Chinese and English words side by side.'

The King had little choice of a vessel to take him on to Thailand, and his stay had to be short as a ship was leaving for Bangkok soon. The Governor therefore decided to give two State banquets for the King. But before these, the American consul, Colonel John S. Mosby, formerly a 'confederate guerilla . . . in the Civil War . . . now as loyal to the Flag as any Union veteran', paid his call, and a rich Indian merchant, Mr Chetar, gave a lavish tiffin in Kowloon, his guests including 'English free traders, American protectionists, large-framed and clever-looking Chinamen, Frenchmen in exile from the Parisian Jerusalem, and Japanese getting into Western ways'.

'In the first toast, after tiffin, "To the Queen!" we saw the impassioned loyalty of the British colonists to their Queen, the centripetal power which makes the British Crown, with its setting of colonial diamonds, the central figure in the world.' The Governor was also present, aluding lightly in a speech to some 'trifling incidents . . . in past years, such as the killing of Captain Cook by his Majesty's predecessor.' But the British government had proposed to the Great Powers that the independence of the islands should be restored and protected. The King's spokesman made the gentle riposte that for three months the King and his suite had been British subjects (when Britain annexed the islands temporarily) 'but were extremely disloyal'. One of the King's ancestors had offered George III, in case he 'ever got into any more wars', to 'go over and help him.'

Then: 'At the two State banquets . . . the dishes, the service, and the wines were such as are found on an English table in London; and coolies patiently pulled the punkas which stirred the lifeless air in which, with the heavy food, one becomes drowsy.'

Events proved too much for the King. At the second banquet, seated on Lady Hennessy's right, with William Armstrong (the writer of the book) beside him to interpret, an amusing scene followed.

'His eyelids drooped . . . and I noticed his hand idly held his fork, and his anointed head slightly nodded . . . . I feared a nasal explosion if the King's doze should deepen . . . . It was a case of emergency.' Armstrong whispered his fears to Lady Hennessy and asked her help. 'She hesitated to break through the divinity that hedges kings, but saw that a crisis was near. Moving her fan with dexterity, she hit the royal shoulder as if accidentally, and the King opened his eyes.'

An American family built one of the early houses on the Peak after the opening of the Peak Tram in 1888

Armstrong explained in the native language that naps were dangerous. The King replied that it was so hot: 'How can I get away?' Then
he dozed off again. The resourceful Governor's lady asked Armstrong
if there was anything that would be sure to awaken the King—music
perhaps?

'She talked quietly to the major-domo, and in a minute the military
band on the balcony filled the air with the music' of the Hawaiian
National Anthem. The King woke up and was advised by Armstrong
later to decorate Lady Hennessy 'who had thrown out a life-line which
saved the royal dignity from shipwreck'.

The Governor's grandson, James Pope-Hennessy, in his book *Half-
Crown Colony*, is of the opinion that the Hennessy administration 'forms
a watershed in the history of Hong Kong.... All this earnest Catholic
Irishman tried to do in this, as in every other Crown Colony entrusted
to him, was to treat the "native races" as human beings with rights equal
to those of the Europeans.'

A dragon dance on the Praya—Des Veoux Road before later reclamation cut it off from the sea

But what was it like to be a Chinese at this time when the earnest Governor of Hong Kong was making a start on giving every one of them some measure of equality with the ruling race? The sources are few. But perhaps we may find hints amid the slightly stilted prose of a Rhennish missionary of this era, J. Nacken, who contributed in 1873, a piece to the *China Review* called 'Chinese Street-Cries in Hongkong'.[2] The editor of the *China Review* was Nicholas Belfield Dennys, a man who (in the usual manner of these days) had been sued for libel by one citizen, and accused in another case of prejudging the case in his paper. But in editorial policy Dennys was a constant and consistant sympathizer with the Chinese. The article is arch enough, but something of truth breaks through now and then:

'My friend was sitting at his desk, busy, no doubt, in framing the best-worded sentence ever penned in the East, when a howl from the street rang through the lofty verandah, and rebounded . . . from the high ceilings of the room. "That's one of those ubiquitous hawkers," said my friend angrily [one may wonder if he *really* said that] springing to his feet and rushing to the verandah. I was just in time to see a pair of broad shoulders raising themselves, and a pig-tailed head bending backwards: and then came a second edition of the howl . . . heard before.

'That was some years ago. In the mean time others like my friend must have suffered from the annoyance which led to the framing of Ordinance No. 8 of 1872, which says that:—

"Every person is liable to a Penalty who shall use or utter Cries for the Purpose of buying or selling any articles whatever . . . within any District or Place not permitted by some Regulation of the Governor in Council." '

'For the hawkers of Hongkong wooden tickets are provided which must be renewed every quarter at a cost of 50 cents. These . . . are signed by the Registrar General' and each had stamped on it a prohibition of streetcrying in Central district, 'on the great road [Queen's Road], and on the sea side. For the first quarter of this year 1082 tickets were issued and for the second 1146.

'Assuming every hawker cries once in a minute (many do it oftener) and that, on an average, his business keeps him out of doors for seven hours a day, this will make about half a million street cries every day.' But there were many others, unlicensed, who also shouted their wares. 'This would give about one million street-cries a day on this Island.'

The writer rejects the idea of translating them all but says he will rather attempt to show the street-cries as the outward 'signs by which we learn the *life* of the Chinese around us, their moral and their domestic habits'.

'The Chinese generally are early risers. Most of them will get up with the sun; then they dress, after which, rich as well as poor, look out for their warm water to wash in and have some tea. But the Congee hawker has been up an hour or two before sunrise; now he sallies forth, two boxes hanging from his shoulder-pole, each containing a large cooking pot and a small wood-fire underneath. Every hawker cooks his own particular brand of Congee. As they pass your door you have your choice. Here comes the first crying *Mai chü hüt chuck* [Buy pig's blood congee]; the next, *Mai yü shang chuck* [Buy fish congee].[3] And you can buy mulberry-root flavoured congee, or barley, or kidney, or pork, or a variety of other congees.

'. . . all street-cries are also heard on the water. When you see a man paddling his own canoe among the Chinese shipping . . . the articles he has for sale are the same as those sold on shore . . . . Their lungs are so good that I hear their cries pretty distinctly in my house up the hill.'

Another batch of hawkers goes out before the two main Chinese meals of nine in the morning and five in the evening. These are the vegetable sellers—with (in spring) celery, coarse greens, watercresses, salad, spinach, and bean sprouts. In summer they have pumpkins, squash, cucumbers, egg-plant, papaya, lotus root, bamboo shoots, and many kinds of beans. And in winter there are mustard plants, 'white greens',[4] colewort, parsley, onions, garlic, scallion, and others.

The squares of bean curd are the subject of another common cry; and after them and the vegetable sellers come the hawkers of meat and fish. 'Dogs are not allowed to be slaughtered in Hongkong [as would be usual in Chinese custom] . . . they are killed and eaten secretly. Salt fish is a common article of diet . . . . A little piece of it is in many cases the only meat on the table.' But then there are vendors of crabs, shrimps, fresh and dried oysters, shark's fin, and 'others go about with baskets of living fowl' while yet others sell these 'dried or cured with oil'. In Canton the hawkers tend to use what the writer calls a 'Western mirror', meaning probably a peepshow; but 'perhaps the Police do not allow them [in Hong Kong] as the . . . pictures are . . . of a licentious character.'

The article goes on to a catalogue of various fruit sellers, some with

Above: An open-air food stall in 1890. *Below:* Chinese watching a theatrical performance in a matshed theatre, *c.* 1890

a 'nicely spread transportable table before them and a basket with stock . . . . The price is marked by little bamboo slips. They will . . . find a shady place and remain there as long as shade and trade are favourable.' You can buy 'loquats, pineapples, mangoes, melons, rose apples, guavas, peaches, lychees, whampees, apples, pears, plums, different plantains, carambola, etc: in autumn . . . persimmons, olives, walnuts, chestnuts, peanuts, lemons etc; and in winter . . . different oranges, sugarcane . . . .

'Of Confucius it is said that he did not eat anything which was not in season. The Chinese . . . do not follow their pattern sage' but pluck and eat fruit still unripe perhaps for fear of thieves.

'At noon . . . tables are set in convenient places shaded by a large umbrella. A bench for guests stands in front, whilst the busy cook stands behind. He cries out his delicacies and the price . . . . Those Chinese who can afford it sit down to *shik an chau* [to eat the noon meal]'[5] Aside from the staple foods, you can get 'several kinds of cooling gelatine or jelly with sugar for 3 cash a bowl, or a glass of lemon water, or cake.'

'In the evenings all the stalls and hawking tables are illuminated by paper lanterns which . . . make the streets look very lively . . . . The Cantonese are gourmands and they pride themselves on their art of cooking.' And the writer quotes the old saying: 'Happy is he who is born in Soochow [where the people, especially the girls, have the fairest skin], who has his meals in Kwong-chow [Canton], and who dies in Laou-chow [where the wood is said to be best for coffins].

'Another class of hawkers are the sellers of articles for daily use. Here is one panting under his load of earthenware; there is another who cries out his bamboo wares . . . baskets, brooms, mats, benches, ginger grinders . . . . Hawkers of fans, pipes, feather-dusters, china, firewood, tobacco, salt, oil, cloth, lanterns . . . . Beautifully arranged bunches of flowers are offered . . . in the street, but happily in a quiet way, because they attract sufficient attention by themselves, I suppose.'

Then there are the men with empty baskets. What do they do? They are refuse buyers and if you hear 'a voice cry out *mai lan tit lan t'ung*[6] [the writer's transliteration of Cantonese sounds is to say the least erratic, but he means: buy old iron and old copper or bronze] you may be sure he will soon be at the back of your house at the servants quarters [where, with his ready supply of money he will extract from the cook] 'bones, feathers (for fans or manure), rags, old cans; and from your coolie, paper, nails, shoes, . . . anything [that has been found on sweeping the house].

106

'Here I must say the Chinese have really acquired *the* art of mending things. In how wretched and clumsy a way are things repaired in Europe! There is not a foreigner in China who has not several testimonials in his house, proving that his servants are very careless in breaking glass and china and that his servants' countrymen are very skilful and careful at mending it. . . .'

And so the writer continues. There are many things he does not mention, things that twenty years ago could still be seen and heard in Hong Kong. But, reading his rather prosaic lists, you get the feeling of a man who loves the ambience of Chinese Hong Kong, and for all his conviction that they are heathens, cannot but be delighted in his bones and in his mind that they are, in daily ways, as they are.

Doubtless there were a few more such Westerners at that time. There are not many more now. But we shall see later how the street scene in Chinese areas changed very little until some years after World War II, and perhaps begin to realize what it is about the life of the Chinese that captivated so many a foreigner in Peking, if not so many in Hong Kong. The exigencies of a spare, lean, living have always made the Chinese an inventive people, a people delighted (as were Westerners of the pre-industrial revolution days in the country) with small but nicely made things, from sweetmeats to ribbons and nosegays. Perhaps it has something to do with the step back in time that makes many a Westerner happy in the Orient. And one senses that something of this appreciation was to be found in Hennessy.

After Hennessy, the Colony entered a period of administrative and gubernatorial change. The new Governor, Sir George F. Bowen, did not arrive until a year after Hennessy left, and the government was meanwhile administered by the Colonial Secretary, Mr W.H. Marsh. Bowen governed for two years and left. Once more Marsh took over, this time for two years, and then a military man for six months, until the arrival of Sir William Des Voeux. He was sick for much of his time in the Colony, and went frequently on leave to indulge his delight in shooting on the Yangtze. He also had one year of home leave during his three and a half years of office.

It would probably be fair to assume that neither Governor had much influence on the Colony, and that during these eight years it was run by the colonial administration and Whitehall. Perhaps the sole exception may be made in favour of Bowen who laid down a principle that was progressive, and therefore made constitutional history in Hong Kong. He stated that the official majority on the Legislative Council 'should

Sir George Ferguson Bowen, Governor
from March 1883 to December 1885

not be used to control an absolutely united unofficial minority, especially
on financial questions'. As to Des Voeux, little can be said in his favour;
and to his eternal shame it must be recorded that he it was who finally
failed to oust the armed services from the very heart of Victoria town,
thus perpetuating what had from the Colony's inception been aptly
called the 'constriction at the waist'. Thus the town was divided into
two parts, tenuously connected by a single road that ran round the
back of the naval dockyard, a situation not really improved until the
early 1960s.

108

What was Hong Kong like from the rulers' point of view in those days of seventy or eighty years ago? We learn a little from the Governor Sir William Des Voeux, who, following precedent, spent his summers in the Governor's retreat, Mountain Lodge, a building of somewhat sterner stuff than that which was all but carried away over the heads of the Kennedy family in the typhoon of 1874. From his own account, it seems Des Voeux found residence there a mixed blessing. During summer, the Peak is frequently obscured by mist and cloud.

'In our second season,' wrote the Governor dejectedly, 'this miserable experience lasted for the greater part of the summer. On one occasion, for several weeks together, the fog was as dense as the worst which afflicts London in November, and only differed from it in being white instead of brown. The damp inside the house was such that water ran down the walls, in streams and collected in pools on the polished floors. . . . At such times one seemed entirely cut off from the world, the existence of which was revealed only at rare intervals by the arrival of a government messenger with papers.' Such were the penalties of governorship in those days—to be divorced in summer not only from the world, and shrouded in fog, but to be more or less cut off from the Colony one was supposed to govern! Mountain Lodge survived the summer laments of damp governors and their families until the Japanese occupation of World War II, when it was destroyed. And no Governor since then has been tempted to exercise the privilege of living on the Peak.

Sir John Pope Hennessy writing of a visit paid by the Queen-Empress Victoria's eighteen-year-old grandson, Prince Henry of Prussia, also reveals attitudes of the times. 'He seems to enjoy his holiday . . . playing lawn tennis with my wife and myself, driving her Sumatra ponies and walking about incognito. . . . He says it is the first time he has tasted fresh butter since leaving Europe. Fortunately it is the coolest month of May we have had here for years, but I have begged him to avoid going out in the middle of the day, and never to do so, when the sun is shining, without his sun-helmet and an umbrella.'

This was in 1880, and in the following year two scions of British royalty arrived aboard HMS *Bacchante*—the sons of the Prince of Wales, Prince Eddy and his younger brother Prince George, later to rule as King George V. They were accompanied by their tutor Mr Dalton, and their valet Fuller, and were spending what were supposed to be three years of normal naval life as part of an innovatory educational programme.

The whole of the town was illuminated and great plans had been made by the enthusiastic Governor Hennessy for brilliant social events. The admiral on board the *Bacchante* had instructions (as did indeed Hennessy, too) that the boys were not to be lionized by Hong Kong people, and in any case they were sitting their midshipman's examinations at the time. Hennessy claimed to have instructions direct from the Queen which overrode all others. No one, least of all Colonial Office in London, believed this, and something of the lustre went out of the affair. As it turned out, the only sight of the two young men was had at a regatta, and at a ball in the city buildings *after* their examinations were over.

Typically, Hennessy sent a bill for £800 for photographs of the royal youngsters' visit, and justified it to incensed Colonial Office officials, when they queried the amount, by replying that every five years or thereabouts it was useful to have photographs to show how tree-planting was progressing. The Princes later published a book of their travels, dedicated to the Queen. It was actually written by their tutor Dalton, and is one of the duller 19th century books of travel, Hong Kong being described as reminding them 'at first sight of Gibraltar, but it is not very like, except that it is a lofty hill with a town at foot and ships in front'. Its streets were 'wide and clean, full of chairs with green canopies and wickerwork sides, on long bamboo carrying-poles.' They evidently did not penetrate far or they would have changed their opinion of the cleanliness of the streets, and would also have discovered their mistake in thinking there were no wheeled vehicles.

They certainly did not appear to understand that there were in reality two towns of Victoria and, like the extremes of East and West which they contained, the twain just didn't meet. One was the filthy, but lively and colourful Chinese town with its overcrowding and absence of sanitation, where most of the populace lived; and the other was official and residential Victoria where Westerners were. But they may be forgiven, for many visitors who stayed longer and were less hedged around with protocol did not know this either.

The Princes' grandmother, Queen Victoria, celebrated her golden jubilee in 1887, and the event was marked in Hong Kong with processions, by the setting up of the Chinese Chamber of Commerce, and the resolve to have a statue of Victoria the Queen suited to the dignity of Victoria the city. In the *China Mail*, however, only two days after the ceremonies, there appeared a letter (22 June 1887) from a citizen of Victoria couched in dignified but indignant language:

'Sir:—Yesterday I got into a street-chair and told the bearers to

110

take me to *Tai-Lai-pai-t'ong*, the Cathedral (i.e. the Large Worship Hall).' After some delay while the bearers consulted together as to where he might be intending to go, he continues: 'When one of them caught the right idea he said to his fellow "It is the *Hung-mo-miu* (the Red-Hair Temple)" [meaning the temple of the red-haired foreigners— a common form of speech indicating all Westerners]. I felt a little disconcerted on that glorious jubilee morning by hearing a nick-name applied to the British people as represented by the august assembly gathering in the Cathedral. . . . How can Her Gracious Majesty's authorities in this great Colony allow such disrespectful terms to be applied to themselves and us all?'

He suggested a fine of ten cents be levied for disrespectful language in the future.

A century and more later, a civil servant recalls seeing a memo in circulation in the Secretariat in Hong Kong to the effect that clerks should be forbidden from writing on the packets of papers destined to be taken to the Governor the words *Ping Tau*[7] (Military Boss). And a common name for the Botanical Gardens adjoining Government House is still *Ping Tau Fa Yuen*[8] (the Military Boss's Flower Garden).

A Chinese family in the Botanic Gardens about the turn of the century

It was in 1888 that one of those ingenious Victorian inventions, the cable car, was applied to the problems of rising from the lower levels of Victoria town to the heights of the Peak—the Peak Tramway, as it was called. There is an aura of mahogany, cast-iron, escaping steam, waxed mustachios, tall starched collars for men, and ample skirts for women, surrounding the later part of Victoria's lengthy and hero-studded colonial reign. Shades of the epicene General Gordon (first, Chinese Gordon, and only later Gordon of Khartoum), of the Prince Edward's pecadilloes (two of the results in the shape of two well-known women lived in Hong Kong for many a decade), the P. and O. (for travel to and from England on whose steamships comes that tremendously *fin de siècle* word 'posh'—composed of the initials for 'port out,' that is toward the East, and 'starboard home', thus keeping the sun on the other side of the ship from that of your cabin, both ways). It was a time, too, of twirling ceiling fans, 'pigtailed' office-boys, the electric telegraph and, at the very end, the 'Kodak' with its tricky black bellows that often spoiled the fun and the film by letting in pinholes of light. It was a time of the confidence of the British that they owned the world. And with the coming 1900 Boxer Siege at Peking and the final penetration of China, the idea that the West, and in particular the British, were the master race, and the Chinese destined (for their good, of course) to join that multi-million strong collection known as the 'subject races', was generally accepted.

Thus the Peak Tramway, when it opened for business on 30 May 1888, was thought of as just one more achievement in the irresistible march of progress. The *Hong Kong Telegraph* wrote that morning about the convenience of the operation with 'the first car leaving St John's Place [opposite St John's Cathedral, as it still does today] punctually at 8 o'clock and the succeeding cars being despatched according to the Company's time table'. The tiny, vociferous universe of Hong Kong took one more metropolitan step. In fact the timetable of the Peak Tramway reveals the interesting point that the 'down' cars between 8 and 10 a.m. were reserved for first class passengers only—for at that time, it must be supposed, the passengers were likely to be exalted gentlemen descending to business. Reaching the lower terminus, they found their chairs, each borne by four liveried coolies, and off they went at a jogtrot to office, with a flourish of shouted warnings to pedestrains to make way. Businessmen were still using the two complementary modes of conveyance in the early 1930s.

The most frequently quoted travellers of this period who sojourned

The Peak Tram on its upward course from a little below the Kennedy Road bridge, 1888

awhile in Hong Kong are Miss Isabella Bird, Lady Brassey, and Lord Ronald Gower. Between them they present a picture of many outward facets. Miss Bird was of that Livingstone breed, only in female form, whose restless motion round the world in the last three decades of the 19th century was stirred by one hardly knows what urge or frustration, stilled for a few years by marriage, and rekindled by (or at least on) her husband's death. Her numerous books on China, Japan, America, Persia and Kurdistan, India, and Malaysia, contain little enough reference to Hong Kong which, she remarks with perhaps unconscious humour, is 'moored to England by the electric cable'. She likens Victoria to Genoa (which, from a study of contemporary prints of both cities, was at least inaccurate). But then she arrived in the Colony, as we already noted, at the height of the great fire, and the general excitement may have unfocussed her usually acute vision.

Lady Brassey, who was in Hong Kong the year before Isabella Bird, thought the place deeply British. It reminded her (as it did the royal Princes) somewhat of Gibraltar. Like Miss Bird, she was visiting in the

113

winter, and both were delighted with the climate (which, during the last three months of the year resembles an English summer). Military men, she wrote, 'abound in the streets', and were it not for 'the sedan chairs and palanquins, in which everybody is carried about by Chinese coolies with enormous hats, one might easily fancy oneself in dear old Gib.' But, young and inclined to romanticism as she was (fittingly she was to die on another voyage in her husband's luxury yacht, *The Sunbeam*, at sea somewhere off Timor), she opens her chapter on Hong Kong with one of those implacable stanzas of deathly verse that the Colony seems to inspire in the breasts of even the best poets:

Sails of silk and ropes of sandal
Such as gleam in ancient lore,
And the singing of the sailors,
And the answer from the shore.

One may hazard a guess (even if this quatrian is a quotation, which it may well be) that the singing of the sailors from the shores of Hong Kong came of an evening from the taverns of Queen's Road, and was moderately raucous.

Like Miss Bird, Lady Brassey was upset at the use of pidgin English. It is hard to see quite why. This translation of Chinese sentence structure into English words was endemic, useful for communication between the English (and others too busy or too lazy or too stupid to learn Chinese), and the Chinese who found correct English hard to manage, and had no experience at all of foreign tongues.

Lord Ronald Gower was another romantically inclined visitor. He found himself, he wrote, 'transported two thousand years back in ancient Rome or glorious Carthage [he was of course a sculptor, and the Roman periods in sculpture were much in vogue at that time in Europe]. This illusion is helped no doubt by the coloured dresses and fanciful drapery of the Chinese, and by the ... classical style of the white houses ... porticoes and collonades ... sparkling under the intensely brilliant sunshine, outlined sharply against the almost purple sky.' The sky in Hong Kong these days is never 'almost purple,' but perhaps the strange colour was due to the dust from the eruption of the volcano island of Krakatoa in August 1883. For years after the event, sunsets round the world were more highly coloured than usual, so Lord Rolald Gower's observation may not be as fanciful as it appears.

A sketch from the Illustrated London News of an open-air ball on the Peak in 1888. The saraonic title, *Roughing it in the Far East*, neatly catches the temper of the times

Roughing it in the Far East

Meet me by Moonlight Alone

Before the Waltz

After the Waltz

Evening Dress in the Tropics

Celestial Attendants

7

PLAGUE AND A REVOLUTIONARY

I T was to a Colony something like the more sober of the foregoing descriptions that the new Governor, Sir William Robinson, was sent in December 1891. Robinson was at the peak of his career, 'very much a Colonial Office man, anxious to keep it well informed, and to be guided by its instructions', as the historian Endacott assesses his character in matters official. But, like all other Governors of Hong Kong or anywhere else, he inherited the legacy of his predecessors in office.

One of the less tractable problems had always been the water supply—or the lack of an adequate one. In this problem the bungling of great schemes under his namesake, Sir Hercules Robinson, had resulted by now in a serious situation in years of little rain, and was to prove in part the cause of a situation of dire calamity.

His other inherited problem of major proportions was the failure to implement the recommendations of the Chadwick Report of 1882. From that report sprang the Sanitary Board (ultimately to become the Urban Services Department). Osbert Chadwick, a former Royal Engineers officer, who was responsible for compiling this massive set of documents, sounds from a perusal of them a man of both insight and humanity. His statements are unequivocal and backed by many a former partial report that told the same unpalatable facts about sanitation, or lack of it, in the Colony. The problem was by no means simple, for the traditions of the Chinese had to be taken into account. Chadwick, in his report, reviewed the whole social problem, remarking that to his surprise he found little opposition from the Chinese. He, too, found water supply inadequate. Neither 'the proposed works, nor works many times larger, would satisfy the wants of the city'. A new building ordinance was urgent as houses were defective and their drainage 'radically bad'. The whole town required new drainage, and scavenging

116

had to be more thorough and entirely separated from the process of collection of night soil. He suggested Chinese district watchmen who should be well paid, to enforce the details, day to day. And so on. He remarks that Chinese themselves often called his attention to abuses, and in his understanding manner Chadwick was keen to go along with their way of thinking on the subject as far as practicable.

Nothing much was done. But one sentence in the report was to prove unerringly true. 'My report will show the necessity for strong and complete measures of sanitation . . . without waiting for the necessity to be demonstrated by the irresistible logic of a severe epidemic.'

It was this 'irresistible logic' in the form of bubonic plague that proved to be the new Governor's second problem. Two and a half years after he arrived, the great plague had Hong Kong in its grip.

Sir William Robinson, Governor from
December 1891 to January 1898

There was no law that required Chinese to register deaths, so it was by accident that in the middle of May 1894, it came to general notice that there seemed to be an unusually large number of deaths occurring in one particular street. By 28 May, 450 people were dead, and the death rate appeared to be rising rapidly.

At this point the cause of bubonic plague was not yet known. The fact that plague is a disease of rats transmitted to human beings by the

117

Victims of bubonic plague lying in the makeshift 'hospital'—in the newly completed glassworks
Opposite: A street doctor of the late 19th century, his sign proclaiming him 'famous for generations, specialist in internal and external diseases . . . cure of knife and bullet wounds . . . haemor-
rhoids . . . venereal and women's diseases,' and much else, including insanity

bite of fleas leaving rats that have died of the disease, was not understood.
Combative measures consisted simply in removing the dead and dying
persons, cleaning and disinfecting premises, and trying to isolate areas
and persons known to be infected. In Hong Kong this was no easy task.
The Chinese deeply distrusted Western medicine—having had their
own, nowadays much respected, systems of treatment for several thousand years—and they even more deeply resented Western troops
forcibly entering their homes, removing dead and sick, evicting families,
cleaning and disinfecting with the crude substances (carbolic and lime)
then available. How essential this operation launched by the authorities
was, can be imagined from the fact that on one day in June, 109 bodies
dead of plague were discovered in the Chinese residential area, the
relatives waiting, as was customary, for the auspicious time for burial.
Well over 300 houses were condemned and the Western area of Hong
Kong was cordoned off as 7,000 Chinese were evicted from their homes.
The new glassworks in the area was turned into a hospital, and even a
collecting place for pigs was pressed into medical service.

Anti-foreign sentiment among the Chinese, then as now never far
beneath the surface (and often with good reason), flared up. Junks from
Canton arrived, attempting to remove the sick and take away the

bodies, but the Governor refused, only later allowing as a 'concession' some 170 striken people to be taken away.

'The plague,' remarks L.C. Arlington who worked in the Chinese Maritime Customs in Canton at the time, 'and the treatment ... accorded to the Chinese inhabitants by the Government [of Hong Kong] caused thousands to flee to Macau and the Hinterland. The specific reasons for this exodus were the house-to-house visitations of the "Whitewash Brigade", the burying of the dead in lime, and the interments higgledy-piggledy at the Western point of the island [all these things anathema to the strict traditional funeral and burial customs of Chinese, to whom the correct treatment of their ancestors was not only a matter of honour but had a direct bearing on their own lives].

Sir William Robinson, Governor, with members of the Legislative Council about 1897. His resemblance

Edward VII is remarkable

The "Whitewash Brigade" used to enter a house and demand a "squeeze" [money]—otherwise the furniture and ... clothing, trunks, etc., were thrown out into the streets and destroyed by fire. The Brigade consisted of foreigners (mostly soldiers) and in greater numbers, Chinese —who, of course, did all the "squeezing", the foreigners being totally ignorant of the matter.'

A large, ponderous query must hang over this last preposterous statement from the book *Through the Dragon's Eyes*. *Of course* the foreigners knew very well about 'squeeze'. They always had known about squeezing, or *cumshaw* as it is often called. They had always been in positions to obtain it readily, had always done so, and continue today to do so like others, irrespective of nationality. Arlington concludes his section on the Hong Kong plague and Chinese actions during it, with a quotation from Bret Harte: 'For ways that are dark, and tricks that are vain the heathen Chinese is peculiar.' But *The Times* of London, referring

The eldest son of a prominent Chinese (in white headband) follows his father's coffin in the funeral procession, c. 1885

basically to the non-Chinese component of Hong Kong, puts the case against what they had made the Colony in more accurate if sonorous terms: 'The name of this noisy, bristling, quarrelsome, discontented little island may not inaptly be used as a euphonious synonym for a place not mentionable to ears polite.'

In Canton, the feelings of the populace ran high, and what would now, after the Cultural Revolution, be called Big Character Posters were to be seen on many buildings telling how Western doctors gouged out the eyes of new-born babies for use in plague treatment. Others warned women not to visit Hong Kong since it was said that the troops in their house to house clean-up raped Chinese women in the process. Hong Kong was declared an infected port, and ships refused to use its harbour.

The Chinese western area of the island, worst affected by plague and called ironically T'ai P'ing Shan, or Peaceful Hill, was taken over by the government, enabling it to be inspected and regulated in various ways. The resentment increased after this measure, which had in fact been opposed by Dr Ho Kai and one other member of the Sanitary Board. There followed a strike of coolies against inspection of their accommodation. The Governor took a tough line and banished several of the strikers' ringleaders. Surprisingly enough, this and an explanation to the Chinese soon ended the strike.

The plague lingered on for several years. Each spring brought its crop of cases. After dying down in 1895, it returned the following year and killed over one thousand people. 1897 showed a mortality of only 17, but again in 1898 it flared up.

Robinson's reaction to his Colony and to the Chinese and the plague, may be summed up by his statement in 1895 that 'it is extraordinary—not to say discreditable—that after fifty-five years of British rule, the vast majority of Chinese in Hong Kong should remain so little anglicized'.

With hindsight, it must appear not extraordinary at all. What possible incentive had they been given to take on the manners and customs of the West—which, for the most part were presented to them by a set of ineffectual rulers and ruffiany merchants whose generally small education and assumption of lordly manners could hardly have been attractive to any Chinese with whom they came in contact? Even Dr Ho Kai, a brilliant Hong Kong Chinese who took the highest degrees in medicine and surgery at Aberdeen University in Scotland, and went on to study law and to become a barrister in London's Lincoln's Inn in 1882, protested at some of the government measures relating to the Chinese. As a member of the Legislative Council, he impressed everyone and led a long and useful public life in Hong Kong, finally resigning from the Council in 1914 after serving 24 years.

Despite the discovery of the plague bacillus by a French bacteriologist named Alexandre Yersin working in the East in 1894, and independently by the Japanese, Kitasato, and the discovery shortly after of its transmission from rats, little that was really decisive was done in Hong Kong. Certainly the long-delayed and bureaucratically strangled Tytam Reservoir scheme got a new lease of life and some more fresh water flowed into the taps and drains of the Colony. But the colonial government of Hong Kong has seldom been distinguished for any radical reform, even when the need for radical reform or action was apparent to all. The Colony 'needed the Chinese', as a speaker at a public meeting admitted during the strike of coolies against inspection of their lodgings. Yet, in its xenophobic Western outlook, Hong Kong was unable to allow the Chinese anything more than the most subservient positions, the most miserable opportunities. Only rich Chinese could afford anything resembling an education, a decent place to live, or any degree of human recognition.

Another traveller, one who seems to have largely escaped quotation but whose picture of Hong Kong is in many ways more considerable than others, is Henry Norman who spent four years journeying in many parts of the Far East, and in 1895 published his long book entitled *The Peoples and Politics of the Far East*. In his preface he remarks: 'The Far East presents itself to the attentive traveller under two aspects. It is the last Wonderland of the World; and it is also the seed-bed of a multitude of new political issues.' Explaining that he has 'endeavoured to reflect . . . this twofold quality', and that his 'record of mere travel is interwoven with that of investigation', he hopes to reproduce in the reader's mind the effect of the Far East on his own. 'It is a picture which is destined, either in bright colours or in sombre, to become increasingly familiar to him in the future.'

Few travellers realized this; probably few really cared: so Henry Norman deserves a little attention.

'The first sight of Hong Kong, the farthest outpost of the British Empire and the fourth port in the world, is disappointing. As you approach it from the north you enter a narrow and unimposing pass

Opposite, above: After church, a stroll on the Parade Ground in 1890. *Below:* Chinese women and children at the race course in Happy Valley

125

[Lei Yue Mun]: then you discover a couple of sugar refineries covering the hills with smoke; and when the city of Victoria lies before you it is only St John's or Vladivostock on a larger scale. It is piled up on the steep sides of the island without apparent purpose or cohesion; few fine buildings detach themselves from the mass; there is no boulevard along the water-front. . . . The face of Hong Kong is not its fortune, and anybody merely steaming by would never guess the marvel it grows on closer acquaintance. For a few weeks' investigation transforms this precipitous island into one of the more astonishing spots on the earth's surface. By an inevitable alchemy, the philosopher's stone of a few correlated facts transforms one's disappointment into stupefaction. Shanghai is a surprise, but Hongkong is a revelation.

'When you land at . . . Victoria . . . the inevitable ricksha carries you through . . . streets far from being beautiful or well-managed, but you forget this in the rush of life about you.' Messengers jostle you, 'rickshas run over your toes, chair-poles dig you in the ribs. The hotel clerk smiles politely as he informs you that there has not been a vacant room for a month. Later on your fellow-passengers envy you the little rabbit-hole of a bedroom you have secured at the top of the Hongkong Club.' Down in the hall 'brokers of many nationalities making notes, laughing, whispering, drinking. . . . The Stock Exchange of Hongkong is the gutter . . . extending from the Club for about a hundred yards down the Queen's Road . . . filled with Britishers, Germans, Anglo-Indians, Chinese from Canton, Armenians from Calcutta, Parsees from Bombay, and Jews from Baghdad . . . . On the Club walls and tables are a dozen printed "Expresses", timed with the minute at which they were issued, and the mail and shipping noon and afternoon "extras" of the daily papers,' with news of shipping, cargoes, auction sales, 'and all the multitudinous movements of a great commercial machine running at high pressure . . . This colony "just hums" all the time.'

'Then the chair a friend has sent to take you to dinner arrives, with its four coolies uniformed in blue and white calico, and . . . you find yourself, three minutes after leaving the club, mounting an asphalte roadway at an angle not far short of forty-five degrees, hemmed in above and on either hand by great green palms and enormous drooping ferns with fronds yards long, among which big butterflies are playing round long scarlet flowers. For as soon as you begin to ascend, the streets of Hongkong might be alleys in the tropical conservatories at Kew.'

Opposite, above: A complicated Chinese kite about to take the air in 1890. *Below:* the shop of a scroll-mounter, similar to some operating today—apart from the shaved heads of the men

127

The old Harbour Office seen from Wing Lock Street. The staff included Westerners, Chinese, and one Sikh. About 1880. *Opposite:* the new Harbour Office, standing gracefully by the water in 1906

The Club at this time was still in Queen's Road, from which the slopes immediately rise—nowadays often by the famous 'ladder streets' that entrance tourists and fatique Hong Kong citizens who now have no carrying chairs.

'Queen's Road is the Broadway of Hongkong, and all business centres upon it. In the middle are the Club, post-office, courts, hotels; then come all the banks and offices and shops; past these to the east are the ... barracks ... parade-ground, cricket-ground, polo-ground, and racecourse, and the wonderfully picturesque and pretty cemetery, the "Happy Valley". In the other direction ... all the Chinese shops for foreigners ... then into Chinatown, a quarter of very narrow streets, extremely dirty, inconceivably crowded, and probably about as insanitary as any place on the globe under civilized rule.'

Henry Norman then goes on: 'I never ceased to prophesy two things about Hongkong, one of which, the epidemic [of bubonic plague, 1894] has come true indeed. The other waits, and as it is rather alarmist it is perhaps better left out of print.' There can probably be only one interpretation of what this sentence means—revolt of the Chinese in

Hong Kong. That too came true, but rather later than Norman anticipated, in 1967.

'. . . . This is all on the island of Hongkong, while across the harbour, in . . . Kowloon, a new city is springing up—a splendid frontage of wharves and warehouses; a collection of docks, one of which will take almost any ship afloat . . . and the pleasure-gardens and kitchen-gardens of the community.'

All this he calls the 'ground floor' of the Colony. 'The second storey of Hongkong lies ten minutes' climb up the steep side of the island. Here nearly everybody lives, and lives, too, in a luxury and ease that are not suspected at home [in England].

'Finally, there is the third layer, the top storey . . . known . . . as "The Peak". The Peak itself is one of the highest . . . hills of the island rising behind the city to the signal station, 1,842 feet above the sea where a gun and a flagstaff announce the arrival of mails and ocean steamers.

But "The Peak" as a residential district means all the hill-tops where cool breezes from the sea blow in summer, where one can sleep under a blanket at night, and where, in a word, one can spend a summer in Hongkong with a reasonable probability of being alive at the end of it. Here everybody who can afford it has a second house . . . . There are two hotels, and a steam tramway [the Peak Tramway] runs up and down every fifteen minutes.' He was startled by the expense of the trip up, although the fare down was only half that amount, and by the necessity to rent your Peak house all year when you inhabited it only in summer. And that it cost about 'a sovereign a day all the year round . . . . Besides this, there is the tramway fare, the cost of coolies to carry your chair . . . and the expense of bringing every item of domestic supplies, from coals to cabbage, a forty minutes' climb uphill.'

Then he asks the question: 'What is the summer climate on the second storey . . . which forces people to flee from it at so much trouble and cost? To be frank, every man I asked . . . described it to me by the monosyllabic appellation of the ultimate destination of the incorrigibly unrighteous.' Perhaps the longest circumlocution for 'hell' in the English language. The author continues: 'One of the chief summer problems of Hongkong is to determine whether the mushrooms which grow on your boots during the night are edible or not'—a flash of humour surfaces now and then. 'The damp is indescribable [as Governor Des Voeux had lamented some years before]. Moisture pours down the walls; anything left for a couple of days—clothes, boots, hats, portmanteaus— is covered with mould. Twenty steps in the open air and you are soaked with perspiration . . . . When the booksellers receive a case of books, the first thing they do is to varnish them . . . with a damp-resisting composition containing corrosive sublimate. Otherwise the cockroaches would eat them before they had time to go mouldy.'

'If you come home at night after dinner, very tired, beware of carelessly throwing your evening clothes over a chair . . . . If you do, the cockroaches will have destroyed them before you wake . . . . It does happen, too, that men die in summer . . . between sunrise and sunset without rhyme or reason. And the community is a pale-faced one. The place used to be known as "the grave of regiments"—a stroll through "Happy Valley" tells you why. [He is referring to the cemetery which does indeed tell a sad story of hundreds of young men and women who died of fever. The headstones are still there.] Now the men are not allowed outside the barracks in summer until five p.m. and there is a regular inspection to see that every man has his cholera-belt on. The

130

"down-side" of Hongkong is damp and hot; the "top-side" is damp and cool. That is the difference for which people are prepared to pay so heavily.'

Staying for the first time on the 'top-side' he noticed here and there in the house numerous large stoppered bottles encased in wicker. To his amazement he discovered they contained things such as cigars, biscuits, writing-paper, the stopper of each bottle filled with 'unslaked lime in filtering paper' to absorb damp. 'These bottles tell the whole tale. People run over to Macau . . . four hours' steaming away, for Sunday, and . . . when their thoughts begin to run on "Happy Valley" and a grave there . . . they just go on board a steamer and disembark at Nagasaki or Yokohama. Japan is the sanatorium of the Far East.'

Some of the doubtful delights of Hong Kong, 'even now . . . not a particularly safe place', befall those who stroll alone at nights. And if you take a sampan to go to dine aboard a ship in harbour, 'the constable at the pier makes a note of its number, in case you should be missing the next day. For these sampan people . . . have a pleasant habit of . . . dropping the mat awning on the head of the passenger, cutting his throat in the ensuing struggle, and dropping his pillaged body overboard.'

The Sikh police are detested by the Chinese. During a spate of burglaries the police were ordered to arrest anyone who did not halt if challenged at night, 'especially if they had ladders. Next night a Sikh saw a Chinaman on the top of a ladder . . . so he challenged the man, who paid no attention, and then he fired and brought him down. It was the lamplighter. Even now no Chinaman is supposed to be out after nine p.m. without a pass.' The nonchalant casualness about Chinese life and death is of course typical of the period. The attitude was shared by most Europeans in the Colony, as one discovers from reading any newspaper of the time.

Writing about the defence of the Colony, Norman says: '. . . Hongkong is more in danger from the Chinese than from any other quarter. Kowloon city is a mass of roughs; Canton is the most turbulent and most foreign-hating city in China; 20,000 Chinese could come down . . . in a few hours; and a strike of Chinese servants would starve out the Colony. Before Kowloon was added to the Colony, a Hongkong head was worth thirty dollars, and "braves" used to come down to try and get them.'

But Hong Kong, he was sure, in spite of its commercial progress and its 'vital position in the Empire', was strangely behind the civilization of its time. Its law was, broadly, that in force in England in 1843 when it was annexed. 'I saw several Europeans in Hongkong gaol for debt.[1]

131

There is no Married Women's Property Act . . . although this actually exists in Chinese law. There is no copyright for British authors under their own flag, and I saw the counters of the foreign booksellers crowded with pirated reprints of contemporary authors.'

It is all hauntingly reminiscent of Hong Kong today when the sale of pirated editions, pirated recordings, and designs of all kinds still goes on, and where any force of Chinese could take Hong Kong in a few hours. The law has been much amended since Norman's time, but not all British law in Hong Kong exists in a Chinese version even today, and the vast number of Chinese who are judged by it would be unable to read it. 'A petition had been presented, signed by all the Chinese merchants of the Colony, but the authorities would have none of them, so it was referred home, and the Secretary of State ordered the suggestions to be introduced. This was already six years ago, and nothing had been done.' That sort of statement is still made, and still valid, today.

Toward the end of his account of Hong Kong the author, like any tourist today, but with a certain feeling for language and for what seemed to him the portentous nature of his subject, waxes lyrical. 'I doubt if there can be a more remarkable view in the world than that of the city of Victoria and the ten square miles of Hongkong harbour from "The Peak". At night it is as if you had mounted above the stars and were looking down upon them, for the riding lights of the ships seem suspended in an infinite gulf of darkness, while every now and then the white beam of an electric searchlight flashes like the track of a meteor across a midnight sky. By day, the city is spread out nearly 2,000 feet directly below you, and only the ships' decks and their foreshortened masts are visible, while the whole surface of the harbour is traversed continually in all directions by fast steam-launches, making a network of tracks like lace-work upon it, as water-spiders skim over a pool in summer-time . . . . The ocean "tramps" ready to . . . carry anything anywhere; the white-winged sailing-vessels resting after their long flights; the innumerable high-sterned junks plying to every port on the China coast; and all the mailed host of men-of-war flying every flag under heaven from the white ensign of the flagship and the black eagle of its Russian rival, to the yellow crown of the tiny Portuguese gunboat or the dragon pennant of China.'

It would be a pity to omit his final sentences. The man who has observed the dirt and injustices, the backwardness in some fields, of the Colony, therein girds himself up and delivers what must be one of the finest and at the same time most typical of all Victorian perorations.

132

'All these vessels cross and recross ceaselessly in Hongkong harbour, living shuttles in the loom of time, bearing the golden strand of human sympathy and co-operation between world and world, or like the Zeitgeist in *Faust*, "weaving the garment divinity wears".' But he sees then he has perhaps gone a little too far, and retrieves himself: 'I am not prepared to say that divinity would always find itself comfortable in the garment that is woven in Hongkong'—then back to the peroration again—'but one thing I can affirm, and that is that a visit to our furthest Colony makes one proud to belong to the nation that has created it from nothing, fills the word "Empire" with a newborn meaning, and crystallizes around it a set of fresh convictions and resolves.'

What precisely these were, he does not tell us—for at the time the answers were self-evident to his proud English readers.

Following the plague, other tensions gripped Hong Kong. The Sino-Japanese war of 1894–5 had ended in defeat for the Chinese and, among other serious matters, the opening of four additional ports to Japanese trade. What has become known as the 'scramble for concessions' by

Central Victoria and the harbour, looking toward the Kowloon Peninsula in the late nineteenth century

133

the Western powers began in earnest, and China became in the period before the turn of the century, virtually a semi-colony of the West.

In Hong Kong a young man named Sun Yat-sen had qualified at the College of Medicine in 1892, one of the first two licentiates, obtaining prizes in hygiene, public health, medicine, and midwifery. But he was not for long to practise as a doctor. By 1894 he was in Hawaii organizing a revolutionary society. Two years later still he was banished from Hong Kong for five years for conspiring against the authorities in Canton. His temperate letter explained that he was only trying to 'emancipate my miserable countrymen from the cruelty of the Tartar Yoke', but did not mollify the Governor, or the Secretary of State in London; and Sun Yat-sen did not return for many a year.

The development of the Kowloon Peninsula from 1864 to 1924

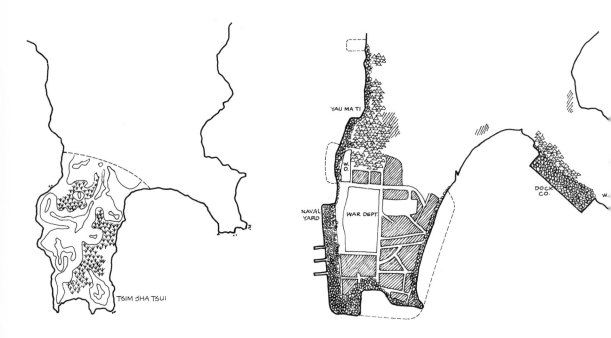

KOWLOON IN 1864
🌱 PRESUMABLY PADDY LAND
◯ ROUGH CONTOURS

KOWLOON IN 1887
🏘 LAND LAID OUT FOR OR ALREADY BUILT WITH HOUSES
/// LAND SOLD BUT NOT HEAVILY BUILT UP
--- PROPOSED RECLAMATIONS
🍀 RECLAIMED LAND

Perhaps he was never aware of the exchanges in the House of Commons on the subject. On 18 July 1898, a member named Davitt asked the Secretary of State for the Colonies the result of enquiries about Dr Sun's banishment from Hong Kong. The Secretary of State replied: '...Sun Yat-sen, not being a naturalized subject of Her Majesty, was...prohibited from residing in the Colony for five years from 4 March 1896, on the ground that he was, in the opinion of the Governor-in-Council, dangerous to the peace and good order of the Colony.... He left the Colony prior to the issue of the order [of banishment] but there seems to have been no doubt that he was implicated in a conspiracy against the Chinese Government which made and makes his presence

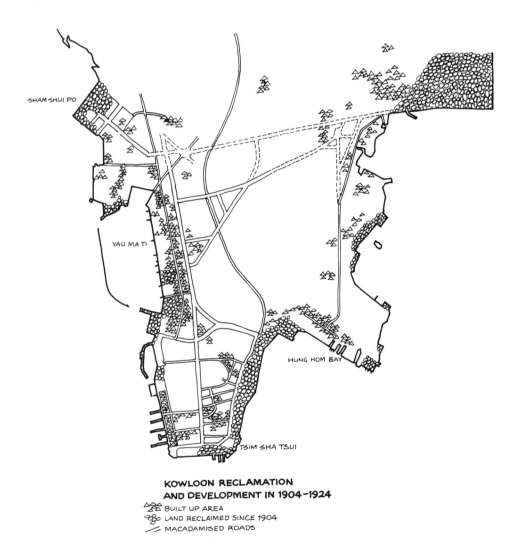

**KOWLOON RECLAMATION
AND DEVELOPMENT IN 1904–1924**
BUILT UP AREA
LAND RECLAIMED SINCE 1904
MACADAMISED ROADS

135

in Hongkong undesirable. I see no reason to interfere with the tempo-rary prohibition of his residence.'

Mr Davitt then asked if the Secretary of State 'is aware that no opportunity has been given to Sun Yat-sen to meet the charges against him.'

The Secretary of State:... 'I think I have seen in the papers that this gentleman is now leading the rebels in China.' (Laughter)

Mr Davitt: I hope he will be successful.

The Secretary of State: If that be true, it will confirm the opinion of the Government of Hongkong.'

When, eventually, Sun Yat-sen did return to Hong Kong, it was 1923, and on 21 February of that year he addressed the students of the University of Hong Kong. He said he would like to answer a question he had many times been asked: 'Where and how did I get my revolu-tionary and modern ideas?' The answer was: 'I got my ideas in this very place; in the Colony of Hong Kong.' (Laughter and applause). '... More than thirty years ago I was studying in Hong Kong and spent a great deal of spare time walking the streets of the Colony. Hong Kong impressed me a great deal because there was orderly calm.... I went to my home fifty miles away in Kwangtung province twice a year and immediately noticed the great difference. There was disorder instead of order, insecurity instead of security.... The difference of the govern-ments impressed me very much.... Afterwards...I began to wonder how it was that foreigners, that Englishmen, could do such things as they had done...with the barren rock of Hong Kong, within seventy or eighty years, while China after four thousand years had no place like Hong Kong.'

He went on to compare official corruption in China with official purity in Hong Kong—a sally that in 1923 provoked patriotic applause for the purity of Hong Kong officials, and would today, in less sub-servient and less conformist times produce a roar of hearty laughter from the majority of the four million citizens. His speech reveals a typical bourgeois reformer. He was apparently unaware that insecurity, rather than security, was the condition of Hong Kong Chinese, and in varying degrees still is to this day for the majority.

Little direct part though it may have in the story of Hong Kong, the development of Dr Sun's ideas, stemming to some degree from his curious misinterpretation of what went on in Hong Kong, is an inter-esting one. Hong Kong at that time was probably as corrupt in many ways as his native China, and that semblance of order was in fact simple colonial control of the voiceless majority by the minority. But out of such random experiences are great movements begun. It required an infinitely more profound mind than that of the Hong Kong doctor to eradicate Chinese corruption in China. Hong Kong itself has yet to find a way to do so within its own microcosm.

The original caption for this sketch from a magazine of the period reads: 'Our latest acquisition in the Far East—Hoisting the British Flag at Taipo.' New Territories, 16 April 1899

137

8

A NEW CENTURY

As Queen Victoria in England celebrated the sixtieth year of her reign over that strange, rag-bag empire her subjects had haphazardly bundled together in her lifetime, Hong Kong and the city of Victoria were not far from their sixtieth year either. The Queen's Diamond Jubilee came in 1897, that of Hong Kong six years later.

'After weeks of strenuous preparation, Hong Kong began to celebrate the royal Diamond Jubilee on Sunday, 21 June. Every church in the Colony was packed for special thanksgiving services.' The Governor and other dignitaries, including the members of Executive and Legislative Councils, walked in a body to the Cathedral for the official thanksgiving. The Roman church was ablaze with the full dress uniforms of the consuls of Spain, France, Austria-Hungary, Belgium, and others, while the Parsee community was praying in its Zoroastrian place of worship in Elgin Street. The Jews, too, were praying for the Queen and royal family, and in the afternoon a special service in Chinese was conducted at the Anglican Cathedral. An amnesty was granted to thirty-three prisoners, who were let out of jail.

The following Tuesday the celebrations began in earnest, the town crowded with visitors from all the southern provinces of China and elsewhere, giving 'the place an unusually animated appearance'. British and foreign warships gathered in the harbour, and the calm of the morning was shattered as their guns roared the Royal Salute of 60 guns. At 10.30 a.m., the gala atmosphere was shattered once more, this time by the roar of one of those violent and earsplitting thunderstorms that punctuate the Hong Kong summer and bring torrents of warm rain. The Governor's reception was due to begin at Government House at 11 a.m., and the guests probably arrived rather wet. But there sat the Governor on a dais, in the midst of the consular body in full uniform. It must have been a splendid sight.

On the 6th of February, 1907, the Duke of Connaught unveiled a statue of the Prince of Wales in Royal (now Statue) Square. Under the cupola is the jubilee statue of Queen Victoria, and the Supreme Court is being built beyond

In the afternoon a grand review of the naval and military forces took place at the race course in Happy Valley. The rain, luckily, this time held off, and following the review a choir of more than 300 voices conducted by Bandmaster Bentley launched into that truly Victorian indulgence—the mass singing of patriotic songs.

The *Hongkong Daily Press* of Friday, 25 June 1897, reports: 'Mr W.G. Bentley, ARCM, the bandmaster of the West Yorkshire Regiment, was the conductor, and as he took up his baton everyone uncovered while the chorus of 300 voices sang the hymn 'Praise the Lord' to the grand

139

old tune 'Austria' .... One of the verses specially composed for the occasion by Miss Danby, was as follows:

Praise to Thee for Her, Thy champion,
Whom our hymns today proclaim,
One whose zeal by the enlightened
Burns anew with nobler flame:
Keep us true to Her allegiance,
Counting life itself less dear,
Standing firmer, holding faster,
As we see the end draw near.

To this lugubrious anticipation, lustily sung as it was, there was added a 'fantasia of British tunes'—*Rule Britannia, The Maple Leaf Forever* (representing Canada), *The Minstrel Boy, St Patrick's Day, Scots wha hae,*

The old Hong Kong Club illuminated for the visit of the Duke of Connaught in 1870

Men of Harlech, Unfurl the Flag (for Australia), *Dear, Sweet Little Isle of Man, Sin-fa* (for Hong Kong),[1] and finally, the audience having by then got well into its sentimental stride—*Aulde Lang Syne*.

As night fell, 'the principal feature of the celebrations was the illumination of the harbour and the procession of launches. Every ship . . . was a blaze of light. The vast fleet of junks and sampans joined in the celebrations. Drifting about the harbour, with strings of lanterns hanging from their masts, they presented a brilliant spectacle.' The fifty launches in procession, all gaily decked with lights, came up the harbour from West Point discharging volleys of rockets and blue and white Very Lights. When they were abreast of the Naval Yard in central Victoria there appeared five or six Chinese fishing junks hung with lanterns in the shape of fish, some bigger than the junks that carried them. The Westerners thought them 'a capital illustration of Chinese skill in this branch of art'. And, far into the night 'bouquets of rockets were discharged, and visitors to Hong Kong were heard to remark that the scene on the harbour could not be surpassed anywhere'.

The city itself was illuminated, and dozens of Chinese arches had been put up. The new Victoria Hotel 'was the cynosure of all eyes. The whole front of the building was outlined with 1,600 fairy lamps and 1,000 pretty Canton lanterns. In the centre was a huge illuminated painting of Her Majesty surmounted by the words *Sixty Years She Has Reigned* in five foot letters.' [sic]

A splendid statue of the Queen, not long unveiled, stood proudly amid the banks and government offices in Statue square; the crowds were immense, joyful, but orderly; and all was right with the world.

In fact, the atmosphere of euphoria reflected in the local (and British) papers of those days, was very far from being justified. While a year later, in 1898, 11,000 ships with a total tonnage of over 13 million cleared Hong Kong harbour, and the Colony's trade was in the region of five million pounds sterling, external events looked like painting a less rosy picture of the future. The Manchu dynasty in China was tottering, alternately stabbed in the back by extortionate Western demands and propped up by Western loans. The Boxer rebels, whose aims at first were to eliminate Manchu rule and to 'drive the foreigners into the sea', were gaining strength and, in 1900, dropping their anti-Manchu stand, were joined by the Imperial Army at the command of the Dowager Empress in their attack on the Peking foreign legations and Roman Catholic Cathedral.[2] These events and others were not without repercussions in Hong Kong. The Boxer Rebellion caused massive unrest in the southern provinces and, according to the shifts of Boxer fortunes, people came and went from Hong Kong. Even after the allied occupation of Peking, the crushing of the Boxers, and the return of the Court to the capital, tension in the East was high. The Russo-Japanese war of 1904–1905 did not lessen it.

The feverish decades of Western dominance by economic and gunboat 'diplomacy' in the Far East were now beginning in earnest, and the pace increased with the melancholy fall of the last dynasty in China in 1911. Again an influx of Chinese, seeking safety from the growing uncertainty of conditions, descended on Hong Kong.

In 1898, the United States navy was operating from Colony waters, and from this haven captured Manila in that year. And on 11 June of the same year the near hinterland of Kowloon, called the New Territories, was ceded to Britain on a ninety-nine year lease. The authorities soon discovered that to occupy and rule this addition of 355 square miles to the Colony's area, was no easy matter. Most of the Chinese inhabitants (who of course had not been consulted by their own or by British authorities on the matter) were violently against British rule, despite the despotic character of Chinese authority. That was the devil they knew, not the 'foreign devil'. It was only with difficulty and sometimes by force of arms that the territory was gradually taken over.

Just after the turn of the century there were still over five hundred people per acre living in the central district of Victoria. The muddled attempts, lamentably too little and too late, at improved sanitation that had been made sporadically for several decades had not yet succeeded in making it a hygienic place to live in. Plague was still endemic (and remained so until at least 1924). The 'irresistible logic of a severe epidemic' as the sanitary report of 1882 had called it, was still just around the corner. An offer of a few cents each for rats caught by the public caused many tens of thousands to be brought in. But it was discovered that numbers of these plague-infected creatures had in fact been brought from over the border in China! The need to clean up the town involved rat-proofing of houses and the spraying of breeding grounds of the anopheles mosquito (just discovered to be the carrier of malaria.) But, in typical Hong Kong style, the officers of the sanitary teams involved in this work were discovered (by an enquiry in 1907) to have been making small fortunes in collusion with property owners and building contractors—and the laws had been massively evaded. One more of Hong Kong's monstrous scandals blew up, and the matter was only slowly rectified.[3]

Top: A customs officer and his wife at an outpost in the New Territories. *Above:* Prince Ch'un of the imperial family with Sir Henry Blake, Governor from November 1898 to November 1903. The photograph was taken in 1901

143

The whole question of education for Chinese, for British, and others, by various agencies and by the government, came under acrimonious dispute. The new Governor, Sir Henry Blake, who had arrived in 1898, set up an enquiry, and the report in 1902 recommended schooling on racial lines, and was a frankly reactionary document even for its times. A wealthy Chinese, Sir Robert Ho Tung, had given the government a school for English teaching that was open to all, regardless of race, but the government (in the light of the report) announced that it would take the school for teaching the British only. Sir Robert had no choice but to agree, regretting a policy 'so much opposed to the spirit which prompted my offer of the school.' Chinese and others were generally more liberal in Hong Kong's history than the ruling British. To be fair, the Secretary of State in London condemned the report and the Hong Kong government's actions in taking over schools for British pupils only. And so the slow fight for education went on. It is still far from won.

The names of Chinese, Parsee traders, Jewish companies and tycoons, coupled with the name of one unique governor, Sir Frederick Lugard, are those which stand out from the miserable story of reluctant British administrations and their rearguard action against worthwhile education. To Lugard, in large measure, the University owes its existence, and however much the Foreign Office might deprecatingly call it 'Sir Frederick's pet lamb', both he and his wife managed to raise large sums for it. And the Parsee merchant H.N. Mody offered vast sums for its building and endowment, and there were many smaller Chinese contributions. Ng Li Hing gave the money for a medical college, and Sir Robert Ho Tung endowed a chair of surgery, while a Straits Chinese called Cheung Pat Sze assisted the arts faculty. It was no thanks at all to the British (with the shining exceptions of Lugard and his wife) that a university came into being.

Oddly enough, the anopheles and its malarial activities when revealed, caused an increase in racial feelings. Never far from the thoughts and lips of the British in Hong Kong, racial prejudice came to the fore with popular demands that separate residential areas be set aside for Westerners and Chinese. Joseph Chamberlain, Foreign Secretary, was only slightly more liberal than the colonists when he approved the principle of an area where 'people of clean habits will be safe from malaria', but added that Chinese of good standing should be permitted residence there too.

It was about this time that an intrepid Englishwoman, Mrs Archibald

Little arrived in Hong Kong.[4] She was President of the Natural Foot Society in China, an association of Western women residing there (mostly the wives of diplomats and merchants) dedicated to abolishing the Chinese custom of binding the feet of girl children so that they did not grow longer than the sexually mind-blowing (to males) 'Three-inch Golden Lily' of tradition. After a successful lecture-tour of many cities in China and a meeting with the great Chinese statesman Li Hung-chang (who teased her, although she did not quite realize it), she descended with undiminished zeal on the Colony and filled the City Hall to capacity for her lecture on the evils of the Chinese custom. The laughter that punctuated her words caused her to write: 'Chinese ... think signs of sorrow unbecoming, and being affected must show it in some way.'

Government House was thrown open for the first time to Chinese women for another meeting. And later still Mrs Little gave a lecture at the Chinese boys school named Queen's College. Over five hundred boys and young men—some of those in the higher grades already married—sat at her feet. At this remove, we can only conjecture what thoughts and emotions affected them as the tall English lady (tightly bound at the waist, be it said) lectured them on this indelicate subject. Doubtless, like other young men confronted by naiveté on sexual topics of which they feel they already know a lot, they were embarrassed. Doubtless, too, their minds drifted to those numerous Chinese drawings and paintings that circulated freely, demonstrating the use of courtesans' bound feet to stimulate their customers. The naive Mrs Little recorded that her audience responded 'with such long-continued waves of applause, and laughed such echoing, rolling peals of laughter, that it was almost impossible to get on with what I was saying.' And when she showed X-ray pictures of bound feet, the youths 'simply stormed the platform.... It must surely be a long time,' Mrs Little suggested later, 'before Queen's College forgets that afternoon.' Doubtless it was. For it would have been hard to hit on a subject more sexually titillating for young male Chinese of those days. After initial surprise, their enthusiasm was understandable.

With such occasional barnstormers as Mrs Little, coming as it were from the outer space of the world, Hong Kong went on its dedicated commercial way.

There were, in the Colony, one or two 'characters' whose oddities of behaviour and outlook caused mirth and sarcastic comment. Mr E.R. Belilios, son of a successful Indian merchant whom Sir John Pope

145

Hennessy had nominated to the Legislative Council in 1881, and who was Chairman of the Hongkong and Shanghai Bank, a philanthropist of no mean standing, and a great drunkard, was one of these urban delights. It is said that people knew precisely how drunk he was at any moment according to the darkness of his face which, in extreme inebriation, became pitch black. He was also fond of animals and had imported a zebra, a llama, and other beasts, including a large camel, all of which he kept in stables on the Peak. Various stories attempt to explain the camel as a response to the poor water supply on the Peak. These are doubtless apocryphal. After years of existence on those dank heights, the poor camel appears to have escaped from its stable one July night in 1907, and to have fallen (or did it jump in final despair with life?) over a precipice not far from the Governor's summer retreat, Mountain Lodge; and died.

It might be supposed that there the matter would have ended. But in Hong Kong it is precisely such trivia that from time to time rend the administration and pit officials and laity with fury and invective against one another. The squabble developed, as the camel rotted under the midsummer sun, between the Public Works Department and the Sanitary Board as to which of them was responsible for its removal. As the tortuous and acrimonious polemic progressed, the stench of decaying camel-flesh grew by the day. And it appears that in the outcome neither department would give way and the animal slowly rotted where it fell. Its owner eventually drank himself to death.

This was the city about which an American at that time went into such raptures. Eliza Ruhamah Scidmore in her book *China—Longlived Empire*, published in 1900, calls the place a 'city of real palaces, more nearly the Magnificent or the Superb than hillside Genoa'. Above the city of Victoria 'there is a second city, a hanging suburb in the clouds of the Peak, and only British dignity could survive being pulled up and dropped down from the clouds backward in those most primitive cable-cars.... Imperial, free, modern, and enlightened Hongkong gives the American citizen cause to consider when he finds himself landing and leaving without having encountered the custom-house. There is none, yet the colony prospers.'

This was the city that to mark the accession of Edward VII in 1901 decided to convert part of a military area in Kowloon into a public park, but was thwarted when the military refused to surrender the land to the authorities.[5] A city where every man's hand was still very often against his neighbour, as *The Times* had said long ago. It was the city

Top: Proclaiming the accession of George V on the Hong Kong Cricket Club's ground. *Above:* the Viceroy of Kwangtung stepping ashore in Hong Kong, 1907

147

where a big new hospital was opened on the Peak, where a big new dock was being laboriously excavated in the granite foreshore, the city where a new newspaper was launched—the *South China Morning Post*, still the leading paper of the Colony seventy years later.

The 70th Anniversary Review of the *S.C.M.P.*, as most people call it with mixed despair and affection, gives in broad terms an interesting picture of the year 1903 when the paper's first edition appeared on 17 November. Early issues are missing, but the front page of the issue of 5 January 1904, contained only advertisements, sometimes curious but often, in this contemporary world of screaming commercialism, dignified announcements of what might be bought. Many companies still in being today were advertising. A.S. Watson promised 'Unique selections of the Purest and best confectionery received from the leading London and Paris houses comprising the simpler kinds to those of recherché description.' Mitsui Bussan Kaisha advertised Japanese coals for steamships, while A. Fong, photographer on Ice House Road, established 1859, advertised 'Photography in all its Branches', and 'Madam Flint & Co., Fashion Parlours, Milliners, and Dressmakers, Latest Paris Fashions, Parisian Hats' were 'at the Connaught Hotel, first floor. Lift available.' And Sien Ting, dentist, advised that his prices were moderate and consultation free; and a delightfully named company, Hang On, were general merchants. Bafflingly enough, since it was 5 January, the Robinson Piano Company, Limited, took a half-column space to state that 'there is no Xmas. Gift [sic] gives so great and permanent pleasure as The "Apollo" Piano-Player.' And they also offered 'Victor Talking Machines, absolute reproduction of the human voice'.

Page two of the newspaper contains reports from the Supreme and other Court proceedings, The Turf, Yachting (in which the Acting Governor, Mr F.H. May came in second in his yacht *Dione*), and Football. Page three has two columns headed Science—a note on the treatment of cancer in France by X-Rays, and a quotation from the British medical journal, *The Lancet*, on the influence of the weather on 'the criminal classes'. Share market reports and more advertisements fill the rest of this page. The Editorial on page four begins: 'Russia and Japan are upon the brink of war.' And under the heading 'Government House', we discover that not only did His Excellency the Acting Governor race his yacht, but he also played polo and was entertained to dinner by the army. This is followed by a series of quotations from newspapers all over the Far East. Page five is frankly a mess. It contains news items of all sorts, from Japanese military purchases, riots in England, football again, news from Canton, celebration at the German Club in Yokohama, and an epidemic of fires in the same city. The following two pages contain only shipping news and advertisements, and the back page deals with mails arrived and expected, and some more advertisements—chiefly for hotels—with lists of the guests staying at each establishment.

It was in this age, too, that the first of the trams, those leisurely clanking old aunts of vehicles, trundled into service—on 4 July 1904. On the inaugural journey the first car was driven by a Mrs Jones, wife of

A third class tramcar in September 1904, two months after the service was initiated

the Director of Public Works, from Arsenal Street, Wanchai, along Hennessy Road to the Bowrington Canal, at what is now the Western border of Victoria Park, her son accompanying her and 'operating the bell continuously'. The waterfront is nowadays much farther from the tramlines than it was then, on the long haul from Kennedy Town in the west to Shaukiwan in the east, and Hennessy Road was still narrow.

In early days the trams were all single-deckers and apparently open to the elements—rather elegant vehicles, conjured up, it seems from the mind of a fine designer to suit the circumstances of Hong Kong, at least in fine weather. The history of the tramways is told in a curious little book, *Hong Kong Tramways*. In 1909, Governor Lugard took the august Viceroy of Kwangtung province for a jaunt in a short procession of two decorated trams, the official party travelling all the way to Quarry Bay to inspect the newly completed Taikoo Docks there.

But the tramway company itself was an enterprising body in earlier years. Advertisements placed in local newspapers carry down the years the authentic whiff of the charming, slightly strange, infinitely leisured past. 'Bathing by Moonlight,' says a headline of 15 July 1913, 'Hong-kong Tramway Co. Bathing by moonlight from the beach at North Point. By kind permission of Capt. Zeeder, the band of HMS *Siberia* will play on the beach from 9.00 p.m. to 11.00 p.m. on Wednesday 16 July. Special cars will run every few minutes from the Post Office.'

Sir Francis Henry May,
Governor from July 1912
to February 1919

And only days later (doubtless in response to the success of the first venture) a similar notice appeared. But, in addition, the company begged 'to inform the general public that twenty-four bathing tents are now available on the beach . . . and with the tides convenient this week, parents with children will find the beach an ideal spot for an afternoon picnic.' Just where North Point beach was located would cause today's traveller some problem, for it has long been built over.

The impression of the early years of the 20th century is of a tamer Hong Kong, of an administration now firmly based and with established ranks and salaries and pensions, constituting a civil service run more or less on the lines of that in other colonies—in the great empire of India, in Malaya, and elsewhere. Public revenue went up—from three and a half million dollars in 1898 to eighteen and a half in 1914. Great tracts of land in the centre of Victoria were reclaimed and on them sprung the Post Office (a vast, architecturally muddled, brick building demolished in 1977), and the domed Supreme Court building—correctly placed between the new Hong Kong Club, the statue of the Queen–Empress, the Bank, and the twirling fans in serried ranks of

150

musty offices that constituted the business district. The 'criminal classes' (aside from the necessary coolies) were still sundered from the body of the town, doubtless under the influence of the particular climate of the slopes of the western part of Victoria as *The Lancet* had confidently predicted, the peninsula of Kowloon, and a scattering of villages here and there. The trams ran conveniently along the length of the town's tentacles, east and west, and the Kowloon–Canton railway was completed, the section from Kowloon to the border in 1905, and to Canton in 1910. Lugard's 'pet lamb'—the University—opened in 1912, with the governor, F.H. May as its first Chancellor.

May, the first Hong Kong cadet to attain the post of Governor, had been in the Colony since 1881, becoming Colonial Secretary in 1902. He had been appointed (for reasons that must always remain a mystery to those of average intelligence) as Governor of Fiji for a short spell before being brought back to Hong Kong where his whole working life had been spent. His return was marked by a dire deed. The *Hong Kong Telegraph* of 5 July 1912 tells the story.

'All records of crime in this Colony were eclipsed yesterday when a daring attempt, miraculously unsuccessful, was made in the presence

The sedans of the Governor, Sir Henry May, and his wife leaving Blake Pier on his arrival on 4 July 1912

of thousands of people to assassinate His Excellency Sir Henry May.' The Governor had just disembarked at Blake Pier on the waterfront in Central and was being carried in his chair, with Lady May in another beside him. 'The red-coated coolies bearing the Governor's chair had just got into their stride when a man was seen to pass rapidly between the soldiers in front of the Post Office. . . . He fired point blank, about 3 feet range. . . .' The would-be assassin was immediately siezed and almost choked, his clothes half torn from him, and beaten by the 'angry witnesses of the narrowly averted tragedy'.

'Sir Henry May preserved a composure which, in the circumstances, was truly remarkable. . . . The bullet whizzed under the cover of the chair . . . splintering the bamboo frame of Lady May's chair. . . . Sir Henry immediately rose from his chair . . . and brushed down his coat. . . . On sitting down again he turned a half-contemptuous, half-sympathetic glance at his assailant.' Lady May was temporarily flustered but was soon 'all smiles as usual'. And the procession continued to City Hall where the majority of those present to tender addresses of welcome had no knowledge of the attempt until later. Thus passed the sole recorded attempt on the life of a Hong Kong governor. The Chinese involved, Li Hon-hung, was an isolated malcontent, and his motives were not political.

Left: The Governor's sedan halted and his would-be assassin on the ground, surrounded by police and others—the old Post Office in the background

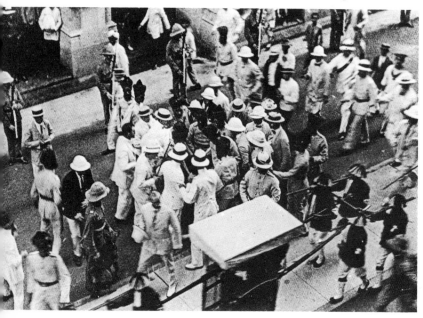

About this time we have another picture of aspects of Hong Kong, from a man who was a scholar in Chinese, and the Colony's Director of Education at his retirement in 1938. In his book *Hong Kong 1862–1919*, apart from details of the scene as he encountered it on his arrival in 1910, G.R. Sayer makes some interesting points that are of more than topographical interest.

It was still a quiet old Hong Kong with Queen Victoria presiding in bronze under a cupola at its centre, the old Hongkong and Shanghai Bank occupying only part of its present site and the old City hall the remainder. The Hong Kong Club had moved to its present building a decade before, and its former premises were occupied by a draper's shop. Shorty after 1910, the Colony's first cinema was to open a few steps up Wyndham Street among the pitches of the flower sellers who, today, have been forced farther up the hill. The Hong Kong Hotel stood on Pedder Street, and Lapraik's Clock Tower was still there impeding traffic. But not impeding it to such an extent as formerly, for (and we have no really valid explanation for the fact) the carriages that various writers noticed in droves in Hong Kong had by this time vanished. The coach houses of great mansions stood empty, and everyone went by rickshaw or sedan chair. Carts were pulled by oxen or water buffalo. The road from central Victoria went as far east as Shaukiwan,

Centre: a closer view as the assailant is heavily surrounded. *Right:* the gunman is dragged away as the Governor's procession prepares to start off again

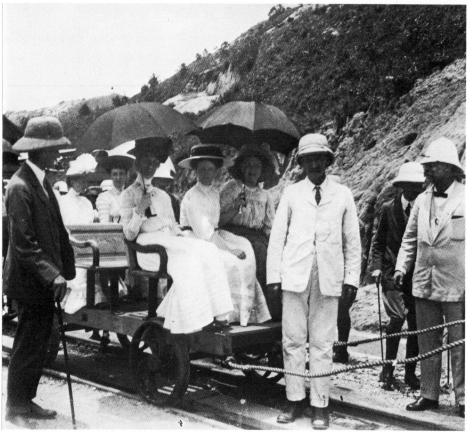

and in the west round to Pokfulam and to Aberdeen. Deepwater Bay was accessible only by a track, or by sea. 'Repulse Bay is remote and unravished. Stanley gradually decays. . . . The village of Tai Tam Tuk still goes about its business unconscious of its coming doom [it was shortly to be covered by the waters of a new resevoir]. Shek-O is still untouched by foreign hands.' The New Territories were almost wholly untouched too, the road to Taipo a zig-zag to the administrative head-quarters, and no further.

The population, doubled in the past two decades, stood at just short of half a million. But in order to enter into the feeling of the Colony in 1910 one of the principal points to remember is that (as Sayer remarks) 'the internal combustion engine has yet to reach Hong Kong. No horn is heard in Victoria's hills and dales. The streets are the unchallenged hunting ground of the pedestrian, the chair-coolie and the common carrier humping his load on his shoulder. . . . The reader must therefore visualize a very different and slower city, a city in which petrol pumps and traffic signals give place to shady banyan trees—and the clatter and screech of gear to the sob of the straining coolie.'

The industrial revolution had not yet hit Hong Kong. Its products, yes: but the thing itself, to all intent, was still a war away.

As for the Chinese: 'With rare exceptions [it was the eve of the revolution in China] every man wears a queue' and with few exceptions none wore Western clothes. The soft black shoes and long gowns of tradition were the order of the day. No Chinese took part in foreign sport and none went swimming. The vast majority, then as now, had no contact

Opposite, above: Terminal buildings of the Kowloon–Canton Railway in 1910. *Left:* Ladies at the opening of the railway riding in a specially designed vehicle. *Above:* a watercolour of the Post Office shortly before it was demolished in 1977

with Europeans at all. 'The elders take their caged birds for an airing on the cricket ground; the youngsters kick a shuttlecock in a back street or furtively fly a kite. At sun-down there is still the same clatter of *mah jong* counters.'

It is a scene familiar today in some ways. The old men air their birds still, the clatter of mahjong is the subject of endless complaints in the local newspapers. But, says Sayer, 'as for the women, excepting the petty hawker, the sampan woman, the scavenger and the seamstress crouching at the foot of a verandah pillar, none yet ventures into the streets.' And there we have a significant difference—the quiet women-less streets.

During the governorship of Sir Henry May the revolution in China brought upheavals which in Hong Kong were thought to be temporary, but which proved but the prelude to the bitterest years of China's history—years of anarchy, of internal chaos, of rampaging armies, and Western nations vying with one another to arm this or that faction in the hope of backing the eventual winner.

Piracy in Hong Kong waters was on the increase, and the Colony was flooded by small silver coins minted in Canton. To suppress the use of these latter, the Tramway Company refused to accept them in payment of fares, thus causing Chinese to feel that their 'lately-deposed Emperor' as well as the newly awakened spirit of nationalism were being affronted. They boycotted the trams, and the company, faced

The house of the Naval Commodore in Hong Kong, built for a German company in 1913. *Opposite, above:* The Cricket Club—United Services *v.* Civilians, 1869. *Below:* the opening of the season, 1889

with great losses, appealed to the Governor. The astute May traced the mainsprings of the boycott to one particular district of the Chinese areas and imposed on it a special 'punitive rate'. Within a few days the Chinese members of the Legislative Council boarded the trams to show their fellow Chinese that 'tram-riding was fashionable again'. The boycott was broken.

The import of private cars had begun by the time May was shot at outside the Post Office, despite the fact that there were hardly ten miles of paved road outside the city. A circular road was built round the island—by 1915 you could drive to Deepwater Bay, and two years later on to Repulse Bay. Similar strides were made in road-building on the mainland.

157

One result was the final demolition of that controversial Clock Tower in Pedder Street, and yet another was the building in 1919 of the Repulse Bay Hotel. Such was the beginning of the 20th century revolution in Hong Kong.

More and more Chinese from the mainland crowded into the Colony. The water supply once more gave serious problems, and new reservoirs were built at great expense. On the lighter side of life (except for the killed and injured) a rampaging tiger was finally killed in the New Territories in 1915 and borne in triumph to the City Hall.

The principal effort of the Colony as far as World War I was concerned was concentrated on raising money in quantity to be sent to Britain; and in putting German merchants in Hong Kong under detention— somewhat reluctantly, be it said—and in passing resolutions to exclude them for a decade after the war from trading.

By the time that most terrible of all wars (in terms of the individual soldier in France) had passed in a welter of blood, the Colony's Chamber of Commerce was pressing for unofficial control of its destinies, and being turned down flat. And on the level of the ordinary man there was the murderous Gresson Street shoot-out between a gang of armed Chinese bandits in Wanchai and the police. And the matshed grandstand at Happy Valley, filled to capacity with Chinese, suddenly burst into

The Ladies' Match teams in December 1924. Mrs Reed, the captain, is seated on the left of the men's team captain in the middle row

The original caption printed on this photograph reads: 'Tiger shot near Fanling on 8 March, 1915, after it had killed an Indian an [sic] European constable aan [sic] a native'

flames engulfing and incinerating six hundred of them in what must be the Colony's largest single tragedy.

In September 1918, Sir Henry May, one of the very few men who had given virtually his whole life to the Colony, could no longer bear the strain. He had not been away from the Colony for seven years, and now he left for Vancouver for a short leave. As soon as he arrived in Canada, the armistice was signed in Europe. Doubtless with relief, he resigned as Governor. His had been a long, unusually strenuous, and much fraught term of office. The words of a Chinese spokesman sum up both the man and his actions very well: 'Sparing of speech and sparing of smiles, he never spared himself in the execution of his duty to the Colony.'

9

COLONY INTO FACTORY

WORLD WAR I in itself had no dire or far-reaching effect on Hong Kong. But its aftermath was much more serious for the Colony. The travesty of justice perpetrated at the Paris Peace Conference in 1919 left China still entirely in thrall to the West and to Japan. It was hardly a matter of surprise to anyone, except Westerners, that with the failure of the agreements (not signed by the Chinese, but signed by everyone else) to abolish Japanese occupation of former German concessions in China, and their failure to abolish the Western concessions, too, the Chinese viewed the whole matter with deepest hostility—knowing they had been sold down the river once more.

The time of China had not yet come. She was still weak, divided, more or less bankrupt; and now brought to her knees by Western and Japanese depredations, and by the social and economic internal convulsions these things brought in their wake. Now the Western world and Japan fed like vultures on the moribund carcass. Few then thought China could ever rise again.

China under Kuomintang rule took once more an anti-foreign stance, something quite understandable in the circumstances. Boycotts of foreign goods, unrest among Hong Kong Chinese, the seamen's strike of 1922, the general strike in the Colony in 1925–6, were all results of the Western 'presence' in China.

For nearly a century the Chinese desire to become once more completely masters in their own house had been growing with each new foreign incursion, but it was still unfocussed. It was an era of warlords dividing the country between them. It was the time of Dr Sun Yat-sen, that product of Hong Kong education, and of the birth of the Chinese Communist Party; and later it was the era of Japanese aggression, and of the Kuomintang 'extermination' campaigns against their own

160

people: it was the time of the Long March. And then of World War II.

Hong Kong was affected in one way and another by the 'spin-off' of most of these processes in China. But it suffered also from the results of that convulsive disease that had racked the Western world increasingly since the 1920s. An unsettled Europe, the General Strike in Britain in 1926, the rise of Hilter and Mussolini, the economic slaughter of undeveloped countries by developed ones, the Depression, rearmament—it was hardly to be wondered that the inter-war years were for the Colony a time of difficulties compounded.

The population rose in steps, each influx occasioned by one more social convulsion in China, from 625,000 in 1921 to 1,639,000 twenty years later on the eve of even more stark events. During that same period exports to China fell from roughly $432 millions in 1921 to $90 millions in 1939. But at the same time Hong Kong industry was beginning to develop. The textile industry (which had been introduced long ago but later removed to Shanghai) was reintroduced, and by the late thirties employed nearly 6,000 people. The older shipbuilding industry expanded and by 1939 had 16,000 employees. And revenue between 1921 and 1940 almost trebled. Despite ups and downs, and there were many, the economy of Hong Kong showed an overall expansion. The resilience of its traders, Chinese and foreigners alike, the prodigious feats of its workers (all Chinese, and most grossly underpaid), the continual stream of new labour fleeing from the uncertainties, the civil strife, the armed Japanese aggressions in China itself; and the unique conditions for trade and commerce in Hong Kong—all these factors kept it bustling, growing, lively, and firmly in British colonial hands.

The University of Hong Kong had held its first congregation in 1916 at which degrees were granted in the presence of the Governor of Kwangtung. Lugard's 'pet lamb' had come of age. But education in general progressed in the usual haphazard manner of non-profit-making activities of the Colony. By 1923 there were nearly 500 schools in urban areas with an enrolment of about 24,000 pupils, some of whom were government subsidized. In the country areas, chiefly in the New Territories, there were 192 schools at this time, with a total of almost 5,000 pupils, of whom about half were subsidized.

The old Sanitary Board, subject of so much debate and so many allegations of corruption in the past, was replaced in 1935 by the Urban Council. This body had hardly any power, and after deliberating was able only to advise the Legislative Council on what bye-laws might be suitable. At that time the Urban Council consisted of five official members and eight unofficials. The curious procedure whereby two of the eight unofficials were elected by those whose names appeared on jury lists, and the six others appointed by the Governor (three were required to be Chinese), was to alter very gradually as years went by.

Water remained a problem—it is charitably said because of the unpredictable influxes of population due to the disturbed conditions in China. Reading the record, however, it is hard to escape the impression that no one ever really envisaged the future demands of an apparently growing population with a tendency to turn toward industrialization. The opening of Tytam Reservoir by the Governor, Sir Henry May, on Saturday, 2 February 1918, went some way to solving the problem temporarily. In his speech as he unveiled a commemorative plaque at the opening, Sir Henry made some pointed remarks, not only on water.

'When one sees so much fresh water around ... one cannot help reflecting what a great pity it is that the residents of this Colony, a thirsty place like this, do not adopt water as a beverage instead of something stronger. It would surprise some of you people to learn the terrible casualties that are inflicted upon the civil servants by too free use of alcoholic beverages.... Out of every two men who arrive here, whether as policemen, overseers on works like this [resevoir], as Sanitary Inspectors, or as Revenue Officers, not more than one lives and remains in the service to earn a pension.'

The Governor went on to say he was talking only of the lower ranks of officers in government service. 'I do not include the upper ranks for I have no figures to go by. (Laughter)'

But Tytam was not followed by much significant progress in water supply until the beginnings of the Shing Mun Valley scheme a decade afterwards; and nine years later still, the Jubilee Reservoir (honouring the reign of King George V), which had the highest dam in the Empire at that time.

The same day as the report of Sir Henry's opening of Tytam Reservoir (in the *South China Morning Post* of Monday, 4 February), a random selection of advertisements in that newspaper adds a little atmosphere to the activities and dreams of the citizens of Victoria. In the 'Wanted' columns someone was advertising for 'A House, with about 10 rooms, in a Central Location ...', something that now does not exist. The Hong Kong Cinematograph Theatre was showing 'the 5th and 6th episodes of "Gloria's Romance", and Keystone Comics.' The equiva-

162

lents are still on the Colony's screens today. Then there were several advertisements of which the following is typical: 'Massage Hall. Miss Han Inokuchi and Miss K. Hanada, Room 19, 2nd Floor, 33, Queen's Road Central. . . .' In 1978, the massage parlours are still flourishing (but not advertising in the *South China Morning Post*—rather in some Chinese newspapers), but we have the escort services to take their place. Life does not change much in some ways.

Hong Kong remained tax-free virtually until the beginning of World War II when taxes on income, salaries, trade and corporation profits, and on property were first introduced. The general buoyancy of the economy—with periodic fluctuations—was somehow maintained right up to the World War II, despite the doubling of police and of sanitary costs, and the tripling of military expenditure.

Hong Kong lived, as ever, for the success of each commercial day. The Colony clung to a theory of society that the World War I in Europe had begun forcibly to sweep away. It was not until the World War II—indeed quite a long time after its end—that Hong Kong began to face reality in terms of the beginnings of social welfare, to choose one among many civic aspects in which it lagged far behind England.

There is a passage in a letter written in later life by the great social reformer of the 11th century in China, Wang An-shih, that strikes to the heart of much that the Hong Kong government lacked then and lacks even now:

'Many are the changes that man must cope with in this world, yet the great men of old had numerous policies to guide them in choosing what to accept, what to keep and what to discard. All these men enjoyed a state of inner preparedness, possessed the wherewithal to act before matters arose, rather than wait for events to determine their action . . . .'[1]

Wise government: not one of Hong Kong's outstanding achievements.

Naturally, the city of Victoria, and also Kowloon, had grown since the palmy days of Edward VII before World War I when it must have seemed to the local British that life and 'progress' would go on forever in much the same way. By the 1920s, some doubts must have crossed even the most patriotic colonial minds, and by the late thirties some people were rather alarmed. Yet the look and the 'feel' of Hong Kong had not grossly altered. In the late 1930s, one could still publish a book entitled *Hong Kong* whose jacket showed a row of happy Jack Tars in whites semaphoring on the bows of a submarine against a brilliant emerald Peak. *Hong Kong* by Ellen Thorbeck, published by that old established Shanghai company, Kelly and Walsh, although not the most penetrating study of the place, achieves the atmosphere very well.

'Nobody,' she writes, 'really could put into words the beauty of its emerald hills and sapphire bays or describe the countless surprises that enchant the eyes in every direction.... The city is modern, noisy, busy and crowded like every other big port .... [yet the photo in her book of a main street reveals a single-deck bus as the only wheeled vehicle in sight]. But close to it, almost without transition, Chinese life spreads its ancient traditions .... Around the City, the Harbour, and the ant-like Chinese town, is the endless space of untouched nature .... Scattered over cliffs and hillsides, the comfortable dwellings of the foreigners and well-to-do Chinese seem to be sown by a giant's hand, linked together by the pale ribbon of beautiful roads.... Nature has poured out all her riches over this small corner of the earth, human genius and British statesmanship have added progress and prosperity and here it is: Hong Kong, beautiful Paradise of Liberty.'

It was still slightly under a hundred years since Captain Elliot annexed the barren island. However much romanticism the author spreads over Hong Kong, from other more sober accounts, from photographs, and from the inference of statements, it seems likely that her picture is basically correct—if only from the viewpoint of its expatriate community.

From the Chinese point of view, another story could be told. Remarking on the over a million Chinese 'who came from all parts of China, poor farmers, refugees from famine and flood' the writer says 'they all found food, shelter, education, hope and future under the British flag. They are all proud of the big town ....' In fact rather few found much but makeshift shelter, most remained too poor to do more than just about feed themselves, and discovered (if indeed most of them had ever given it a thought) that all education, with tiny exceptions, had to be paid for in money they could not earn. Hope—hope is an emotion that humanity requires to survive the vile circumstances that most of its members have known most of the time. There was certainly not less hope in Hong Kong than under the feet of warlord troops, the depredations of KMT armies, or in the vice of extortionate landlords. Yet Chinese pride in Hong Kong is still barely a reality, except among those who can afford civic pride. For Hong Kong is still a place divided.

But, for those who had means, and an underdeveloped social sense, the Colony of the thirties must have been a pleasant enough place. The automobile and the airplane had not yet made it a respiratory trap and an auditory horror. In fact as late as 1912, when, after the attempt on Sir Henry May's life he was given a motor car and no Governor ever rode again in a sedan, scions of the Chinese community were petitioning him with objections to the 'coughing, spluttering, and honking demons', and asking for their total prohibition. But they were not slow to learn to love those same demons.

The Chinese, and the British too, were never slow to learn anything when it became inevitable, or profitable, or pleasurable. A report in the London *Daily Express* in November 1925, records that the Hong Kong Telephone Company had issued a warning against attempts to flirt with its operators. 'Chinese . . . subscribers who flirt over the wires with the telephone girls more than three times will have their numbers cancelled.' Such goings-on were described in the same article, however, as 'honourable, if invisible, celestial amatory overtures'. It is hard now to imagine any Chinese attempting flirtation with the operator. They took to the telephone like ducks to water and, were charges to be made by number of calls, Hong Kong would probably be among the world-beaters.

For Westerners these were days of leisure. There was golf in the New Territories at Fanling. There was even, briefly, a hunt in the English style, hounds and all. A local doctor started it—he was generally known as the 'Father and Founder of the Fanling Hunt'—but the hounds couldn't stand the heat of summer, and a trail laid by dragging an aniseed bag proved less than exciting. There was tennis, and swimming at many an almost deserted 'sapphire bay' where the water was yet unpolluted. There was the fashionable dinner-dance of a Saturday night in the restaurant called (for reasons that are obscure) 'The Gripps' on the top of the Hong Kong Hotel in central town. There was the Lido on the beach at Repulse Bay, and the grandmotherly Repulse Bay Hotel herself, squatting on a rise with flights of steps leading down to the straw huts on the beach, its twirling fans and white-clad 'boys' equally active in cooling brows and quenching West-ern thirsts.

'It was before the days of drycleaning, and nylon and drip-dry hadn't been invented,' an old resident recalls. 'You had seven or eight suits of Shantung silk. One was washed at the end of each day. Then sharkskin cloth came in. We thought that was very smart.'

The British were still in the last flush of what they felt to be greatness; if not the master race of Asia, then something rather like it. 'People of mixed blood were beyond the pale,' the same resident recalls. 'You couldn't afford to know them. I was a young doctor straight out from medical school. Patients over forty just wouldn't accept me. But I used to spend a lot of time with the Chinese. I wanted to learn the language, for one thing. The "number one" of the firm, as they still said in those days, the senior partner in the group of doctors, said to me one day: "Don't you think you're seeing rather a lot of the Chinese?" I said: "Quite frankly I prefer them." Now it so happened that my father was a highly respected member of the community, or—well, if I had been in the Bank, or one of the big Hongs, I'd have found myself smartly on the next boat back to England.'

'Life was really inexpensive then. I remember a subaltern in the army—paid almost nothing in those days—telling me he could take a girl out most nights of the week and still have lots of money left over. Drink was so cheap that when you asked for a gin and lime in a bar— they served them then in flat champagne-type glasses, it was the cock-tail era—the barman just went on pouring gin until you told him to stop. Gimlets, we called them. They were just pure gin. People drank themselves stupid in those days—there was nothing else to do. Hardly anyone drank wine. You drank gin before dinner, whisky with the food, and brandy after.

'It was before airconditioning and the popular refrigerator. The variety of food was very restricted. The food was really quite inadequate in some ways. Between July and late September the only fresh vegetable was the Chinese bean grown locally, and very slimy when cooked. There were few oranges, and all the chickens were of the Olympic champion variety. Most people suffered from prickly heat, Hong Kong blisters, and even boils were quite common.

'We all dressed inappropriately—clothes were far too thick. I remember my main impression when I came out in the thirties was of how incredibly hot it was. But perhaps the greatest change between those days and now is the *pace* of life. It used to be an incredibly leisurely existence. You had leisure, and more leisure.'

Early in 1938, W.H. Auden and Christopher Isherwood were on their way to the war in China and stayed awhile in Hong Kong. Like most others who attempted to write poetry about the place, the result, in this case from their book *Journey to a War*, if little more than the usual verse, does at least catch an aspect of the Colony.

Its leading characters are wise and witty,
Their suits well-tailored, and they wear them well,
Have many a polished parable to tell
About the mores of a trading city.
Only the servants enter unexpected,
Their silent movements make dramatic news;
Here in the East our bankers have erected
A worthy temple to the Comic Muse.
Ten thousand miles from home and What's-Her-Name
A bugle on this Late Victorian hill
Puts out the soldier's light; off-stage, a war
Thuds like the slamming of a distant door:
Each has his comic role in life to fill,
Though Life be neither comic nor a game.

The voyage out from London to Hong Kong had seemed to them like a dream. 'At Hongkong, we had said to each other, we shall wake up, everything will come true. But we hadn't woken; only the dream had changed. The new dream was more confused than the old, less soothing, even slightly alarming. It was all about dinner parties at very long tables, and meetings with grotesquely famous newspaper-characters —the British Ambassador, the Governor [Sir Geoffry Northcote], Sir Victor Sassoon. We seemed to be perpetually in a hurry, struggling into our dinner-jackets, racing off in taxis to keep appointments for which we were already hopelessly late. . . .' Thus, in *Journey to a War*, Hong Kong seemed to them.

By late November 1938, Kwangtung province had been overrun and there were Japanese faces in uniform on the far side of Hong Kong's border. Apparently unsuspected by the Hong Kong government, Japanese intelligence in Hong Kong was informed of every item of any importance. The defensive 'line' of tunnels in the New Territory hills, locally known as Gin-drinkers Line, existed in all its details in Japanese plans as soon as it was built, as did details of ammunition, and manpower of the army and the various volunteer defence corps that were got together.

The colonial government's intelligence came from Singapore, from an organization named the Far East Combined Bureau, whose estimate of Japanese army and air force strength and capability up to and after the outbreak of World War II was that Japanese troops were incapable of night movements, and that they only seemed good because they had been pitted against inferior opponents; that the Japanese air force could not cope with night flying, and that their bomb-aiming was bad. This not only effectively lulled the Hong Kong government into rapturous sleep but deceived Winston Churchill in London. He remarked: 'The probability of the Japanese undertaking an attack on Singapore is remote; in fact, nothing could be more foolish from their point of view.' He said nothing about Hong Kong until later.

In January 1941, Hong Kong under British rule reached its centenary. The war in Europe had raged for over a year, so celebrations were muted. The two leading newspapers got together and published a joint supplement. 'Conditions in a war-torn world prevent fitting celebration of a great historic event in the Colony's history. Nevertheless, Hong Kong stands today a monument to British foresight [in what precise way it did not specify], enterprise, and stamina; it is still a haven of refuge, a symbol of democratic freedom, and a beacon for many who falter in these troubled and uncertain times.' Just where democracy entered the Hong Kong picture for an unfranchized population basically ruled by politicians and civil servants in Whitehall, it is hard to understand. But the editorial continued: 'It stands as a bastion of civilization, as democratic peoples translate that term; perhaps a challenge. Whatever the next hundred years may hold for Hong Kong, its first century is a glorious one, and the tale of its development . . . should form an inspiration to any who came after us.' Allowing for some hyperbole on the occasion of a centenary, this must still be one of the more demonstrably untrue statements made about the Colony.

Less than twelve months later, the Colony surrendered unconditionally to the Japanese, on Christmas Day, 1941, after just over two weeks' resistance. Churchill, in the third volume of his history of World War II, states: 'I had no illusions about the fate of Hong Kong under the overwhelming impact of Japanese power. But the finer the British resistance, the better for all.' One may doubt this bland bit of wall-papering also. It would seem at least dubious whether the expenditure of life incurred in the hopeless military situation in Hong Kong— which had no air defence, only token armed forces, and all its big guns placed to ward off attack from the sea—was in any way justifiable. The heroic efforts of the defenders were not only in vain but suicidal, and the resistance ordered from London had probably no effect at all on the course of the war.

On 8 December, it was a fine clear and sunny morning. Pearl Harbour was under attack. A Hong Kong businessman, Benjamin Proulx, recalls that he was at the Jockey Club about to do a practice ride. Like other private citizens in those days he was an amateur jockey.[2] When the first Japanese bombs fell on Kai Tak airport over the harbour from Happy Valley about 8 a.m., his horse went out of control for a time, but he managed to finish the circuit.

A teenage schoolboy remembers he had just got to school in Wanchai and was in the classroom taking his books out of his case when he heard the sound of bombs. The school was dismissed and they all ran home as fast as they could. A Portuguese lady was at Mass in St Teresa's Church in Kowloon—it was the Feast of the Immaculate Conception —when the sound of bombs and machine-gun fire caused her to look out of the windows. She saw 'planes darting about like silver fish. They flew quite low over the church and I noticed on their wings the full red discs. This was the way it began for me and hundreds of others.' An understatement—for hundreds of thousands of others. For the population of Hong Kong had been given no warning at all.

The heroic, muddled, pathetic, and pointless epic of the defence of Hong Kong had started. Just over a couple of weeks later it was all over. The armed services and the administration had surrendered, and the Colony began its three and a half years of painful Japanese occupation.

A reasonably objective guess made at the time of the fall of Hong Kong to the Japanese would surely have come up with the answer that this—the centenary of the Colony—must surely prove to be its end. The same educated guessing might well have predicted the end of Britain's (and other Western powers') colonial empire in the East. For the Japanese, who had been the first Oriental power to rout a Western power, in 1905, had now shown they could rout the forces of all Western powers in the East. The fact that they were reconquered in a matter of three years, radically altered Japan and the Japanese attitude to the rest of the world: but it also perhaps even more deeply changed the attitude of the Eastern peoples as a whole to the rule of Western powers. That the latter filtered back and tried to take over, to replicate the societies and the hegemony they had for many a pre-war year known in the East, proved everywhere quite a brief interregnum. And the Eastern peoples in varying ways removed Western powers from their ruling positions. Except in Hong Kong.

The reasons why are extremely complex and have geographical, industrial, practical, political, and other aspects that require at least a volume to themselves for adequate elucidation. Suffice it to say that Hong Kong with, as in former times, more luck than good guidance, remained a colony of Britain, and in fact (due to these curious, all but unique circumstances in which she found herself) went on to change as if the first century had been one of embryonic life, and the end of World War II the moment of birth.

Meanwhile, under Japanese occupation, Japanese brutality and Japanese administrative inefficiency and callousness were the main factors that affected those caught in Hong Kong. The worst sufferers were the captured armed forces whose condition in internment camps was terrible indeed. Civilians fared on the whole better in the famous Stanley Camp where, on a peninsula on the southern aspect of the island they were herded together and made the best of what little they found there. Some of Japan's major weaknesses as a conqueror were vividly demonstrated in its occupation of Hong Kong. The victors completely failed to administer the Colony in any rational way. Their answer to food and other shortages was to deport a million of the population. They failed even to get the basic utilities such as water and electricity running in a reasonable manner. A tram driver remembers that 'when the war came, the tramways ran for a few months. And then most of them stopped. I was out of a job and had a wife and children to feed. I joined forces with a friend of mine and we got a three-wheeler [a pedicab, or trishaw, or pousse-pousse, depending on your language]. 'I used to peddle passengers along the tram routes, or anywhere else they wanted to go. Then we decided to branch out. We got two axles and four wheels and made a wooden platform to fit on top of them. This was a kind of passenger cart, and one or other of us used to drag it by a rope with the passengers crouched on top. There were hardly any buses, not many trams, and really no other means of getting about except by bicycle. So we were usually quite busy.'

The teenage schoolboy, his sister killed in an air raid, his family dispersed, went with his father to a small property they had on an island. There they spent the war growing vegetables and chickens to eke out an existence.

The Japanese completely failed to win over the population—partly because they had no idea how to do so, and partly because all Chinese knew from long years of Japanese erosion of Chinese territory, that they had little but oppression, brutality, extortion, and forced labour to look forward to from the conquerors.

On the Japanese surrender, Hong Kong was re-occupied by the British on 30 August 1945. It was not too long before the Colony was running again. But in fact the old Hong Kong, although it seemed

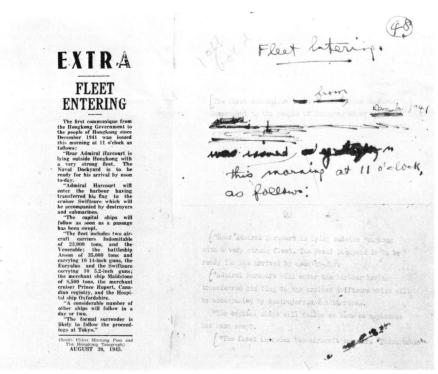

The first issue of the South China Morning Post (a single sheet) following the liberation of Hong Kong, with part of the corrected 'copy'

outwardly to have taken up its life again, had vanished. Rather in the way that traditional leisure vanished from the life of the well-to-do in England after World War I, never to come back: it was no longer a Western world of leisure because it was a world that had been saved from its enemies by the unleisured poor.

So, in Hong Kong, if leisure lingered on a little longer, the pace of living, forced by the accelerating pace of life elsewhere when it inevitably caught up with the Colony, rapidly increased. A new face replaced the old shipping and entrepôt face, and industrialization began in earnest. The effect was a revolution, and if it was a long-delayed one it was all the more sweeping. The city, essentially of the past, and the attitudes of its rulers and its ruled, were swept into the history books within a few years so that now, three decades later, one already looks at them much in the manner in which one looks at the events of much earlier times. Doubtless this abrupt shift can be discerned in the postwar life of many another city, but in Hong Kong it was all the more dramatic because of the particular circumstances of a colony which has continued to *exist*, but in a very different form.

171

The Japanese War Memorial on Hong Kong Island was demolished in 1946

10

HONG KONG TODAY
THE KALEIDOSCOPE

Hong kong, from its very inception, had more luck than its government had foresight. And so it proved again after World War II. Luck, this time, came chiefly in the form of people, and to some extent in the expanding economies of Southeast Asian and other countries as they recovered from the ravages of war.

The factors that a newly industrializing city or state must initially look for would pre-eminently be just those—a fairly cheap work-force of large proportions, together with expanding markets. The other two requirements must be an innate intelligence and adaptability at all levels, and capital investment. Hong Kong was indeed in luck, for all these factors were present soon after the end of the war. The influx of Chinese from over the border was considerable, varying with the events of the Civil War in China, final victory of the Communist forces, and the establishment of the People's Republic. The constituents of this human tide were as various, from peasants to semi-skilled and skilled labour, and wealthy industrialists from Shanghai and elsewhere who brought not only their fortunes with them but in some cases their machinery as well.

The result, accompanied by the usual fluctuations of fortune to which Hong Kong had long been accustomed, and to which it adapted with what was at first a basically Chinese resilience but is now characteristic of most expatriate businesses as well, was the growth of one of the world's small industrial giants within a few years. In a sense, because it lacks a hinterland from which raw materials could come, and lacks also a large population to absorb most of its products, Hong Kong is even more of an industrial miracle than post-war Japan.

There had often been, in the past, influxes of people to Hong Kong. The causes were unrest in China and real or apparent economic

173

Part of one of the older resettlement estates. *Right:* The Ngau Tau Kok resettlement estate. Low structures are remnant squatter areas

174

opportunity in the Colony. But the phenomenal numbers of people arriving in post-war years had no equal. At the end of the war there were about 600,000 people in Hong Kong. This quickly grew as former residents returned. The civil war in China brought, with each city and especially each southern area that fell to the Communists, a body of 'refugees,' larger or smaller—the fall of Canton in 1949 added 700,000 mouths to those the Colony somehow had to feed. By 1950 there were 2,360,000 people in the Colony, and by 1956 at least two and a half million. In 1950, entry at the border was restricted to a daily quota.

Conditions verged on the chaotic. A rise of almost a million in the population of a colony whose existing population was only a million and a half, and that in five years, spelled urban squalor, human misery, a potential health hazard—perhaps even in the shape of that old 'irresistible logic' of overcrowding and lack of sanitation—plague.

The majority of the million newcomers had no place to go. On the steep hillsides all over Hong Kong and in the vicinity of Kowloon, they put up their pathetic little shacks, their ingeniously perched, laboriously contrived huts of waste timber, tar-paper, old corrugated iron, cardboard cartons, bits of sheet plastic—all held together with wire and nails.

Faced with a million homeless in huts on the hills, without water or sanitation, and others on rooftops where a space cost a little money in rent; faced with thousands of pavement-dwellers for whom it cost money even for a space to lie on—the government appeared not to know what to do. One can hardly blame it. In fact one of those heart-rending events, a huge fire on Christmas Day, 1953, that destroyed the squatter homes of 53,000 people in a few hours, was required to rouse the authorities from bewilderment and apathy.

Sir Ronald Holmes, on the eve of his retirement from Hong Kong in 1977 after forty years of service, tells the story of these days somewhat differently.[1]

'The key change came . . . at the end of 1953 with the enormous fire at Shek Kip Mei, which must have been one of the worst fires in history from the point of view of numbers made homeless. It started on the evening of Christmas Day and by the next morning an estimated 60,000 people had lost their homes—personally I think the figure was a good deal higher. But fortunately there was an extraordinarily small loss of life.

'The fire brought home to us [the Hong Kong government] that the problem simply couldn't be solved by any of the means that had

The view in late afternoon from Causeway Bay towards central Victoria and the Peak

been tried up to that time. So the basic descision was taken that the only way . . . was by Government building accommodation. In the time between then and now—that is, less than 25 years—we have reached the stage when nearly half the population is living in public housing. I should think that is a higher proportion than in any country in the Western world.

'The Government set up a Resettlement Department in April 1954 and I was the first Commissioner for Resettlement. As a first step a lot of temporary two-storey structures were erected on part of Shek Kip Mei. A remarkable number of the fire victims were absorbed into the city, taken in by their friends and relatives. But there were still whole sections of Shamshuipo where perhaps 20,000 people were camping on the streets in little huts made of fibre-board or asbestos. It was an incredible sight.

'I can clearly remember appearing before the Executive Council when our multi-storey resettlement plan was first put to them. . . . The Governor, Sir Alexander Grantham, said to me: "Well, Holmes, what do you think? Is this the best we can do?" I said that we couldn't think of anything better. Then he asked the Director of Medical and Health Services, who said, "Sir, I feel bound to oppose it. These are standards of overcrowding which are simply intolerable and we shall be criticized all over the world." So the Governor asked him: "Well, what would you do?" He replied: I don't know, sir." And that was the key.'

What was done at first was to build seven-storey barracks, long rows of rooms with communal washing and toilet facilities. These were undoubtedly better than flimsy huts on the stinking hillsides—huts that were fire-traps and blew away in typhoons. But of course they were potential, and are now real, slums. Since those early panic days much better has been done, and Hong Kong now bristles with blocks twenty and more storeys high in which families are resettled in rooms and small apartments. In 1964 there were 411,060 squatters. In 1976 this figure had dropped to 274,427 (about 33 per cent fewer). And fewer people on average inhabit each apartment or room.

While the government record in rehousing is good, perhaps un-equalled anywhere in comparable conditions, it is now becoming apparent that those complexes of resettlement blocks pose as many hazards and problems as they were supposed solve. One of the most frightening is violent crime. But in the long term perhaps another, connected but more fundamental, is the question of not belonging.

Especially for people who a few years ago were mostly villagers, the impersonality of life in a forest of high-rise buildings (ill-equipped with shopping, transport, amusement, and other communal facilities) is humanly destructive. For those born and brought up in such an environment the results are unknowable but probably menacing. The problem is not unique to Hong Kong, but in the Colony it is more acute than in many other places because of the high density of people in any given room-space, and because of the basically rural background of the over-twenty-five age-group.

The population density in areas that house the majority of persons living in Hong Kong produces human problems of alarming proportions. Most families in the city live in an area not as big as a good-sized bedroom in an ordinary Western apartment. Into that space, perhaps divided to form a separate cubicle for the husband and wife, but not always, the parents, possibly one or more grandparent or other relative, and several children may have to live. There is generally a tiny kitchen that holds a kerosene burner, a sink (at which personal as well as culinary washing must be performed). The lavatory, which may have a shower in it, is often communal. Two and even three levels of bunks, one on top of the other, serve not only for sleeping, but for sitting on, and for storage space as well when not in use. A small round table, metal folding chairs, or stools, fill the floor space along with boxes, suitcases, and trunks standing in piles up to the ceiling and containing the family's belongings, apart from what they are wearing and using. In summer the boxes must contain winter bedding, the heavier clothes. A single electric light bulb hangs from the middle of the ceiling, serving to light an area generally poorly supplied with window space and in which, in summer, the intense noise of the living-activities of neighbours on either side, above and below, and across the narrow street that is in any case emitting its own cacophony of revving motors, klaxons, bicycle bells, and the accumulated roar of the surrounding city, cannot be excluded because the heat is as intense as the noise, and the window must be open. A Japanese table fan, perched on one of those piles of boxes, stirs the humid air and flutters the leaves of exercise books as the children do their homework round the table or on the floor. The radio, the radios of all the neighbours, the T.V. sets of the better-off, chatter their Chinese, jangle and bang and screech out their Cantonese opera, with remorseless advertising punctuating the programmes every few moments. And the machine-gun clatter of mahjong played at speed and with a verve only the southern Chinese manage to work up, forms

179

Aberdeen harbour with Apleichau on the right, an industrial estate beyond, and Deepwater Bay in the distance

a kind of ground base of sound like that in a textile factory. There may indeed be several small factories nearby adding their quota of noise.

In older resettlement blocks, conditions may be even worse, while even in the newest it is open to some doubt whether conditions are better in fundamental ways. The living space may be larger, the windows bigger, the general state of the buildings cleaner, and the air less burdened with pollutants than in the crowded city tenements. But other things have gone with the older form of slum dwelling. The old friendliness that comes of meeting your neighbours in local shops and markets, the feeling of a community, however beleagered by poverty and abominable conditions of living, the comparative ease with which children could be looked after—within sight or within hail—the proximity (often) of places of work and places of amusement such as the cinema; these are gone.

Virtually all these accustomed amenities and humanizing factors disappear when several tens of thousands of people are settled in high-rise, high density blocks. The markets and shops that spring up around such new complexes are generally dearer than the old ones, have less variety in the thousand and one little things that a Chinese housewife wants for cooking. The cinemas are far away, and so, often, is work. Transport costs more money and entails endless hours per week of standing in line for the overburdened bus services run under government franchise in both the Island and the Kowloon areas. The children playing in the area set aside for them down on the ground, are out of sight, out of hearing. Someone has to go and fetch them, down perhaps twenty storeys in not very convenient and overcrowded elevators, for meals. The former role of grandparents in looking after the children is limited by this concrete environment where there is little shade to sit in as the children play. Gangs of youths terrorize the populace, monopolize play areas to the exclusion of younger children, or of rival gangs. The incidence of robberies, murders, and rape rises sharply as old living customs and familiar ways break down under unaccustomed and inconvenient new conditions.

Hong Kong, like other places, but here very acutely because of the sudden translation of a basically villager-populace to high-rise, has simply created vast new slums, forcing-grounds for crime, for communal discontent that springs in part from family disharmony—so often itself the result of industrial and living conditions that verge on the unsupportable. However much it may be said that the Chinese have been accustomed to squeeze into small living spaces, the equating of those

181

Above: The Lantau countryside with Silvermine Bay at the left and the bulk of Lantau Peak in the distance. *Below:* The press of fishing junks in Aberdeen Harbour at the Lunar New Year.

182

conditions in villages with constricted living space in great concrete hives often placed in the middle of nowhere is a gross error.

One of the completely new towns has been built at Kwun Tong, east of the Kowloon Peninsula, most of it on reclaimed land. On 913 acres a highly industrialized satelite town of over half a million people now stands. In haste, and without, it would seem, real thought or intelligent research on the questions involved—questions of consciously making a new environment for that huge number of people—Kwun Tong was rushed up and sprang into strident, crime-ridden, polluted life. It is simply an industrial slum—little better except in sanitation than those of Midland England in the 18th and 19th centuries. A vast maze of desolate concrete canyons that serve as streets, forests of barren apartment blocks, great raw, clattering factories where, despite 'laws' that forbid a shift of more than eight hours duration, it is often more than a man's or girl's job is worth not to submit to a 9–hour shift and overtime too. The communal facilities are extremely poor, the transportation inefficient, unplanned for this size of community in its need to reach other parts of Hong Kong for shopping, for visiting friends, or any other normal recreation.

It is likely that the environmental horror of artificial fabrications like Kwun Tong is worse in human terms than that of the old-fashioned slums. At least the old slums had grown over years, and provided a sense of identity within the framework of small associations and local shops, and the like. With half a million people jettisoned into a new and totally untried way of living, a place studded with factories and screaming with heavy goods traffic day and night, none of these things happens.

Yet further new towns are rising. While the authorities say guardedly that they have learned from Kwun Tong (you may pause to wonder, incidentally, why it required an experiment with half a million lives to provide a lesson for a few bureaucrats), there is little reason to hope that much better things are in store for the working people of Hong Kong. The problems are admittedly immense; but perhaps the intelligence and empathy applied to their solution has been less than sufficient.

Hong Kong—happily—is not comparable in human misery and in squalor and degredation to the horrors of Calcutta. The average income is much higher and there are almost no inhabitants now without a roof over their heads, even if it is one they built for themselves out of oil drums and tar-paper on a dangerous hillside, and without water or

Opposite page, top: Central Victoria, the harbour, Botanical Gardens centre, Government House right, *Below:* Victoria, looking west to the Peak.
Left: Western district with a ferry, a hydrofoil, and old and new buildings. *Below:* Against a background of resettlement blocks a small dyeing industry continues

185

sanitation. But Hong Kong is—here lies the nub of potential trouble, of man's inhumanity to man, of other human uglinesses—infinitely richer than Calcutta. There are no real excuses in Hong Kong.

*   *   *   *   *   *

From the Hong Kong conglomerate of randomly gathered humanity numbering in 1976 about four and a half million, which until very recently largely kept itself to itself, like the poor in the West until the last war, has now sprung a mass of young people. In 1976 about 42 per cent of the total population was below the age of 20. But the birth rate is falling and is now low when compared to some developed countries, having fallen from 35.5 per thousand in 1961 to 17.7 per thousand in 1976. About 59 per cent of the population is now of Hong Kong birth.

This large (and more or less captive) labour force is undoubtedly the Colony's greatest single asset. From its work in post-war years industry has grown miraculously, and prospered. In the process, the financial picture of the Colony has also altered from the old one of rich-employer ruling-class and poor most of the rest. There are now even more millionaires than before (probably more per square mile in Hong Kong than in most other places in the world) and a dense mass of working class. But there is now also a growing, significantly large, and vociferous, middle class—the product of Hong Kong's own industrial revolution—with money, with social pretensions and a marked absence, on the whole, of social conscience.

As far as the Chinese middle class[2] is concerned its members are largely interested in the good life for themselves and their families. And they can increasingly afford to buy what they see as its ingredients. They are aggressive, often poorly educated, opinionated, not co-operative in public schemes. Their children form the majority of the student population at both the University of Hong Kong and the Chinese University of Hong Kong. These students mostly want to become lawyers, doctors, architects, and business managers; and many of them hope to emigrate as soon as possible, the favoured destinations being the United States and Canada. The anachronism of the 'professions' viewed as being quite distinct from and superior to other means of employment is accepted without thought. Society, in this aspect, demonstrates its backwardness. In the schools children are for the most part taught 'facts' and learn skills rather than being educated in the modern sense of the word. The whole aim is to pass examinations and thus obtain the passport to that 'good life'. This is broadly a traditional Chinese educational outlook. But in the framework of twentieth-century Hong Kong it is most unsuitable.

For the European who does not wholly subscribe to the anachronism of much of life in the Colony, the spectacle of that life is often painful, angering, dismaying. What is billed as a tourist paradise (for reasons that remain somewhat obscure but with results that are effective in luring the world to the Colony) is a social cesspool. The statement by a Secretary of State in London back in 1843, that 'methods of proceeding unknown in other British Colonies must be followed in Hong Kong' has been faithfully followed down the years.

Hong Kong is a city that from its very birth was artificial. This is the root of its present and the story of its past. Its initial incentive was gain from the wilful illegality of smuggling opium into China. Its adolescence was conditioned by a buccaneering spirit among a great diversity of people drawn to the place by the excitement, the lure of that illegal commerce and the subsidiary activities required by a growing population. As various administrators discovered, it was hardly a place conducive to the evolution of a society, in the traditional sense of one that evolves naturally in response to its own needs, exploiting its own environment, and amenable to law and order.

With variations on the theme, Hong Kong has remained basically just what it was. Its social conscience is not in the hands of its citizens (who are not interested), but in the hands of various unofficial organizations without whose ministrations in various fields of need, the Colony would be a much harsher place. In the last quarter of the twentieth century Hong Kong is a city without cohesion. Its sophistication is surface, its heart somewhat stony; and its government *follows* events with legislation rather than legislating for the future.

Yet, despite these strictures and problems, on a human level there is much that makes life in Hong Kong rewarding. The warmth of ordinary Chinese, their still country-style friendliness on a personal level, their freshness of response to a direct approach. Where there is little justice, there is at least a lot of goodwill, among the indifference and hostility of both foreigners and the Chinese.

*   *   *   *   *   *

The sole body concerned with the government of the people of Hong Kong that contains popularly elected members is the Urban Council.

187

It has 24 members, of whom 12 are elected. But in the 1972 elections, when the franchise had been considerably widened to include about 300,000 worthy residents, only a total of 23,000 actually put their names on the electoral roll, and of these only one-third actually exercised their right to vote. In 1977 the turnout was even less. Hong Kong, remarked the editorial in the current *South China Morning Post*, when these damning figures were released, 'just isn't interested' in even this mite of democratic process.

It used to be said, unkindly but with a grain of truth, that the Urban Council was responsible only for garbage collection, and not very good at it. In fact its areas of power cover the provision of many other urban services, both cultural and otherwise. These include the licensing of factories and food premises, the running of markets and abattoirs, libraries and car parks, of museums, and a grandiose future 'Cultural Complex'.

Apart from such matters, its deliberations and its decisions have almost no effect on the broader government of Hong Kong, which remains resolutely colonial in structure and practice. The Governor, appointed from London, presides at meetings of an Executive Council,

A newspaper stall

must seek their advice but need not follow it. And there is one other body, the Legislative Council, of whom the Governor is head, whose principal functions are to control public expenditure and to enact laws. But the Queen, sitting in state in London, and advised by Parliament there, can negate any law passed in Hong Kong and can pass laws applicable to the Colony. So rule is finally in the hands of Britain which, of course, also controls the Colony's foreign policy—its relations with China, for example, being dealt with from Whitehall.

In the context of this 'unabashedly colonial' structure, the frenetic commerce of Hong Kong is carried on largely without British restrictions. Without, shall we say, the refinements that have been evolved by trade union movements and gradually thrust down the throats of employers; and without those other refinements that have been squeezed out of the long struggle to establish and make workable some form of democracy—those that attempt to curb the machinations of financiers and monopolistic international company operators. In Hong Kong, just as in the heyday of Victorian capitalist expansion during that seemingly eternal and God-countersigned sunshine of the peak of empire, if you can do it and have enough money to do it, then you can

People with peach blossom bought at Victoria Park for the Lunar New Year

probably get away with it. This is an aspect of Hong Kong that presents an unpleasing sight to the democratic eye, and an even less pleasing picture to employees who have to work under the system.

It is for such reasons as these, and because of their attitude of superiority (quite unconscious in many cases) that Westerners and extortionate Chinese are disliked in varying degrees even in the Hong Kong of 1977. Most of the foreigners don't know this because their contacts with Chinese are limited to those at the employee level, or to the business or social level where Chinese either don't find the British unendurable because they are in the same income-bracket, or because they would like to be, and therefore find the exemplars exemplary. As with contact adhesive, when you put the surfaces together as instructed, the rich Western and rich Chinese parts of life adhere so firmly there's no prying them apart.

Possibly the other circumstance, aside from their lack of Cantonese language, that causes the British to assume they are loved (and like most Western expatriates they *do* want to be loved) is the host of cookboys and amahs, most of whom are as conservative and at least as snobbish as their masters and mistresses. However much they may squabble and quibble, this tribe is on the Western side when it comes to relationships with other Chinese. Butlers were always embryonic dukes. And in fact the history of Sino-Western relations over the last century in this particular tells the same story. To work for or with a Westerner, put you in your own eyes several rungs up the ladder from your fellows; and from their point of view, generally it put you several rungs down. The majority hold the latter opinion.

* * * * * *

Official figures confirm what anyone with eyes in his head and a mind to step off the beaten track of main streets can hardly avoid seeing. Hong Kong's success in terms of money has been achieved at considerable human cost. More than three-quarters of a million people live in conditions that one of the Colony's leading figures once described as more suited to cattle than to human beings. 68,000 people live on verandahs or in cocklofts—the storage space above work areas and below the ceiling. About 100,000 people have no home, only a bedspace for an eight-hour stretch which is all they can afford in rent. A further 138,000 inhabit the shops, workshops, small factories, or garages where they work; or sleep in corridors, even on staircases.

In this land
There shall be one cigarette to two men,
To two women one half pint of bitter
Ale....

Sometimes the lines of T.S. Eliot come forcefully to mind. For in this city of Hong Kong, one of the richest in the world, about one fifteenth of the people—nearly 300,000 souls—still live as 'squatters', on barren hillsides, on forgotten corners of land, on the roofs of decaying tenements, anywhere they can find a few square feet to construct their pathetic homes. Some of them are termed 'legal squatters' and live on land set aside by a thoughtful government for just such a purpose, until the time eventually may come when rehousing can be carried out. Much has been done, of course, but so much more is still to be done that rehousing, like the water supply, is never going to catch up with the natural increase in the population, which includes a natural increase in the number of squatters.

The squatters are hopelessly at the mercy of at least two other things: the weather, and themselves. In the mercifully short but quite chilly winter they shiver. In summer they bake. Their ingeniously erected huts clinging to the slopes of Hong Kong's decomposing granite hills are hardly built to withstand heat or cold, and certainly not the typhoons that flay the Colony most summers, bringing torrential rains and pitiless winds that rip the roofs off many a conventional building. A direct hit by a typhoon leaves a squatter area a mass of smashed and sodden planks and corrugated iron sheeting, a jumble of rubbish uninhabitable until the huts are rebuilt.

Perhaps the chief hazard is fire. It is generally started by one member of the community cooking on a makeshift stove in or beside a hut, in winter tinder-dry like all the others. A spark in the breeze, and flames spring up and engulf within moments a whole colony of little homes. The inferno can rarely be checked early enough for there is no running water near, and it generally claims several lives—often those who dash into it to try and rescue some precious belongings. In a few hours from tens to thousands of people are made completely destitute, possessing only what they may be wearing.

Charity plays an active, God-sent role in Hong Kong life. This is fortunate, for without it many many people would be closer to the condition of the poor in India. Both Christian and secular organizations annually contribute immense sums and expend equally huge efforts to relieve the plight of the needy and the helpless, and to educate.

191

Left : Early each morning Chinese practice the ancient exercises called *t'ai chi ch'üan* in the Botanical Gardens
Below : Summer afternoon on Repulse Bay beach

But it remains a curious fact that among dozens of hospitals, clinics, and other charitable institutions named after generous, if sometimes also honour-seeking Chinese millionaires, it is hard to think of one such place donated by a Western millionaire. Probably the largest overall benefactor is the Jockey Club whose vast gambling profits, in a city filled with a race of born gamblers and, moreover, with people who have rather scant other forms of adding a little zest to life, are mostly ploughed back into the pastures whence they were so easily extracted—the Chinese community as a whole.

Bereft of the ministrations of these often disguised angels, the government would have to dig much deeper into its richly lined pockets than it has so far shown any intention of doing.

* * * * * *

Any wide-ranging and intelligent assessment of Hong Kong in the year 1977, would surely be forced to sum it up as rather a doubtful bet.[3] The lease on the major portion of it, the part that contains virtually all the industry, a very large proportion of its population, its airport, all its agricultural land, its container port, practically all its water supply, expires in 1997. After that, all that will be left of the Colony will be the small island of Hong Kong (29.2 square miles of mountain and reclaimed coastal land) a sliver of mainland territory the shape of a pen nib and hardly as big as an ordinary airport, and one or two insignificant, waterless lumps of rock and scrub in the adjacent seas.

The events that may be pending when (and if) China with perfect legality resumes the 370.5 square miles of the Colony called the New Territories that is merely leased land, would normally frighten the commercial guts out of any self-respecting capitalist. But in *laissez-faire* capitalist Hong Kong, so far there are few signs of lack of confidence. The economy booms, super-booms, sags a bit, and booms again. The stock exchanges (four of them) in 1972–3 rocketed in a way that no stock market in the world has ever rocketed and survived the trip to the sobriety of the morning after without a major depression as hangover. Not even the fact that the stock market stagnated thereafter seems to have dampened the fire in the bankers' and commercial gentlemen's eyes, or curbed the crazed exuberance of builders of more and more office blocks.

193

The cost of living spirals upward and there are still perhaps two million or more quite poor people in the city who work long hours for incredibly low wages. The poor do not really get poorer, but their lot has not greatly improved of recent years, although better than it was two decades ago. The rich, on the other hand, get richer and more numerous, and the middling rich get more nearly really rich. There is nothing like the prospect of making a lot of money, or of being destitute, for engendering hard work. And those prospects are both acutely present. So Hong Kong is on the whole one of the hardworking cities of the world. The contrast is sharply observable when you spend some time in the West, in London, for example, where it is impossible to starve, and rare to become as rich as that large segment of Hong Kong Chinese and Westerners who have bottomless bank balances. The pace of work on average in the West is easier, and people there emanate an aura of security, however ephemeral that may prove to be.

The frenzied hunt for money or more money that is such an obvious aspect of Hong Kong, is all the more curious in the geographical and political context of the Colony. Over a little river and bit of wire fencing, is China with 800 million probably even more hard-working citizens. But over there everything that Hong Kong is, is everything that China wants the Chinese not to turn into. They have a point, apart from sheer ideological matters. For, in order to conjure up something like what Hong Kong is, you have to make a civic mixture of the decadent public *mores* of 19th century China and those of prohibition Chicago, add the *laissez-faire* capitalism of 19th century England, the wealth of Manhattan today, and the condition of the poor in London at the time of Karl Marx and Prince Albert's Crystal Palace. It is at least an improbable social cocktail, tending to be unpotable for those not endowed, by familiarity, with strong mental stomachs.

Yet people escape here (still) from China. That many of them quickly end up as undesirables in the Colony's criminal courts may have something to do with why they escaped, but does not explain all escapers. After the massive exodus of April and May 1962, when 60,000 people managed to cross into the Colony, the figures have fallen, but even now with fairly prosperous and controlled conditions in China, 27,000 arrived in 1976. The number is approximate since it is not impossible to reach Hong Kong without being discovered, and to be absorbed into that great network of family and clan alliances and allegiances, protections and obligations, that is part and parcel of the 19th century Chinese society fossilized in Hong Kong in the twentieth. Illegal im-

Illegally crossing the border, often to end up in squatter conditions like these

migrants, if found, are now generally returned to China.

All but 70,000 of the Colony's people are Chinese. Most of them were born in China, or their parents were, and only a few families have lived for generations in the Colony. There are, for that matter, old Portuguese families who have lived here since Captain Elliot took the law into his own hands in annexing the island in 1841, and called for young Portuguese from prominent families living in Macau to come and help him with the administration. Macau, of course, has a history of Western occupation dating much farther back—the first Portuguese to arrive in the vicinity, Jorge Alvares, was in the Canton Delta in 1513, only a little over a decade after Columbus set sail for what turned out to be the New World. But those Portuguese, and the perhaps even rarer English families who have been in the Colony for a century or more, are insignificant in numbers compared to the rest of their Western compatriots who come and go on commercial assignments, on tours of government service, some, though not many, spending the best part of their working lives here before retiring to native Scotland, or England, to Bermuda, Spain, or elsewhere. In comparison to the great bulk of the Chinese, the Western population is infinitesimal.

The Chinese are mostly from adjacent Canton province—Hong Kong was a part of the Po On district of Kwangtung (Canton) province before it was taken by the British. But there are sizeable communities from other southern provinces and, since the advent of the Communist regime in China, strong contingents of Shanghai and northern people. The Cantonese are a tough, sentimental, pleasure-loving, immensely hard-working people with the liveliest sense of humour of all the Chinese. History records few outstanding Cantonese intellectuals, several outstanding revolutionaries, the most recent of whom was Dr Sun Yat-sen (who was more nearly a radical reformer), and millions of small, persevering, natural businessmen. They are also gourmets to a man and woman. Cantonese food is regarded even by Chinese from other parts of that great continent of eaters, as being the most succulent, the most sensuous.

Hong Kong is one of the few places in the world where food is one of the important pleasures of life. Even in these days of inflation you can still eat magnificently, memorably.

But there is something else in the air of Chinese Hong Kong—the inbuilt desire to go somewhere else. To Canada, to the States, to England, or Australia. Anywhere. But away from Hong Kong. Hong Kong is like a telephone wire on which birds perch, listening perhaps to the

196

hum of world communication, getting the message—to move on when times become propitious to do so. For there is an insidious feeling of impermanence, of uncertainty in Hong Kong. There is, too, among the Chinese, a certain ambivalence in relation to their compatriots over the border in the Peoples' Republic. First and foremost, the Chinese are Chinese (or Cantonese, or Szechuan, or Fukien, depending on what is there province of origin); and belonging to Hong Kong is so far a secondary consideration. The needle of the seismograph registering political unrest swayed violently in China in 1967, and in Hong Kong it moved too.

In that year the spin-off from the Cultural Revolution arrived, and a surge of ill-organized, ill-treated, antagonistic citizens rioted in the streets of Hong Kong for several months.

It was a hot summer. All summers in the Colony are hot and nerve-frayingly humid. Most people have no air-conditioning either at home or at work. Many have electric fans, but not all. Most live and work in areas too small for human beings in this climate, in conditions that are in many cases, industrially, a disgrace. The history of employment of labour has on the whole been a disgrace to humanity, but even in Hong Kong with no effectual trade union, conditions are not nearly as bad as in other Eastern places—South Korea, for example.

So the Chinese in Hong Kong rioted. And as the clerks in a post office urged us to come behind the counter and get among some stuffed mailbags, a riot passed outside with a flurry of helmeted police with shields (how medieval it looked!), and sirens screaming, in chase of a bottle-throwing group. There were many riots, this was just a minor skirmish.

Things had started with the dismissal of workers from a plastics factory, not an unusual event in times of fluctuating markets. But in the context of the Chinese Cultural Revolution raging over the border, and of what had happened to Macau the year before, Hong Kong authorities were naive in not having anticipated what a labour dispute might do at that time.

In Macau, similar demonstrations led by the local Communists virtually removed governing power from the Portuguese who—it has been said—offered to return the peninsula and its two little islands to China, but were turned down. They offered because Macau was at that time a mere backwater of no value to Portugal, and looked like becoming a headache of migraine dimensions. They were turned down by China (always presuming that the offer *was* made) because the Chinese had

Demonstrating at the gate of Government House. Tear gas had to be used to disperse rioters in some places

enough on their hands at that time, because some foreign capital accrued to them through the overseas province—as the Portuguese insist on calling all their colonies—and, to accept the opinion of veteran correspondent Richard Hughes, because the Chinese wished merely to humiliate the colonial government. The relevance of those events ought to have been plain to the Hong Kong authorities.

The crackling fires of the Cultural Revolution over the border undoubtedly created the draft that reinforced the at first small conflagration in Hong Kong. The local Communist press and popular leadership did the rest. A bloody period ensued in which many people were killed, maimed, and otherwise injured—police, public, rioters. The rioters, unfortunately for them, were as ineptly led as the Hong Kong government was unprepared for their exploits, and it was not long before they lost the most important asset workers in revolt can have—popular sympathy. The loss was partly their own fault (it doesn't gain sympathy to gouge out policemen's eyes in front of news cameras), and partly the comeback in intelligence (or cunning) that was evinced by the authorities who made the very most of every bloody incident through all the media.

Unlike Macau at that time, Hong Kong was then, and is so even more today, a vital economic link in the inflow of foreign currency, as far as the Government of China is concerned. The Chinese, in spite of all the ideological impulsions of the Cultural Revolution, simply could not afford (for the sake of gaining what must have seemed to them not a pimple but a festering sore with four million unruly inhabitants and built-in ideological problems on a gigantic scale, and the bubble reputation that such a gain would produce) to take over Hong Kong at that moment. That the time will come when the Chinese *can* afford to do so, goes without saying. There are factors that may make this event less certain as to timing and less traumatic than it might seem to be, factors accumulating, belonging to the future, where we can consider them in their proper place (see pages 259–65).

The shock that Hong Kong experienced, however, belonged to that time in 1967. Numerous wealthy inhabitants, Chinese and Western, left immediately with their more valuable possessions. Doubtless the wires were hot between the great banks in the Colony and those of the West as money was transferred in haste. And, to be fair, if you had been caught in Shanghai by the Communist Revolution, with money and the things it had bought and could buy, no doubt you think twice about being caught again.

Perhaps it was too soon, perhaps it is still too soon, but in the press or in the various books published about those blood-letting months, there has not been much written that even tries to understand the deeper causes of the popular revolt of that year. The conditions the Chinese had to live and work in were certainly abysmal, although slightly improving. But the improvement was not enough to invalidate the accumulation of resentment, hate, frustration, the despair generated by hopelessness and helplessness, before it exploded on the streets in blood. The inhumanity of a rich administration and a well-heeled society that just didn't care to know about the conditions of its work force and their dependents, seemed then, as it does now, a classic case of political blindness. The Vice-Minister for Foreign Affairs of the Peking Government described it in inflamatory but accurate terms to the British *chargé d'affaires*. He was referring to prisoners taken and people killed and injured during the revolt in Hong Kong, but his words describe also what the policies of an autocratic government had produced in terms of life for the governed. 'Sanguinary atrocities,' he said, 'and barbarous murders.'

The revolt jolted the government into some action. Quelled, it was not allowed to rise again. But the seeds of violence are all too evident a decade and more afterward. Obviously, the days of colonialism, even with the tacit agreement of the Peking Government, are coming to an end.

*   *   *   *   *   *

From almost every vantage point overlooking the harbour of Hong Kong the visitor has to remind himself that this is the East and that he is gazing on an oriental city. Almost everything in sight is occidental. Scattered about the grand harbour, whose natural configuration and sheltered position in a region torn by typhoons was, (we must remind ourselves) something over a century ago the principal reason for the choice of Hong Kong as a British foothold on the South China coast, are scores of merchant ships, their masts and derricks glinting in the sun. Sometimes there are more ships in harbour than there are days in the year. Fat black-and-white ferries, some carrying passengers, some cars, and some both, bumble across the water like beetles, from the island to this or that part of the opposite Kowloon shore. And practially all the shorelines in sight are lined by tall buildings, office blocks forming canyons in whose depths run city streets. More distantly great clumps

Above: Victoria in the early 1970s. *Below:* Looking from mid-levels on the island to Kowloon, in 1974

of high-rise buildings demonstrate a questionable government policy of housing as many people as possible on the smallest possible area. In the midst of densely populated areas smoke-stacks emit smoke and fumes (even nowadays when it is forbidden), not continuously, but in what seem occasional irrepressible belches.

From Victoria Peak, highest point on the island, the hillsides fall sharply to the north, toward the harbour, in bristling ranks of multi-storey blocks where many Western and Chinese residents are boxed in a high-class urban ghetto not dissimilar except in the larger floor area to the lower-income high-rise ghettos over the water, visible from the same vantage point. Those concrete-peopled slopes run down to the city of Victoria itself where more orderly lines of even higher close-packed buildings contain in larger or smaller series of cubicles, the commercial nerve-centres of the city. The lines of the city streets follow the historic contours of, first, the original shore, and then a number of successive land reclamations.

Two walled villages first established about 500 years ago at Kam Tin in the New Territories

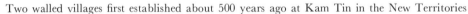

Until about two decades ago the Hong Kong Club, a charming late 19th century building, stood almost on the shore. Now it is far from the sea. On land reclamations of former days the buildings that were first put up have long since gone, torn down to make way for others. Jon Prescott, a well-known Hong Kong architect, remarks: 'Central,' the local term for Central District of Victoria, 'had a lot of lovely domed buildings . . . cupolas above and setts let diagonally into the pavement. They all had projecting verandahs so that pedestrians were protected from the rain . . . . At that time [1958] there were so many marvellous buildings . . . .'

New reclamations starting on a large scale about the time when Prescott came to the Colony obliterated what was left of the original harbour contours. Districts still called by names such as Wanchai (meaning Little Bay) are no longer recognizable except when you look down on them from a height such as the Peak or a plane, when the old shoreside path that became a road and was later engulfed by re-claimed land, still shows as an irregular curve, inland from the newer grid pattern of streets.

Across the harbour to the north, the beak of Kowloon peninsula prods into the ship-infested waters, a long triangle of tall concrete, rutted by the tracks of its main roads fanning out east and west toward subsidiary centres where the industrial estates and resettlement com-plexes stand in severe clumps of concrete forest. And behind this Manhattan-like scene rises the bare face of the Kau Lung—Nine Dragons—mountains from whose Chinese name the English made 'Kowloon'. They stand, often sharp and unreal against the skies, like cutouts, vaguely green in summer and burned ochre for the rest of the year.

But in Kowloon, a long way before you reach the Nine Dragons you pass Boundary Street, and with it pass out of British land into leased land—the New Territories. The general impression of Kowloon and the New Territories where they meet, and when you look north beyond the Nine Dragons barrier, is of some odd coalescence of Manhattan and the Scottish Highlands at their barest. All is Western, the vast, brand-new but already shoddy commercial and industrial city backed by Scottish-looking hills and, once over that first row, by rolling Scottish country not unlike parts of Argyllshire. True, from the heights here and there, with powerful binoculars, one tolerable Chinese pagoda (of recent growth) and several hipped, green-tiled Chinese curly roofs may be discerned, lurking poetically amid the prose, the often exceedingly bad prose, of the urban landscape. All is Western. To any ordinary observer standing on the Peak or on some point on the Nine Dragons, this must be the conclusion. Where, you might ask, is the exotic, the oriental, opium-ridden, colonial, and above all the *Chinese* Hong Kong?

That most of the four million Hong Kong people are Chinese is quite obvious when you descend from the heights. While the pavements in Central district contain Westerners by the hundred among the crowd of Chinese, half a mile or so in either direction a Western face is a rarity. Tourists mostly keep to the areas where all the shop signs are in English and the shop assistants comfortingly speak something like it. Surprisingly, in the late seventies, most foreign residents tend not to stray much further. You will not in any case find much that is exotic in Central, but from time to time in the year, and from place to place in Hong Kong, in Kowloon, and in the New Territories, you still may.

* * * * * *

Looking around in any main street in a Chinese district such as Causeway Bay or North Point on an evening or on Sunday you wouldn't guess that wages for most people are still very low. The Chinese have the knack of emerging from conditions of overcrowding, of enforced squalor, looking fresh, clean, carefully pressed, immaculate. Even in days before 1967 when those living conditions were on the whole worse, many visitors to the Colony remarked on this. Chinese have not only a universal respect for personal cleanliness, but a kind of *amour propre* that simply does not allow them be out and about looking less than their best.

The streets between the tall buildings bristling with immense neon signs that stretch often more than halfway across the thoroughfare, are jammed with a moving mass of people and vehicles. There are so many people that it is sometimes nearly impossible to go in a direction other than that of the majority. But it is an orderly, smartly dressed, somehow eager-looking crowd. When Chinese in Hong Kong want to go some-where, even if it's only to buy some vegetables for supper, they go with a certain spirit, often with friends, chattering and laughing as if they had had no opportunity of talking to each other for weeks. They are gregarious and garulous—like Neapolitans or Romans, but infinitely less aggressive, infinitely neater, and more patient with each other, and with things and with the world in general. Life, with the Chinese, is much more deeply a matter of accommodation, of finding the mean, the middle way where tempers and feelings are not ruffled, antagonisms not generated, 'face' not lost. You can see this sometimes when two Chinese get very angry with each other. There is always some person, or maybe a group from their workmates or friends, who physically intervene, interpose themselves between the combatants before the deeper aggressions become overt. This is true also in less dire circumstances. The art of compromise is more highly developed in the most illiterate Chinese than in many Westerners.

Per head of the population, there must be more shops in Hong Kong than in most other places. Each little shop is crammed with goods, its cheap imitations of Western current fashion that exaggerate stylish cut in inferior material, just as is done, or was done, in cheap clothes in the West, before the fashions of the adolescents themselves took over. Since men began to wear wide trousers again, and Hong Kong caught on a year or so later (the normal time-lag in fashion), there are no louder or wider trousers anywhere in the world than here. And when fashion decrees that a girl's face should resemble a mask with a doll's eyes and lacquered spirals of hair jiggling in front of the ears—the young Chinese out-does her Western counterpart with ease. The Chinese face is susceptible of almost any make-up change—its lack of indentation or pronounced features has the potential of a blank page. You may write anything there, not only with pigment.

Various time-honoured and baseless Western ideas are readily scotched by an hour's observant drifting with this Chinese crowd. The Chinese face is seldom impassive. On the contrary, it is more often animated than Western faces in the same sort of crowd. The Chinese don't like and therefore don't seek solitude. They hate to be alone for any length of time. They love going about in big groups (like the Japanese, but for slightly different reasons), they don't care much for quietude except in small doses when enjoying the beauties of nature in some hallowed spot. They appear to be largely insensitive to noise, doubtless because noise is the usual context of Chinese living.

A Chinese from a large family visiting Western friends some years ago for the first time, was given a moderate-size bedroom all to himself. The following morning his hosts thought he looked a little pale and asked if he had slept well. 'Not very well,' he said (with candour, another Chinese attribute), 'You see I never slept in such a big room before, or alone either. It was uncomfortable.' (Understatement, balancing the candor. He had, it was learned later, not slept at all because of the agony of loneliness.)

The night market at Temple Street, Yau Ma Tei. Large signs read from left: Plastic Utensils
(with A), Tai Sung Furniture Company, Women's hairdresser (vertical)

206

Contrary, too, to Western ideas of Chinese character, taken perforce from Chinese literature in translation, and from paintings, the Chinese are probably less a race of dreamers than many another. The literature of the past, and much of the painting too, reflects the ideas, ideals, the life of the intellectual or *literati* few, and has about as much to do with ninety-five per cent of the Chinese in the past as the writings of Marcel Proust had to do with French peasants of the turn of the century—rather less, perhaps. Learning is respected, but rather as a commodity that every child should be given the opportunity to acquire, because its acquisition leads to greater earning power, than for any intrinsic cultural worth.

Things are changing fast in Hong Kong, partly as a reflection of what is going on over the border in China where the emphasis is on work and practical learning and the abolition of ideas necessarily embodied in the literature of the past; but partly also because of close contact with the outer apparel of Western culture in the form of technology, life-styles, and such aspects as Western pop music and art, and Western movies. As usual, of course, culture is not readily exportable, so that little of Chinese and little of Western culture has penetrated the understanding of the other group in any significant way. What has rubbed off are the more gaudy or exotic aspects of both.

You have to remember that parts of Western life appear quite as exotic to the Chinese, as do parts of their traditional ways to the West. The worst possible Western 'taste' in interior decoration and furnishing is regarded in Hong Kong by Chinese with a little money as being 'smart'. And you don't have to look far in Western homes in Hong Kong for examples of the most decadent Ch'ing bric-a-brac, indicating an equal lack, not only of fundamental 'taste,' but of understanding of what is good in another culture.

On that stroll with the crowds of Causeway Bay—or, for that matter, of a poorer district such as Mongkok at the far end of interminable Nathan Road on the Kowloon side—practically everyone you see who is over twenty-five is likely to have been born and brought up in the country, not in a town. Quite a proportion of the younger people, too, have country origins, having come from southern Chinese provinces as small children. The town, the rawness, the glitter, the fundamental cheat of big city life, is their context now. But only recently. It is this which accounts for the fact that, until the last decade, Hong Kong had one of the lowest crime rates for a city of its size in the whole world. People were straightforward like country folk are in most places. Travellers to China since the Revolution have consistently returned with tales of the (to them) amazing honesty they encountered at all levels. All that happened in China was the encouragement of an already native peasant honesty and the suppression, by a process of shaming them, of those who transgressed that country code. What happened in Hong Kong was the reverse. The city slicker mentality, the secret society, the embalmed 19th century decadence of Chinese *mores*, all combined with a wide-open *laissez-faire* outlook in which to get away with as much money as possible is so evidently the credo of the successful, that old virtues like honesty quickly fell victim.

The break-up of the old Confucian code—total, in effect, in China during this century—has not been followed in Hong Kong by the insertion of any substitute other than the struggle for money. Much more so than in the countries of Europe, for example, what you see in Hong Kong today is a society in disarray, in the throes of moral corruption which has engendered a frightening crime rate, and a network of graft that runs from top to bottom, involving the highest and the lowest in the social and income brackets.

The depths of this corruption have only in the past two years or so begun to be exposed, begun to be accepted as fact by responsible opinion. Despite the revelations of conscientious people in the years before, despite the fact that everyone knew about corruption, the authorities would not face it as an important issue. One suspects that they, like most of the citizens of Hong Kong, feel the exposure is slightly dangerous, because so many people are bound at least to know someone involved. The affair has a disgust-fascination aura, like some unnatural birth. But it is probable that varying degrees of corruption will continue. Stranded like a sandbank in a great river, between the political and cultural streams of East and West, Hong Kong is at the mercy of the opportunist eddies of both.

The vast majority of its Chinese people have no real hand in major corruption—they just have to live with a corrupt financial and human environment. They pay a dollar here and there to get what they need, if and when they have to. Some, like the hawkers with their mushrooming and importunate stalls making chaos of traffic in streets, get the heavy end of the stick. They either pay the police, the hawker control force, or are extinguished, their stalls demolished. And so it goes on, the patient many and the swarming parasites living on the many, and (even) on each other.

Meanwhile, a basically peasant population, whose outlook, rhythms, speech, lingering country lore, and lingering conservatism also, is form-ing itself painfully into a city community. No wonder it still finds the purely surface sophistication and excitements of city life attractive. No village lad ever had such a choice of girls—and such provocative girls taking their manners from Taiwan actresses—to ogle at. While the sexual permissiveness of the West is still curbed in Hong Kong by various family (Confucian-type) taboos, the classical prudery of ten years ago has almost vanished. A decade is a short span of time for such radical changes in morality to take place.

In all this change, several things have not changed much. Chinese practicality, the facing of an issue with down-to-earth common sense, is rooted in Chinese tradition, expressed in a thousand pithy aphorisms, part of the general outlook. Not long ago, after a day in Lantau with a Chinese and an Austrian friend, we returned by one of Hong Kong's cheap and efficient ferries. The boat called at the island of Peng Chau where two or three passengers boarded. We cast off at once and were soon pushing out towards distant Hong Kong. The Austrian, echoing my own thought, exclaimed: 'Well, that was a speedy turn-around!' The Chinese said: 'What use to wait, no more passengers.'

Also unchanged is the delight in small pleasures. Hong Kong is a collection of villages, however artificial, that happen to have coalesced (and have been taken over by big business). There are resemblances in this respect to London of a couple of centuries ago, and to Manila today. For Chinese, the family outing is still cherished. On any Sunday morning from quite early until well into the afternoon the 'teahouses' as the larger restaurants of a certain type are called, are crammed to capacity by families of up to twelve—babies in diapers and grandfathers with thin beards—having Chinese brunch, called *dim sum*. Members of the family not living under the same roof will be telephoned and asked to *yam cha*—literally 'drink tea'. The meaning of the characters *dim sum* is literally, *dim* a mite or tiny piece, and *sum* the heart, but like our word tidbit, there is little point in dissecting it. *Dim sum* simply means this type of meal consisting of numerous dishes of 'bite-size' morsels of a large variety of ingredients—accompanied, of course, by libations of tea, generally the common bland *heung pin*, or 'fragrant flakes'.

Each one of these varieties of food used to be carried by a young girl in a tray slung by a band round the neck. Nowadays they push trolleys. Each of those young girls has a more piercing voice than the next, and all outscream the general uproar of Cantonese conversation that animates the aromatic air of the restaurant. Ordinary conversation on a Western level is impossible, everyone forces everyone else to scream; but you become used to it after a while.

Many of the most delicious dishes are those steamed in circular wooden baskets which, as they are emptied, pile up on the table along with the emptied saucers and plates, large and small, that contained other delicacies. By the time it comes to getting the bill the table is an untidy but happy mess of tiers of baskets and dishes which the waiter simply counts. The bill is a multiple of the price of a basket, a plate of this or that size.

Dim Sum[4]

The range of dishes that can be ordered at an ordinary *dim sum* meal include the following:

Siu mai—a mixture of minced pork and flavouring topped with egg yolk, steamed in a purse made of rice flour and water

Ha gao—shrimps, bamboo shoots, and flavouring enclosed in a purse of semi-translucent rice flour and water paste, and steamed

Cha siu bao—morsels of pork roasted in a kind of barbecue sauce and then wrapped in a bulb-shaped lumps of steamed Chinese bread. In the old days you peeled away the 'skin' of this bread before eating—a measure of hygiene not now necessary

Ngau yok—minced beef mixed with fatty pork, made into a ball and steamed

Wu go—mashed boiled taro, with bamboo shoots and shrimp forming the stuffing. The ball of stuffed taro is then fried

Pai kwat—pork ribs cut into short pieces and then steamed with pepper and a sauce of black bean

Chun gün—the familiar 'spring roll'

Fung chao—literally 'phoenix claws,' but in fact chicken feet

Ham sui kok—pork and bamboo shoots fried in a pastry case

Lang cheung min—cold noodles with shredded chicken and spicy sauce

And for a concluding sweet:

Lin yung bao—mashed lotus nuts sweetened and used as a stuffing for steamed bread

Chi ma gün—black sesame seeds and rice flour pounded together with sugar, made into a paste, and steamed

Ma tai go—pounded chestnut with rice flour made into a paste with white sugar and steamed in a tray. The resulting mass is cut into squares and fried

210

The bill settled, the waiter will cross two chopsticks on top of one pile of baskets, and bring another graceless brown pot of tea and a basket of steaming towels wrung out of a solution of boiling water laced with a particularly hospital-smelling disinfectant. Quickly, for the Chinese generally don't care to linger over the table, the party gets up and goes, abandoning a scene of gastronomic carnage that has to be seen to be believed. In the Orient, there is none of our Western prissiness about fine eating manners. The more succulent the food the richer the noises of eating. It is not impolite to spit out bits of bone, to spill sauces on the tablecloth, to slurp soups with relish. And so the table is cleared—with a fine disregard for the brittleness of porcelain that you would expect from a nation that invented it so many many centuries ago, before the West had begun to refine its manners at table and was still eating from wooden bowls.[5]

*   *   *   *   *   *

There are times, by the grace of some Chinese god, when the brutal concrete of Hong Kong and its soulless commercialism give place to things so entirely out of keeping with high-rise blocks and the frenzy of multi-million dollar international mergers, that it is hard to credit the evidence of your eyes. One such magical time comes in September at the point when the Chinese lunar calendar reaches the fifteenth day of its eighth month—the Mid-Autumn Festival, or what in the West we used to call Harvest Moon. As dusk falls, gathering round the trees in Victoria Park on Hong Kong island, and obscuring the concrete teeth of North Point blocks, all eyes turn toward the southeast. For there soars the great Chinese Autumn Moon. It rises portensously like some cool queen, the giver of auspicious gifts, seen, as it were, through the window of the eastern air, remote, yet somehow on this special evening attached to human destinies.

Perhaps it is rather odd that a Westerner should be susceptible to this Oriental experience, but many are. And certainly the Chinese sense a climatic point in the concatenation of heaven and earth. In the dark, the roads leading to the park are glow-wormed with bobbing lanterns —red, orange, lemon, green, tallow-colored—each one or two carried by an excited child. Once inside the park the glow-worms turn into fireflies, darting here and there, becoming encrustations of lights on the slopes and summit of the artificial hill in this piece of reclaimed land that was once a shallow bay shaped like a type of basket (the

Chinese name of which, *Tung Lo Wan*,[6] it still bears). Cicadas and children's voices coalesce in the dark humid air. And the moon hovers, phosphorescent, imperturbable above—a celestial lantern suspended by the forces of the universe.

The scene is repeated in many another place, especially on high ground; because, as every Chinese child knows, for the family to stay at home on this Mid-Autumn Moon evening is to risk dire troubles befalling them. The story is as old as most folktales and appears to be a Han dynasty rationalization of a more primitive myth. A soothsayer warned a virtuous scholar of impending calamity. 'Hasten!' said he to his friend, 'take all your kith and kin, climb to the shelter of the mountains until there is nothing between you and the sky; and take with you food and drink.' The scholar thanked his counsellor and followed his advice, carrying with him a bag of food and a jug of chrysanthemum wine, believed to prolong life. Returning at the end of the day, he discovered his cattle and poultry had died a violent death. 'That,' he said to his family, 'would probably have been our fate, but for the warning.'

For weeks before the festival, shops have been selling great numbers of 'moon cakes'—round pastry-covered pies of several kinds containing such ingredients as whole boiled eggs, nuts, several kinds of dried fruit, all mixed into a savoury or sweet paste. Nowadays moon cakes come in boxes decorated with numerous characters of good luck and other propitious emblems embossed on the lids and gaily coloured in reds and golds. Everyone gives everyone else so many mooncakes that even the hearty Cantonese don't always manage to ingest them all, and Western friends tend to get the overflow. Delicious to taste, they sink like lead to the stomach and abolish further appetite for many hours to come.

* * * * * *

The day after Autumn Moon the city, surprisingly, looks as though no Chinese festival had ever been celebrated there. Its frenetic activity continues as usual, seeming more prosaic by contrast. The tramcars, bursting with passengers, clatter along the streets, another reminder of the history of Hong Kong. In 1906 the trams carried seven million passengers and covered 1.1 million miles. In 1963 they carried 191 million passengers and ran 7.6 million miles. First and second class have been abolished and the fare for the total run of nearly seven miles along the northern coast of Hong Kong Island is still extremely cheap, and an average of over 400,000 people take advantage of it every day.

Each morning as the trams, the buses, the 14-seat mini-buses, and the private cars disgorge their hundreds of thousands in the business districts of Hong Kong and Kowloon, and as the crocodiles of humanity move along the pavements to their offices, the town slowly gets into gear. By 10 o'clock it is even possible to walk without taking too much notice of other people's movements. And by that time the shops of central town are lethargically opening.

Hong Kong is in some ways a faceless place. Its architecture and its attitudes seem non-committal. There is no expression of a unified culture because there is no such thing. Rather there is a multiplicity of expressions of the fringes of two cultures—the Chinese and that (or those) of the West. Embedded in these are fragments of Indian life, small particles of Pakistan, of Korea, of Japan, and of other Eastern places.

Perhaps the sole coherent aspect is the firm Chinese-ness of the Chinese. Like the English in the late nineteenth century at the height of Empire and world domination, when every man jack of them felt passionately and proudly English, the Chinese are intensely Chinese. This not specially new, they always have been when confronted with other people. But they are Chinese in a different way from the patriotic English of great moments in British history. The roots of their clannishness are deep in history, in the sharing of the most ancient form of written language still in use, and in their unique form of civilization. These things are about all the Chinese share, but they are more than sufficient to make of them a race consciously apart from others. Not, it should be added, unpleasantly so. But apart, all the same.

In fact the Chinese, whether in Hong Kong or elsewhere, are quite as racially mixed as the English (which is to say, extremely), and by speech large masses of them cannot understand other large numbers. Yet somehow—perhaps because of that exclusive and brilliant implement of culture, calligraphy, that makes every literate Chinese comprehensible to every other, and at the same time incomprehensible to almost every other living soul apart from Japanese—every Chinese feels he is a member of a special group of humanity.

It is fundamentally this that makes muddled, frenetic, venal, boisterous, vulgar, and in many ways charming Hong Kong so Chinese, so basically non-Western despite its aggressively occidental envelope.

213

The outward expressions of this Chinese-ness can be amusing, startling, baffling, irritating, by turns.

Most large, and many small businesses employ a heavy majority of Chinese and a tiny number of Westerners. In large open-plan offices, if you disregard the faces behind the graveyard of typewriters and desks, the scene might, superficially, be anywhere in the West. Closer familiarity reveals differences. Among other strange customs, the system of messenger 'boys' (any age from fifteen up to seventy or so) whose job in life it is to deliver by hand all local correspondence of the company with other companies or persons in the business areas. These messengers often wear a uniform of sorts with the company's name on a pocket, and are a feature of Hong Kong streets, each with his ledger, his sheaf of letters or rolled drawings or both. At each port of call he hands over the letter and gets a signature against the entry in the ledger referring to it, before going on to the next office for the same procedure. The custom is probably European in origin. It was useful in times past, but became quite pointless in recent years when the postal service was both cheap and fast. Now, once again, it is useful since the post has slowed down.

In those same Western-looking offices, there are yet other arcane activities to be observed by the diligent sociologist. Enquiry will reveal that many, if not most, of the clerks and office boys have relatives, or close friends of relatives, already working for the company. The attaining of the job of office boy (such is the intensity of job competition in the over-populated, statistically young, community) means in most cases that the relative who obtains the job for the boy will extract 'tea-money'—in the shape of, perhaps, a month's wages—from the new employee.

Nowadays it is not so common, as customs break down a little, but formerly an executive appointing an office boy without the recommendation of a person already employed in his company, was likely to have his decision reversed as the new boy left after a week or two—unable to stand up to the pressures brought to bear on him by others who wished to have one of their relatives given the job.

This Chinese clannish loyalty can be matched in many another circumstance of business and personal life in Hong Kong. It has its good and also its less desirable aspects. At a Chinese wedding it is virtually obligatory for the groom and the bride to invite all their relatives and friends. This means frequently a crippling debt for a dinner party for several hundred people, incurred by the groom or his parents. It is

214

only partially offset by the custom of giving 'lucky' money at the banquet.

Until very recently one of the sights of Hong Kong around midday was the sudden appearance in the streets of the business and shopping districts of numerous strong women carrying at the ends of bamboo shoulder-poles stacks of containers often wrapped in blue cloth, and of men bearing on their heads equally loaded wooden trays. This was lunch for many thousands of office and shop workers, ordered and brought in to their place of employment. It was incredibly cheap and generally quite nourishing—noodles, fried rice with shrimp and bits of meat and some vegetable in it, and other such filling foods. At that time of day the already crowded pavements became dangerous, for all those trays had stout metal corners which, with a backing of twenty or thirty pounds of porcelain and food and the momentum of a hurrying delivery man, have been known to inflict bloody wounds at forehead level on incautious pedestrians. Now, to the annoyance of many an underpaid worker, a government ruling has prohibited the operation of 'unlicensed catering establishments', and the trade has virtually stopped. Office workers must now either bring sandwiches (which the Chinese, like the French, don't find a rewarding substitute for a meal) or go out and join the crowds struggling for a place in one of the multi-storey teahouses, where they can afford a few *dim sum* dishes.

*   *   *   *   *   *

The twin cities of Victoria and Kowloon, separated by the grand harbour, are really Western places peopled largely by Chinese. It has always been so since Victoria was founded by the British for the further-ance of British trade.

Possession Street, running uphill to the place where the flag was first hoisted, is a steep narrow way hardly a carriage-width across, rising from the area of Western Market and Bonham Strand (called after the third Governor of the Colony), lined at its lower end by vegetable stalls, crossing half-way up an area of abundant vegetables and cooked meat, live chickens and ducks that came quacking all the way from China in flat wicker baskets; and ending in a steep pull up to Hollywood Road, a twisted thoroughfare of variable width, lined by tottering four- and five-storey buildings whose ground floors are shops and upper storeys dwelling places. Possession Point, as we already noted, lies in a yard down the road a little, a mess of scabrous buildings, a couple of enigmatic octagons, and a broken iron object of unknown purpose. Tempting to carry the analogy somewhat further into the state of Hong Kong's corporate being. Like Possession Point and its once proud Western buildings, the lease on life is running out and those hormones that invigorated the colonial tissues should be trickling uncertainly now. But it is doubtful if the geriatric process is definitely under way in this unnatural city.

The whole area of Western district is full of strange sights, deeply rotting in its very bones, intensely picturesque, and of a medieval insanitariness. In the streets above lie such white elephants as the decaying family mansions of wealthy Chinese families, dating from the turn of the century and before—one of them for many years inhabited by a single old servant, and still standing only because the grandfather who is head of the family cannot bring himself to knock it down. The land on which it stands is worth at least a couple of million US dollars. Below are streets and streets of shops selling the improbable ingredients of the vast (remarkably efficacious) Chinese pharmacopoeia, especially in Bonham Strand.

Aerial view of Victoria, looking west, in 1935

216

There, too, until lately, was at least one shop selling porcelain, often hard to enter because of the delivery boys' bicycles stacked outside, and because of the (in summer) semi-naked youths dripping with blood, carrying carcases of meat to the Western Market nearby. Once inside the building, its walls slightly askew, its shelves stacked with teetering piles of porcelain of every imaginable shape, size, design—you mounted the stairway past a patchwork of glazed tiles with feeble Ch'ing landscapes in *famille rose*[7] enamels and emerged into the warren of the first floor. Here the porcelain was piled even higher, here were large tubs of antique design made yesterday in imitation of Sung garden seats, here were vast cauldrons of brown with yellow rampant dragons playfully clawing their way round the outside—destined for goldfish in former days, and now for ornamental plants.

But here, too, were the most practical and cheapest forms of Chinese-made European-style cups, saucers, plates, bowls, and every other dish necessary for either a Western or a Chinese meal.

At a vast desk sat an old man who seemed to have been there as long as time, whose smile was not easily conjured up except upon lengthy acquaintance. He wrote the accounts in Chinese characters—not the

A view of the central portion of the previous photograph in summer, 1974. In the foreground is Garden Terrace and older houses

simple numeral characters but the other set used in business, which cannot be altered for fraudulent purposes. In winter he wore a beret and grey woollen mittens against the chill that hung in the air and dropped like an invisible waterfall from the cold stacked goods that surrounded him. Now the shop has gone, relocated in a brand new building. And the old man and the charm of the place have disappeared too.

In this area is a street almost entirely lined by shops that sell cloth, gimp, and other such trimmings; and a long stretch of Queen's Road West consists almost solely of gold and jewelery shops with the occasional small shop that sells Chinese fans, brushes, and ink, with the grinding slabs for the ink in various carved shapes; and numerous tea shops. These are a special delight, an acquired taste in shops. Most of the employees are on the elderly side, not given to great talk. In sharp contrast are their wares, housed in glass tanks, each labelled with such whimsical and echoing names as Dragon's Well, Ten League Fragrance, The Iron Goddess of Mercy, and (supreme fantasy) Long Life Eyebrows.

Much of this part of Western Victoria is due for demolition, the two streets known to tourists the world over as Cat Street, just south of Hollywood Road, even now gone. No one seems to know the reason for the appellation Cat Street, since their names were officially Upper and Lower Lascar Row, and the local Chinese called them both Mo-lo Gai (Indian Lane) with historical justification since many Indians lived in this quarter long ago. The streets were the centre of the antique and junk trade, and also of the stolen property exchange. Ten and more years ago there was marvellous Chinese porcelain there, but latterly the contents of the dark and cockroach-ridden shops held little but third-rate rubbish.

In a sense, as the scaffolding of bamboos went up in front of those old facades and was covered over with *rattan* matting, and as the sounds of demolition began within, one felt a pang of sadness. Another little corner of a more intimate and more personal relationship between people was disappearing. It is one thing to enter an air-conditioned shop with immaculate glass cases and carefully dressed assistants where the goods are all highly priced and probably all authentic; and quite another to know over the years this and that old man in his dusty old shop where the front room contained what he wanted to sell to undiscriminating buyers, and in the back room, once you penetrated there, box after box of surprises—good and bad—was brought out. You didn't have to buy, very often made no purchase. But as an adjunct to the training of the eye by study of authentic great works in museums and perhaps in private collections, the gradual acquisition of the 'feel' of Chinese wares was enjoyable and worthwhile. And the sharing of the experience with others whose experience was greater than yours, was a valuable thing.

It is this, perhaps more than the loss of what were insanitary structures of merely superficial picturesqueness, that is now gone. The city is the poorer for such loss of human contacts in particular areas.

A decade or so is not really long in urban history, but in the history of Hong Kong as an urban complex it is like a transformation scene in some not altogether edifying theatrical performance. And twenty years seem, in the addition in changes, a startling and rather vulgar miracle —at least visually.

The past two decades of Hong Kong have to be regarded as contemporary Hong Kong, since change in the city in almost every aspect of life has proceded so fast and in such a manner that alterations in one aspect are inextricably entangled with those in others. The dramatic growth in population from 1962 onward, is paralleled by the dramatic increase in the rate of building. Perhaps in these twenty years the city has built more than in all its previous history. Parallel with those factors is the sharp rise in crime rate and the alteration in types of crime.

The staggering increase in business, in exports, in manufacture, and in affluence all come into the picture of a couple of decades of change from which any city would be reeling. And Hong Kong, far from being an ordinary city in world terms, is an extremely unusual one. It reels under the impact of these obtrusive facts and their often nefarious side-effects, and—like the breeding lemmings whose numbers occasionally get so out of all sense of proportion, that they rush at the prompting of some biological urge headlong to cast themselves into the sea and death—Hong Kong as if at the behest of some such genetic and social urge would appear to be heading in that same general direction. On the other hand it may not.

*　*　*　*　*　*

The writer James Pope-Hennessy, grandson of Governor Hennessy, called his Hong Kong book *Half-Crown Colony*—a biting reference to an old British coin, and also to the fact that under the British crown colonialism is on its very last legs. Nonetheless, it has to be recognized

219

that Hong Kong has a remarkable capacity for survival. Here we might look briefly at the transformation since World War II. Prior to the War the wages of the Colony were earned principally from its position in the oriental entrepôt trade. It served as a trans-shipment point and a place where processing of cargo could be carried out speedily and with efficiency and safety. Goods destined for China came, admittedly, to Shanghai and Canton in vastly greater quantities, but Hong Kong processed its share. Trans-shipment to other parts of the Far East accounted for a large part of the commerce.

All this was smashed by the Japanese as they enclosed the Colony in their so-called Greater East Asia Co-prosperity Sphere. By the end of the War and the hermetic sealing of China by the Communist regime, Hong Kong had to look around fast for other means of subsistence. The statistics demonstrate more dramatically than description the abrupt and astonishingly successful manner in which the Colony altered its role.

In 1950 only 25 per cent of exports were Hong Kong-made, the bulk of the remainder being imported, processed, or trans-shipped, and re-exported. By 1976, the miracle had been fully achieved and Hong Kong manufactures formed almost 80 per cent of total exports, worth US$7 billion.

The factors in this astonishing feat were several: the influx of hundreds of thousands of Chinese from the pre-1949 horrors of a land torn by civil war; political stability in Hong Kong that encouraged the influx of foreign capital—from lands as diverse as India, Britain, America, later Japan and the Middle East—to a city where the *laissez-faire* policies of the government promised the minimum of interference, and the maximum mobility and manoeuverability of that money. There is virtually no governmental distinction between Hong Kong and foreign companies, the minimum of bureaucratic paperwork. For a registration fee of under US$20 you can incorporate a business in Hong Kong. Taxation is at a standard maximum rate of fifteen per cent, and Hong Kong is a free port—only five commodities being subject to a small duty.

Added to these attractions in a world of increasing red tape and tighter control on capital and profit, is the efficient infra-structure, an inheritance from earlier days of difficult trade, in the form of banking, insurance, warehousing, and shipping.

The basic expansion in industry involved the textile sector. Today, 53 per cent of the Colony's domestic exports are textiles, and the industry

Fisher-people in small boats. *Below:* A girl made homeless by a landslide in 1972, doing home-work in a temporary camp

In a village market in the New Territories an old woman with her traditional pipe buys fish

employs about 48 per cent of the workforce. The plastics and the electronics industries account for another very large chunk of Hong Kong
products, US$1.4 billion in 1976. Both industries were new to the Colony
in the late 1950s. In 1960, four thousand transistor radios made chiefly
of imported parts were exported. By 1969, 21 million units were exported, of which most parts were manufactured in Hong Kong. And
in 1976 the electronics industry accounted for almost US$870 million
in export value. Recently, the toy industry has become a factor to watch.

The other big money-spinner is the tourist trade—the inexplicable
attraction of Hong Kong for (in 1976) a million and a half people who
stayed an average of about 3 days each and spent US$815 million on
things they could mostly buy at home for very little more.

Various economists and others have attempted to fill out the picture
of how all this was achieved in so short a time. And the answer seems
to be, broadly, the immense capacity the Chinese have shown (and
passed on to their English colleagues) to adapt to whatever the commercial needs of the world were at any moment or looked like being
in the near future. Suddenly, some years ago, people in the West began
to wear wigs again—a fashion phase that boomed for a few years and
passed. And suddenly Hong Kong had dozens of wig factories supplying,
cheaper than the rest of the world could, excellent wigs in every category. If in the near future the world wakes up to the idea that the air
we all breathe is becoming dangerous to health, and the world population takes to wearing respirators—doubtless Hong Kong will be in on
the ground floor with more and cheaper varieties than anywhere else.
That is essentially what made the boom in Hong Kong—flexibility,
and the unfettered manipulation of capital plus comparatively low
wages that (if we cast our minds back to 19th century England) seem
to be the essentials of booming industrial economy.

In 1976 there were 678 miles of roads in the whole Colony, but 283
vehicles for every mile. The nature of much terrain in Hong Kong
Island and some of the New Territories is such that to expand the road
system significantly is difficult in the very places where expansion is
needed most.[8]

Of the four and a half million population, increasing on conservative
estimate at the rate of at least 60,000, and probably more like 80,000,
every year, the New Territories at the last (1976) by-census held nearly
940,000 people, with an additional almost thirty thousand Tanka and
Hoklo people who live out their lives on fishing boats. The population
density of the urban areas (Hong Kong Island, Kowloon, New Kowloon,

and Tsuen Wan) was calculated at about 25,000 per square kilometre. But the density of population in one of the more crowded parts of Kowloon is approximately 144,000 per square kilometre. There is a government sponsored 10-year housing plan for the New Territories that will rehouse and relocate over two millions before 1983, converting several existing townships into large cities. Shatin, until recently an agglomeration of villages with a population of 50,000, will multiply ten times to half a million souls.

We have glanced at the miracle, and also at the human debris, the human misery, the breakdown of traditional codes, and the spreading affluence in some sectors of the population, which the Hong Kong industrial miracle (like the Industrial Revolution in the West) threw up in its ruthless progress. It is such factors as these that have made of Hong Kong in a matter of twenty years the bizarre city it is today.

*   *   *   *   *   *

This bizarre quality is best appreciated by noting the enormous changes in two decades, and at the same time observing the contemporaneous disparities in various aspects of the Colony's life.

Fifteen years ago, perhaps even more recently—it is not crucial—the Star Ferry that traverses the harbour from Kowloon to Hong Kong Island and back, was still a little tub of a thing. It left from and arrived at wooden jetties through whose old slatted floors you lost coins if you dropped them.

In those days the tourist trade had not profoundly affected the Colony. The airport buildings were housed in large Nissen-type 'huts'—almost incredible as it may now seem—and in fact in 1962 passengers still passed through the same stifling, and by that date densely crowded set of buildings. In 1976 the airport cleared over four million passengers, and was capable in 1977 of handing 5,000 an hour.

Crossing the harbour to the Hong Kong side, as local people always say in order to differentiate the Island from Kowloon, the view in the early 1960s, was of a waterfront still chiefly composed of four- and five-storey buildings of that slowly evolved blend of European styles, but with basically good proportions, adapted to the tropics—almost all of them with a covered pavement on all street sides, the first floor being supported on pillars. Hardly any examples remain nowadays, but they had charm, and a certain dignity. Inside, the staircases were anything up to ten feet broad, made of solid teak, often with fine bannisters polished by generations of hands. Office workers all worked by the light of day and under the twirl of great white ceiling fans. The rooms of executives faced the waterfront with a fine view of the harbour and the ships that until two or three decades ago were the main source of Hong Kong's wealth.

Far across the harbour the view was of the rather flat area of the city of Kowloon, dominated by a few taller and bulkier buildings such as the Peninsula Hotel, built in response to the completion of the railway from Hong Kong to Shanghai. Its main lobby rose through three storeys with white columns and gilded capitols, ancient black-wood chairs, potted palms and an orchestra playing Franz Lehar at teatime. Away to the east, along a shoreline that was green scrub in summer rains, and brown in winter drought, there was hardly a building to be seen. One small shipbreaking yard was virtually the only sign of commercial activity, and it was not until about 1957 that the first factories began to rise in the district, which is now a industrial and resettlement housing area stretching from the airport for several miles along that coast to Kwun Tong.

The view of Victoria and the Island in 1957 as you crossed from Kowloon, was dominated by the Peak above the town, a dense pack of buildings rising at first gently and then steeply up the hillsides. Only the tall Bank of China building, that of the Hongkong and Shanghai Bank, and one or two others, rose above the general level. The Hong Kong Club with the slightly feminine elegance of late Victorian colonial style used to sit primly in the sun beside the gardens fronting the Bank. The other flank of the gardens of Statue Square (from which Queen Victoria in bronze was removed by the Japanese in World War II and now stands in Victoria Park a couple of miles to the east) was formed by two not dissimilar colonial-style edifices—one on the site now occupied by the Mandarin Hotel, and the other, called like its successor, Prince's Building. Slightly inland, above what used to be the old shoreline of the 1840s, stood Murray Barracks with the Parade Ground on a mound to the West, and the Cathedral just a little higher. The residence of the Commander-in-Chief, Flagstaff House, stood comfortably close to all three, ensuring a spiritual and a defence proximity for the original occupant and his successors since 1846.

To the west there stretched out along the water progressively less elegant buildings of nineteenth and early twentieth century styles, while east of the central district was a small naval dockyard and a row of similar buildings fronting Wanchai and Causeway Bay. Up the hill above the town centre the buildings mounted some considerable way and the houses of Mid-levels, as this elevation is called, were established, with a few blocks rising several storeys high. Further up, the buildings thinned out and the fine white houses of the Colonial Secretary and other government functionaries, of *taipans* (the heads of rich *hongs*, or companies) stood mostly in isolated splendour. Finally, around that place where the Peak Tram reaches the saddle of the hill, a good number of fine residences were perched. By the late fifties, a few multistorey residential blocks sprang up in Mid-levels, but even then the view from the harbour bore some resemblance to that of long before World War II, and indeed to the scene at much earlier periods.

In under a decade from then, today's forest of concrete harshness, has sprung like a crop of mighty fungi, and the well-to-do have placed themselves inside—in boxes often so small and so low of ceiling that in the long, humid, and very hot summer, air-conditioning is obligatory. And yet, in the same locations, in houses designed up to a century ago, and even much more recently, good tropical architecture had permitted comfortable living with no more than one of those silent and slowly twirling ceiling fans for aeration. The quality of life—another instance —has really diminished while its costs have immensely risen.

Along the glades of this concrete forest there still exist some old and graceful houses, their view over the grand harbour long obscured by the kitchens and servants quarters of towering blocks on whose unplanned posterior elevations all the plumbing rises (or, if you like, falls) like creepers of varying thickness in a tangle of monstrous hideosity. * Murray Barracks, that graceful old colonial structure with its black Chinese roof, is still there, saved by the protests of a few conservationists, but standing in something of a hole formed by overpasses. Flagstaff House is still there too, in a bosky clearing with some fine Victorian barrack buildings near it (soon to be demolished). Over the road the Cathedral is still there, lost amid highrise. It no longer looks over the Parade Ground, whose excavation from a hill served, incidentally, to fill the bay where the Cricket Club was established in 1851. For the Parade Ground gave way some time ago to the Hilton Hotel. The Cricket Club with its square of impeccable lawn, practice nets, occasional lawn tennis tournaments, and its dreary little clubhouse at one corner, still clung to its multi-million dollar site until in 1976 it removed to a newly prepared ground at the Wongneichong Gap, when the original ground was resumed by the government.

The once tranquil space of Statue Square, with its lawns and palms was 'redesigned' some years ago. Levels were raised, tame little patches of lawn planted, pools sunk, coloured underwater lights put in to show the water jets hosing the graceless slabs of 'sculpture' standing in the water. And, ultimate horror, the erection of what became locally known as the Thai bus shelters from their ressemblance to Thai steep-pitched, curled-end roofs and the general form of Western bus shelters.

Time and a tropical climate have mercifully covered up for rude mankind, and the area is less hideous now—and much used by the people for sitting and reading newspapers, and taking photographs of proud fathers, mothers, and children.

There always was a snob-value in the district in which people lived in Victoria, as in other cities. In the early days, the best area was on the slopes to the west of Central district. By the 1950s and sixties it had long been in Mid-levels and upward—the higher, the more elevated in social status. So that the phrase, 'Peak ladies' came into being as a term of derision used by those who could not or did not aspire to life on the heights. In fact, until 1946, you could not take up residence on the Peak without the express permission of the Governor himself. But oddly enough, Government House, the residence of the Governor, has always been where it now is in low Mid-levels, with summer retreats for Governors built on the Peak in the past.

In the years before the last war 'Peak ladies'—the hostesses of those palmy days—were inclined to inquire, looking cooly from the spiritual stockade of society at some luckless new male arrival in what was still a restricted community of expatriates: 'Are you married? Or do you live in Kowloon?' For at that time the other side of the harbour was regarded as territory beyond the pale of polite society, its reputed charms of a type fit only for the unattached male.

Wanchai, the home of Suzie Wong—archetype of Cantonese prostitutes—was for many years a household word of sailors and soldiers the world round. At one time or another, hundreds of thousands of naval personnel have enjoyed its drink, drugs, and girls. Nightfall in Wanchai until only a few years ago was the signal for the lights to go on, for those vast neon signs that used to stretch more than half way across the street at the level of the second floor to blaze, and to sizzle in the rainy season, announcing bars and 'nightclubs', dancing bars and ballrooms, tattooing, massage of all known and invented varieties from Japanese to French, quick tailoring, and a host of other attractions.

The gusts of 'rock' and other forms of pop music in vogue from time to time struck from the swing doors as the drunken patrons rolled in or out, or were occasionally thrown out. Tall sailors disappeared up narrow stairways between shops and bars with small Chinese girls. The numerous sleasy rooming houses did a roaring trade, rates by the hour.

It was an area that younger residents used occasionally to take selected visitors to see, because for everyone who had ever heard of Hong Kong, 'Chinatown' was located in the area of Suzie Wong. But most Westerners, and most Chinese other than those who worked there or had the misfortune to have to live in the district, did not frequent the place after dark. The exotic aspects of Wanchai were nicely calculated to suit the tastes of 'lonely' servicemen. For the resident of the Colony, Wanchai had a kind of underlying sadness with its raucous music and girls for sale, the atmosphere Graham Greene catches so well when he writes of the emptiness of lust and its eternal need to be casually satisfied. Long ago, just after the Japanese surrender in Singapore, that broken city still had its areas of similar joys—the Great World and the New World, now so tamed and prim, and Lavendar Street and Bugis Street, the former no longer a red light area. Wanchai was no more than a bigger, more brightly neon-lit version in the era of permissiveness and electronics.

Since the termination of the war in Vietnam and of American troop involvement there, and since a quiet agreement between the British Government and Peking not to re-supply the American fleet in Hong Kong, Wanchai has faltered, flickered, and faded. Now it is in full decline. The area is fast becoming an annexe of the business district of Central, with new office blocks rising on the sites of the old rotting tenements.

The town is expanding east, and new reclamations made in conjunction with the building of the harbour tunnel in the first years of the 1970s, looping 'spaghetti' overpasses and freeways, have opened up the waterfront area and completely altered the old character. At the same time the building of huge new tourist hotels farther east at Causeway Bay, has sent the rents there rocketing, pushed many a small shopkeeper out of business, and is fast making this area with its dozens of Chinese restaurants conveniently near, its dozen or so cinemas, and its excellent markets here and there, into an middle-class Chinese district.

Once more the quality of living has diminished. A sprinkling of boutiques, interspersed with radio and TV stores, shops full of smart clothes, have displaced the food stores, the local hardware stores, the

Dragon Boat races are held round the coasts annually. *Below:* The container terminal at Kwai Chung in the New Territories

booths in little alleys where you could have a key cut while you waited, or a shoe repaired in a few hours. Luckily the finest restaurants in the Colony—though there are some who would dispute this and vouch for others on the Kowloon side—are still there and flourishing in the new affluence of Chinese and Western society.

But Suzie Wong died some time ago in Wanchai. Her reincarnations in the shape of topless Australian girls and little Chinese 'hostesses' whose part-time occupations are the same as that of Suzie, can be easily discovered in a thousand bars, nightclubs, discotheques, and boarding houses up and down Nathan Road, Kowloon. The clients for private sex shows, blue films, and the charms of latter-day Suzies, are now tourists and not sailors, and the services exceedingly expensive. You can take you choice, from pornography to pep pills and passion. It's all there in the new Wanchai in Kowloon. Soon, perhaps, those matrons on the Peak will once more be asking the old question: 'Are you married, or do you live in Kowloon?'—ignorant of the fact that today one could be (and do) both for varying reasons and in varying degrees.

*   *   *   *   *   *

The southern aspect of Hong Kong Island offers still a rather different picture from that of the wholly built-up northern shores. The port of Aberdeen (still termed Little Hong Kong by Chinese) was fortunate in the Colony's beginnings not to have been named Queenstown and become the city Victoria now is—when Captain Elliot changed his mind on the subject. It remained until the last two decades one of the most picturesque, but also one of the livliest villages, the home of thousands of boat people.

The boat people are a race apart. Many of them are Hoklo people whose language and customs and traditions differ considerably from those of the Cantonese as a whole. 'They are a tougher, sturdier people who for centuries have fished and pirated up down the coast of China. They are . . . proud of their distinctive characteristics, worshipping their own gods, of which the Queen of Heaven is the chief. She sits in many temples round the coast gazing out over the water where her people fish and live and die.' F.D. Ommanney, whose book *Fragrant Harbour* contains this passage, worked with them for years and has the greatest admiration for them.

Tough they certainly are, the men walking with a swagger, half

The congestion in Aberdeen harbour, with resettlement blocks beyond

An ocean-going junk on the slips at Apleichau for repairs

seaman's roll and half abounding self-assurance, when they come ashore. The women too have a solidity reminiscent of peasant women from the countryside of China, a firmness of body, leg, and arm that speaks of generations of sculling the little boats called *sampan* (literally, three planks) and assisting in the arduous work of deep-sea and coastal fishing.

Between the village on shore, which has now developed into a town with big resettlement estates and streets of thriving shops replacing the old chandlers' stores where all the necessities of life and work on the junks could be bought for next to nothing, and the small island of Apleichau (Duck's Tongue Island), the water is always crowded with the strong shapes of anchored junks. There are many types, according to which area of the South China coast they originated in, and between those intended for estuarine, river, and coastal work, and deep-sea fishing. The whole subject has been written about in depth.

A *sampan* trip from the shore at Aberdeen among the fishing fleet in the harbour gives some slight impression of the life of the junk people. Most *sampan* women naturally assume that any *kwei-lo* (foreign devil— a common term for Westerners) wants to visit one of the three floating restaurants. Avoiding this, it is interesting to wander on the strong-smelling water between the great wooden walls of the junks, to watch families at work, or eating in a circle of squatting forms on the deck, the dogs sleeping, grandmother in the poop cooking, potted plants tied down and flowering gaily, and all the net-mending and gear-checking activities of a fisher-family's life.

Around you not long ago, in that wooden, slope-masted village on the water, was a scene that had little changed for many a decade. The cliff where the water of the fragrant stream fell is still there, high above the harbour and a little to the west. And the conoid shapes of the mountains are still evident, although slightly cluttered with the houses of the great. Through the forest of masts, looking south, lies Apleichau, not long ago a mere hump with some interesting old Chinese tombs on it, a straggle of village, and boatbuilding yards. The tombs are like a hundred thousand others set on propitious slopes where the *feng shui* is good. They are semicircular, the shape that results when you cut vertically into a slope, the wall curling round, embracing a stele with inscriptions.

The village on Apleichau long ago became a centre for maintainance of the diesel engines that for more than a decade all big junks have used as main motive power, relying on their wing-like boned sails, part

Repairing a junk. The electric drill has largely replaced the traditional bow-drill

bird and part Chinese fan, as adjuvants on breezy days. The repair shops of Apleichau are a clutter of rusting or oil-dripping parts, engine-casings, propellors, shafts, and cylinders of dismembered engines. The labour force seems mostly to be composed of youths between fourteen and twenty, dressed in the summer in cotton pants, but oiled from eyebrows to toes in black. But they are a cheerful lot, plunged all day and half the night in the sump-oil and steel of dissected machines.

In China from time immemorial the art of carpentry included the art of architecture. Formal plans with measurements were not made, and if you intended to build a house you specified how many 'bays' you wanted. These, like the Japanese *tatami*, were the module, and their proliferation produced a larger house. This was all carpenter's work; and so is the building of a junk. Elevations and sections do not exist except in the head of the man with the saw and the awl.

There is a profound pleasure to be had in watching such skilled carpenters at work. The profession—that of a cabinetmaker and marine architect rolled into one—is handed down from father to sons. The tools are simple—hammers, bucksaws, bow-drills, various planes. Nowadays they still use bow-drills for making smaller holes, although the brace and bit, and the electric drill are supplanting them for bigger work. On the slips you can stand for hours and watch as the pinkish butter-coloured wood of a rib takes springing shape, or watch the blading of that Chinese object the fenestrated rudder, one among many early Chinese inventions in nautical technology.

In other yards on the Apleichau waterfront the great bulk of the big junks can be appreciated as they are hauled up the slips by cable for repairs to be made. Twice a year most of these and other wooden craft have to be taken out of the water, their bottoms scraped and fired with a flash of brushwood before being coated with a barnacle- and wood-worm-preventing paint.

But Apleichau, alas, and Aberdeen as a whole, is now disfigured by the new electricity generating station with its silver oil tanks, tall smokestacks, and the great straddling pylons that tie the island to the place where of old the fragrant stream casaded 'in one grand and graceful lapse' down the mountainous terrain of Hong Kong. Soon, a bridge will connect with Hong Kong. Aberdeen and its harbour are undoubtedly cleaner and better places to live in, and Hong Kong is more plentifully supplied with power, but the ancient charm of the place, except for the detail, has disappeared. In Hong Kong you find yourself voicing all too frequently such small laments; because the process, unlike much of a similar nature that slowly happened in the West, goes on daily before your eyes.

Another Chinese skill worth watching is the erecting of bamboo scaffolding. You can see this any day, since Hong Kong is in a perpetual state of demolition and massive reconstruction. The old skills—again passed down through generations of the same families—that were sufficient to tie together the bamboo scaffolding for a two-storey building or the construction of a great temple of the past, have been adapted by the workers to suit the construction of the highest buildings. The resulting lattice of poles tied together with rattan strips may look precarious, but is as strong and possibly more resilient than the Western tubular version.

At Aberdeen and in many another place before Chinese New Year there comes the chance to observe a wonder of construction verging in its beauty on that of the groining of some Gothic cathedral. It forms the skeleton of the temporary theatre from which for a week or two the assorted bangs, and warbling, declamation, and *recitativo* of Cantonese Opera, emanate until far into the night. The theatres are often quite large, perhaps a hundred feet across by a hundred-and-fifty long, and the roof is supported without the use of pillars. The intricacy of the structure has to be seen to be appreciated. The same care and intelligence go into a similar structure erected over the foundations of a new building that must be prepared during the rainy season.

While the Chinese New Year is the climatic annual event for all Chinese, the boat people have festivals of their own, one of the most colourful being the celebration of the birthday of their own goddess, Tin Hau, that mistress of the oceans and arbitress of the destinies of all who sail them. She is a manifestation of the Buddhist goddess Kuan Yin (in Cantonese, Gun Yam) who in turn was once male but, by one of those not infrequent sex-changes that occur in Oriental religions, at some point in history became the sweet-smiling Goddess of Mercy.

As for all major Chinese festivals, great preparations are made in advance, and when the fleets of junks weigh anchor in the morning sun, all fluttering with magnificent *tong* (co-operative association) and other banners, long floating pennants, and every inch of cordage flapping with bunting, a lion dance in progress on the deck, it is obvious how much has gone into the day's event.

By mid-morning at Joss House Bay, called Fat Tong Mun, (the Gate of Buddha's Hall) the waters are congested with junks from all round the Colony, thwart to thwart, all of a riot of colour and with the noise of clashing cymbals and rolling drums as many dances are performed. Up the hill stands Tai Miu—the Great Temple—usually almost deserted, but on this twenty-third day of the third lunar month (generally about the third week in May, by Western reckoning) the focus of crowds of fishing people. The temple is embowered in clouds of incense, as though some romantic film director had ordered it thus. From the boats come parties of fishing people all dressed in their best, the men bearing shoulder-high on a litter a brown and succulent roast pig. Struggling through the press of others, they ascend the hill to the temple, there to offer it to Tin Hau, to burn incense, to make their kowtows before her.

Then off down the hill again through the crowds and the noise and incense smoke, with that rumbustious jollity that the convivial souls of Chinese love. The pig, having been offered in a side-temple, now goes back to the boat where the whole family sit down to a bumper meal, the rice and vegetables cooked and ready for their return.

Before the 1967 riots, when firecrackers were made illegal, the noise at Tin Hau Festival was even greater and incense smoke mingled with

Fishing junks decorated in celebration of the birthday of Tin Hau, the Queen of Heaven, the patron diety of fisher-people

237

that of the 'bursting bamboos'—the written term for fireworks[9] that comes from long ago when gunpowder (which they invented) was stuffed into a hollow bamboo, the end sealed, and the bamboo cast on a fire.

After eating, the family settles down to play mahjong, the clash of the bricks making up for whatever devil-scaring effect was lost with the demise of the firecracker. Late in the afternoon they set off back to their anchorage, wherever it may be. Through the narrow straits of Lei Yue Mun leading into the great harbour they come in dozens, silk flags and long pennants fluttering, making a somehow medieval sight of great splendour as they sail into the orange eye of the sun way down to the west among the first evening mists between the islands.

Nothing could be more typical of Hong Kong than this heraldic sight of Chinese ships in all their festival finery breasting the choppy harbour waves, against a backdrop of the rawest concrete sprouting beneath the cardboard cutout of the Nine Dragons that rear beyond against the sky. It's a great sight, provocative, and one that in time will disappear like all the rest. The Chinese will doubtless invent new festivals (they have already, over the border, thrown up a few) just as the West has done, and it is perhaps foolish to regret the vanishing pageantry of the old. But that is not the emotion you experience as those strong, purposeful boats with their gaudy flags nose up the harbour all gilded in the radiance of the setting sun.

* * * * * *

Christmas is as commercial and frenzied a festival in the Colony among the Western population, and also with a large number of Chinese who can afford it, as it is in the West. But the real, the deeply felt events of Hong Kong's year are not unnaturally all Chinese.

When the Mid-autumn Festival is over so are several other things. The real fire of summer and early autumn heat diminishes. The Chinese mostly stop swimming (because, they say, and it is often correct, that at this time the inshore waters of the Colony become filled with tiny red organisms called *sui chi*[10] which cuase a slight tingling rash on the skin of many people). The beaches which have been crammed with Chinese since April and May—another phenomenon that has really come into being only in the last two decades, before which few Chinese could swim and not very many went to the beaches—now look deserted by comparison, and the density of the Western population on them rises rapidly. People begin to take out winter clothes and look them over for the ravages of moth and cockroach, to think about what new clothes and new bedding will be necessary in a month or two. The shops that sell bedding—the roseate and sharp-coloured quilts and the bright checkered blankets—begin to rearrange their stocks in gaudy piles. Lacquered hollow pillows sold throughout summer suddenly disappear from the shops. Everyone who takes exercise now thinks of weekend walks on the hills, of barbecues (although these are a summer feature as well), of taking a ferry to some outlying island and exploring a little. The exhausting humidity of summer begins slowly to fall and drier air comes with vacant skies and a progressive browning of the grass, and riots of colour as the more than seventy varieties of bougainvilea in the Colony shoot out bursts of scarlet, orange, lemon white, and shades of flame.

The days are like days in remembered childhood summers of Europe as the weeks go on through October and November into December. Sometimes a few grey days intervene, and everyone feels miserable and talks about how unseasonable such weather is. It may even shower a little during these days, thin gently-falling rain, a mist that has become too dense to hold up. The trees that did not flower in spring and summer now bloom, and with the slow disappearance of the flaunting red and yellow hibiscus whose vast petals now refuse to unfold as the sun and the humidity grow less to their liking, and hang like red puppy-tongues, with the stamen protruding, the colder evenings of late November and December arrive. And about the end of December even the days are not very warm in the sun. By January it is often overcast, by February it is generally overcast, and by Chinese New Year which falls in late January or in February it is generally cold. You can see your breath even at midday sometimes, and nearly always after dark.

These colder days bring with them a flurry of preparations by the Chinese inhabitants for their great pivotal festival—the New Year.

One of the astonishing things about it is that even the poorest Chinese manage somehow to find a little money to spend on extra food, and on a sort of undiluted enjoyment that shines on most Chinese faces at these times. In days between the Wars, with even more conviction in Victorian times, those who could afford the luxury talked of Christmas as a time of joy. And it is something like the childish joy of Christmases long ago, translated into another culture, that is so obvious at the Chinese New Year.

239

For a week or two before, you can see people in the market gardens of Hong Kong and the New Territories observing the young peach and plum blossom on tender trees, trying to assess whether this or that one it will actually come out at New Year. For by custom the family whose tree fails to blossom by that day is doomed to bad luck in the coming year. In the same gardens banks of miniature orange trees are heavily loaded with kumquats of two different kinds,[11] the little inch-diameter fruit that are also lucky omens. They are inedible, but kumquats preserved later yield a liquid said to cure sore throats.

The back streets of old and new Hong Kong are all pasted with strips of bright red paper inscribed with the black or gold characters of lucky slogans, one on either side of each doorway. In the villages each narrow street is festive with them, and as the great junks whose home is one or other typhoon shelter come in for their week-long holiday, they too are fluttering with multitudinous leaves of red. The whole stretch of water at Aberdeen is solid with junks packed side by side with only narrow channels between blocks of them forming lanes in which sampans pole and collide in cheerful abandon.

A week before New Year the Kitchen God has been despatched to Heaven from his place above the stove, to recount the family's deeds in the past year. Food stalls and markets and stores are at their busiest. The amount of food eaten in the week before and the week following New Year must be nearly double the normal. Restaurants are choked with diners ploughing through gargantuan meals and pouring libations of brandy by the tumblerful. Brandy, in Hong Kong, has quite ousted Chinese wine among the Chinese, and is drunk with the same abandon as if its alcohol content were as low as that of the wine—which is not the case. But most Chinese are not drinkers, except of the traditional tea.

By New Year all debts must, traditionally, be settled, everyone must have a haircut (which, by the last possible day, doubles the price the barbers' charge) and everyone must have new clothes. Until recently when it was forbidden to reward public servants, all the messengers, mail men, meter readers, and even now all children and all unmarried people have to be given *lai see*[12] meaning approximately 'auspicious money', but often called *hung chi*,[13] literally 'red paper'. The street stalls are stacked with wads of those little envelopes, small shops are carmine with piles of red paper, and old men sit in corners brushing in gold and black the characters of good omens that—among a people whose calligraphy means much more than just communication—are

The doors of an ancestral hall in a New Territories village decorated with a pair of military figures with flags bearing the word '*ling*'—'command'

241

essential to the smooth passage of the old into the new.

A great flower market is set up in Victoria Park, and in the evening thousands of people struggle through it buying blossoming branches, the little lily called crabs claws, and other flowers, and bear them home swathed in bright pink tissue paper.

The family is still the focus of celebrations. All over Hong Kong, New Year's Eve is celebrated at home with a feast. Traditionally the foods at New Year are those whose characters, or the sounds of whose characters, resemble those of felicitous things. Once again the complex and subtle depths of an ancient civilization show themselves, this time in the midst of simple jollity.

New Year's day is set aside for visiting close relatives and wishing them *Kung Hei Fat Choy*[14] (literally: Respectfully wishing you prosperity), and for eating further sustaining delicacies such as cake (*lo bak go*)[15] made with turnip, rice flour, and dried pork, fried and eaten hot in half-inch thick slices. The second day of the New Year is a general visiting day when you see friends near and far, bearing gifts of fruit and sweets. The streets are full of families dressed in obviously new clothes; and at this time the size of many a Chinese family becomes apparent. Father carries the tiniest baby, mother another who may just be able to walk but not far, the elder two children hold the hands of the intermediate two or three.

The third day of New Year is not for visiting, and is said to be a quarrelsome time. But on the fourth the outgoing nature of the Chinese takes over again. The fifth day is the birthday of Kuan Kung the merchants' god, and shops open again. Business and ordinary life take a turn to normality. But this is somewhat interrupted by the feasts of the 7th day which is celebrated as Everybody's Birthday, and when special foods are eaten to ward off sickness in the coming year.

While the traditional festivities in the city, and especially among the well-to-do, have nowadays taken on a rather brassy air like Christmas in the West, in the poorer quarters, in villages, and among the fishing people on their junks the happiness that the rituals and traditions of the season bring are just as evident as ever. The Chinese have a capacity within the structure of their traditions and superstitions to extract easily the maximum joy from the minimum material input. What they give in warmth, in an outgoing and spontaneous gregariousness, they recapture in this communal happiness and human joy.

Perhaps this process, this capacity for simplicity, warmth, and enjoyment of life and its accepted feasts in a year whose events basically reflect the needs and the fruits of the soil and its crops, may in some ways resemble (if only we could take our time machine back there) the atmosphere of country people of Europe before the industrial revolution. And it may be that this is the charm and the comfort in living among the Chinese today. You have the chance, now brief perhaps, of feeling what it was like in the days before steam and electricity, in times when at its best life had long produced profound philosophers, but also a human accommodation to the tyranny and the felicities of the natural environment.

* * * * * *

There are, however, times when, in the apt words of a recent satirical article, Hong Kong becomes 'not so much a Colony as a punishment'. This catches the spirit of the situation very neatly. At such times, when desperation looks like taking over, escape is essential. In fact, a periodic escape from the urban madness of Hong Kong—a phenomenon that has no parallel except in Tokyo—is almost a prerequisite of sanity.

This has become more than ever true since the government decided to build a Mass Transit Railway—Hong Kong's first underground transport system—at a cost of $5,000 million. The Mass Transit Railway Corporation was set up, and at the peak of construction activity in 1977, employed about 4,500 workers on all aspects of its burrowing and station construction activities. This is to result, in Spring 1980, in a limited version of the first overambitious scheme, and will consist of one line with fifteen stations. The Chater terminal station on Hong Kong Island is set right under the heart of central Victoria, and the chaos involved in its construction for many months was such that at times traffic came to a virtual halt, pedestrians were shunted round and up and over the various holes, pits, mechanical monsters; and the Central district suffered a virtually continuous cacophony very hard to bear.

The line will proceed to Admiralty station (fortunately constructed beneath a vacant lot to the east of Central) and then under the harbour in tubes to the Kowloon peninsula where the remaining thirteen stations are in the process of construction—those which lie along the main traffic arteries of Kowloon causing even more appalling disruption in construction.

243

The scene in Chater Road, Central, in January 1977, from the roof of the Hong Kong Club.
Left, the Supreme Court with Prince's Building and the new Alexandra House beyond it.
Construction of the Mass Transit Railway in progress

244

A further extension of the system will doubtless be attempted when this line is complete. Hong Kong will have, even with the modified initial line, one of the most modern underground railways in the world in every sense, with air-conditioned stations and cars, two-minute train frequency at peak hours, a nineteen-hour daily operating period, to carry a maximum expected one million passengers a day by the mid-1980s.

In sociological terms it is hard to decide what this ease of locomotion from residential to work areas for a very large number of the lower income groups of the population will mean. The introduction of the Peak Tram in 1888 caused a revolution in ideas of where the wealthy wanted to live. The introduction of the tramways running the length of the Island's northern coast has tended to make accessible areas of residence that were before that too far away from work to be practical. And the introduction of the motor vehicle opened up many parts of the Colony to both public and private movement not otherwise easy.

Now the possibility of getting from Kwun Tong's industrial-cum-residential area to Central Hong Kong in twenty-eight minutes, will mark another transport revolution. The journey at peak hours now could not possibly take less that about an hour by any means of public transport, and often takes much more.

For the fortunate few residents, and of course for any tourist, who can leave the hubbub and congestion of urban areas, the weekday escape routes are many and comparatively easy to follow, and still delightful. Even on Hong Kong island itself it is possible to walk for several hours among the hills amid scenery reminiscent of parts of Scotland alternating with breath-taking views over the South China Sea and the islands to the south, of reservoirs and catchments, and to hear nothing at all but the calls of the scanty bird population and the sawing of cicadas in the rough grass.

The New Territories offer much wider fields for country adventure. You could in fact walk for several days at a stretch among its hills and valleys, among rice paddies and vegetable gardens, passing villages that are still connected to the outer world only by a path, and some only by boat. You would have to choose the route carefully to avoid such formerly charming and now horribly urbanized villages as Tai-po where only one street of ancient shops remains intact like a small dream of 19th century South China; and to avoid others such as Fanling which is now reduced to the environment of a major crossroads, but has the Colony's best golf course as dubious compensation.

Some children have to play with what they can find. *Below:* A village in the New Territories after Lunar New Year with *t'o fu* either side of the doors, and printed door gods pasted on. Characters on the left hand door mean: 'Opening flowers bring wealth; the family's future is peaceful.'

246

Ploughing with water buffalo. *Below:* Hakka women form a significant part of Hong Kong's work force

247

A bride in the New Territories, preceded by a lion dancer and music, goes to her wedding in a sedan. *Below:* Visiting ancestral graves at the Ch'ing Ming festival

248

There are still villages nestling in front of their sacred groves of trees—camphor laurels, tall sprays of whispering bamboo—in ancient peace. The wood is a part of the village, supplying from its fruit trees the papayas, the bananas, the *lung nan*,[16] or dragons eyes, a fruit so called perhaps because of its large shiny brown stone. But even more essentially the function of the grove is protective. The *feng shui*,[17] the good auspices, embodied in it as in many another natural and man-made feature, and even in the direction that things and people face, are still deeply important to villagers. In the grove are often shrines to various spirits, set at the base of some particularly venerable tree, neglected most of the year but cleaned and furnished with burning incense sticks at appropriate times such as Chinese New Year.

There are other places where outcropping rocks are the site of curious scenes of worship of ancient spirits; and one 'matrimonial rock' where women go periodically on certain calendrical days to burn incense for married felicity, to prevent a husband taking a second wife, to make the auspices good for a daughter of marriageable age.

For the majority of Hong Kong people, whose free time comes at weekends as elsewhere in the world, those avenues of country charm are fairly inaccessible since the routes leading to them are as clogged at weekends. It can take anything up to three hours on a Sunday to drive the thirty miles from Kowloon to Fanling where the golfers swing. The roads are long snakes of hot metal on wheels, bursting with Chinese families and emitting a just sub-lethal effluent of part-combusted fuel. The journey that used to be so charming a mere decade ago is now inadvisable. Except on weekdays.

There are other places to go,—Lantau Island is one. On weekdays, the first ferry to the islands of Peng Chau and Lantau is not crowded. From the Outlying Districts Pier, it leaves an oddly quiet, somehow secret Hong Kong at 7.10. Most of the passengers have stretched out on the benches to complete the night's sleep in the fifty-minute voyage. Across the gangway a young man lies with head pillowed on elbow, his ear resting on a small transistor radio whose sounds appear to assist his sleep. In front is an old woman returning to the island after a visit to relatives combined with Hong Kong shopping. She lurches and nods half asleep over a stack of plastic bags and brown-wrapped parcels. Almost the only wakeful passengers are a bunch of workmen squatting together in a circle on the deck playing with narrow, sticklike Chinese cards that are much easier to handle than the Western variety.

It has dawned by the time we reach Peng Chau. Peng Chau looks grey-green, the village huddled and darker grey, dolefully decorated with ads for cigarettes in grey-orange and grey-pink on walls that are some solidified grey substance. A few of the ferry passengers cross the jetty to a battered old junk on the other side, to go to Lantau. The ferry, too, goes to Lantau, but to Silvermine Bay which is not where we want to go at the moment. Five minutes over the grey water lies the jetty of the Trappist monastery of Our Lady of Joy. A narrow road winds up the hill, lush greens on either hand, the unaccustomed, pungent smells of countryside in the nostrils as you mount, and the splash of water tumbling over stones.

The monastery is halfway to the top of a ravine, on a knoll—a chapel with a stub of a tower, long two-storeyed monks' quarters, the new guesthouse in what might be called Hong Kong functional style. Notices meant for weekend invaders forbid radios and request no loud noise be made. Inside the guesthouse it is pleasantly cool and spartan. It is around 8.30, and we feel we have already accomplished something by reaching this oasis of quiet across the water so early.

The good abbot and his nineteen monks, however, have accomplished much more. They rose at 3.15 a.m., and a quarter of an hour later began Vigil and Mass. From 5.0 o'clock they were at prayer, and then at devotional reading until breakfast at 6.30. This was followed by Morning Office at 7.0, and by the beginning of the day's manual work at 7.30.

One of the monks, Father Benedict, comes to talk. In his white soutane and black scapular of the Trappist order, he radiates goodwill, and also a kind of Chinese joy. The smoother, less indented Chinese face makes interior peace and benevolence look different from their appearance on a Western face. If their cheerless architecture hardly recommends itself, the cheerful earnestness of the Trappists of Lantau does. Their farm lies a little up the valley—cowsheds full of cows, clean long milking sheds, and huts of battery hens.

'The cows stay in their sheds year in year out. It is too hot for them in the sun,' Father Benedict said. 'Except twice a day when they walk down the hill to be milked. Poor things,' he added. 'In recent years, since we came here in 1951, only two of the boys from Hong Kong have stayed on with us. Many come for a month or two, some for years. Then they go away. Here,' he continued with a gesture, as if all life was integrated 'is the pasteurization plant, the bottling machine. The cows give us between fifteen hundred and two thousand half-pint bottles a day.' It was as if this were some marked favour.

'So we support ourselves more or less on selling milk to Hong Kong and Lantau. And our thousand hens help us with six or seven hundred eggs every day. The older Brothers look after the hens, it is lighter work for them.'

'Some monasteries are still silent,' he said. 'But we have recognized the changing world, and changed a little. We talk to communicate useful information to each other. But that is all.'

He showed the path leading to the brow of the hill, waving until we were out of sight. Not a lonely figure but a man content. Up the path tall grasses planted for cow fodder are eye-high, and the sun seeps down through a flat gold-clouded sky. It is hot and silent. You might be in the heart of China. Half an hour to the top. Suddenly the sky breaks. A torrent of sunlight floods the flank of Lantau Peak far over the valley and makes the sea shimmer and the semicircle of Silvermine Bay's sand glisten a moment or two. A huge view, as if life had opened out, still in silence, the silence deepened by the call of a bird or two and the passing of a little swarm of dragonflies.

Down the twisting hill path in the full scent of the country, and along to a restaurant by the beach and huge helpings of freshly made fried rice with shrimps and little bits of savoury fried pork and specks of Chinese chives in it. The proprietor comes and talks. He laughs when we tell him how we saw a fat male tourist softly whistling, over and over again, to encourage a stolid rump-presenting buffalo to turn and have its photo taken.

Then the small country bus with twenty or so people talking volubly in Cantonese starts off with verve from the ferry pier and plunges down valleys and bounces across the dam of Shek Pik Reservoir, flat sheet of steel water to the right and the gentle sea not far on the other hand. Up and up, winding like a bee among banks of flowers, among the hills, with grindings of worn gears, and valleys dropping on either side filled with lightly heat-misted air, far above the reservoir. And Lantau Peak, three thousand and sixty-four feet of it, still towers above. Then the bus trundles into a small plateau called Ngong Ping. Buddhist stupas and an ugly new white *p'ai-lo*, or ceremonial gateway, made of concrete in place of stone, herald the Po Lin Chi, or Precious Lotus Monastery.

Now that you can reach it by bus instead of arduously on foot, the place is flooded with noisy visitors from Hong Kong every weekend, and its old wooden Vegetarian Hall, as the fading characters inform you above its leaning portal, where they serve succulent meals, is hard put to it to cope with the influx. And there is no peace.

But on weekdays when every part of Hong Kong's countryside is at its best—and Lantau Island is more than twice the area of Hong Kong Island—rather few people come who do not have some business to bring them there. A rustic peace settles around shrines embellished with the vulgarity of later Ch'ing decadent elegance. It is hard to put aside the intrusive feeling that this humble little plain, formerly the site of some old broken buildings, now bristling with way-out Buddhist trimmings in blue and imperial yellow and gilt, all curly and contorted like arthritic feet turned into porcelain—has suffered an affront. But the merciful trees are fast sprouting against the yellow of the roofs, dropping their leaves on the new marble of the courts; and the vegetable and flower gardens, smelling bucolically of night-soil and rapid chlorophillic proliferation, assist in ridding the mind of the good Buddhists' mindless architectural aberrations.

The monks themselves seem not to welcome enquiries about their life. There are many of them, mostly rotund, clad in grey; and nuns too, sweetfaced and also grey-garbed, with shorn heads. Probably they all spend aeons chanting the sutras in the desolate gaudiness of those new halls, as good monks should.

Lantau is another world. The machine of Hong Kong commerce and Hong Kong society that grinds the inhabitants in various ways on that startling island has, still, no moving parts on Lantau.

An American Buddhist monk got on the return bus at the monastery, and an ancient lady of that fragile type with wide flat lips that slightly tremble, and large finger joints; also three young Chinese men and two Chinese girls who had sensibly enough spent their sojourn at the monastery taking pictures of each other against its more obvious vulgarities.

The sky at this end of the afternoon had loosened up, and we rolled over the little plain. Then over the lip of the chasm below, lurching and swiftly speeding like a bird from the thin-aired mountains to Silvermine Bay, stopping only once to pick up a party of tough men with red plastic buckets filled with big mussels they had gathered from the foreshore.

And, waiting for the ferry which was late, there were pears, the hard watery not very sweet pears of the orient, and coffee with condensed milk, which is as oriental as can be. Everything was still casual and not very ordered, and human and non-machine; and just as life should be.

Then came the ferry, importantly, round a spit of land to the right, and we called in briefly at Peng Chau. After that, round the corner of the island and, headed toward the east, Hong Kong was rising, glistening, fabulous like some wonderland, some latter-day Island of the Blessed that Chinese myths have always placed in the Eastern Seas. There it was, bathed in that falsifying and glamourizing light of the falling sun. Behind lay the serenity and the unpretentiousness of Lantau —a place, perhaps, much like the Hong Kong no one is now old enough to remember, before its slopes sprouted concrete and an infestation of steel ships invaded its great harbour. Then, on that hump of granite, there was only a village or two, the haunt of pirates and the despair of shipwrecked junkmen. And there was a Buddhist temple or two, a faint memory of the last stand of the last Sung emperor and his death at sea; and the peace of an ancient shore.

By coincidence, it was then, at the birth of the Colony, that the Trappists were making their oriental start in remote Peking.

* * * * * *

The cliché 'a cultural desert' is often applied to Hong Kong. In many ways it is true, for the arts in the strict sense have little following and few competent practitioners. But in a community almost exclusively composed of merchants and industrialists and their work-forces, buttressed by hordes of clerks in government and commercial offices, all of them living in the context of a traditionally aggressive business community, it is hardly surprising that the arts have not exactly flowered until recently.

Easily the most popular form of entertainment is TV, whose content in Hong Kong, where both English and Chinese channels transmit, is if anything more dismal and puerile than in other major cities of the world. Most of the material is canned, and what little is transmitted live is not distinguished for its intelligence.

The cinema comes next. The film business, as far as attendances go, is enjoying a boom that resembles the film fever of the thirties in the West. New cinemas open every year, the local Chinese film industry is one of the largest producers in terms of numbers of feature films in the world (and also one of the worst)—its markets being in Southeast Asia among the local and overseas Chinese communities there. Most of the films shown in Hong Kong, whether Chinese- or Western-made, are of that shoddy quality associated with routine epics from Italian studios and the inane sex-fumblings of less reputable European and

American producers. The rest is a diet of action-packed, violence-contorted, expensive movies whose only redeeming feature is the slickness of the technique employed that partially masks the incredibility of the plots and the total absence of anything to do with cinematic art at its best. These films generally have long runs, the more sex and violence they contain being the test of how many weeks a film can be profitably retained on the local screens. More intelligent films may last two days, a week, hardly ever more. You have to act quickly if you want to see them.

The reasons are not hard to discover. First, films that deal in a subtle or intellectual way with Western subjects are not specially interesting to the mass of Chinese whose life-style is completely different. Second, if there is much talk and little action or music the sub-titles in Chinese cannot cope with giving rapidly enough a sensible and at the same time readable impression of what is happening. So the bulk of the audience may be forgiven for finding such films boring. The Western audience is so small that no cinema could subsist on it alone.

In a public sense, the artistic life of Hong Kong might be said to have begun in 1962 with the opening of the City Hall—a name that conjures up municipal offices but in Hong Kong is something else. The name derives from its predecessor whose demolition in 1933 went unlamented because the building had fallen into disuse—a comment on the Colony's cultural life. Characteristically, it was demolished to make way for the new Hongkong and Shanghai Bank. So for three decades the city was without any suitable public place where large numbers of people could congregate for any other purpose than sport which, again characteristically, was well provided for.

The new City Hall was formally opened by the Governor, Sir Robert Black. In his speech he referred to the opening of its predecessor in 1869 by the first royal visitor to Hong Kong, His Royal Highness, the then Duke of Edinburgh, and to the continuance of a name with connotations other than the arts. 'Here, in these buildings which I am opening today, there will be a welcome for the citizen not as a bearer of his rates and taxes, but as a partner in the artistic and social life of the city . . . .' He continued, hyperbolically, quoting Shelley on Athens, doubtless to the astonishment of nearly all his audience:

> '. . . a city such as vision
> Builds from the purple crags and silver towers
> Of battlemented cloud.'

'Here in this Colony, upon barren rocks through the joint labours of

254

people of many races, one of the great metropolises of the world has risen, and surely no one, a hundred years ago, even when dreaming dreams and seeing visions and with all the purple crags and silver towers of the clouds to inspire him, would have dared to prophesy such a transformation. . . . ' Resoundingly true, indeed.

Predictably, the Governor continued by pointing to the difference between the towers of Hong Kong's commerce and this new building dedicated to the arts. Whatever the City Hall as a building leaves to be desired, it has served as a focus for the development of the arts in the city. And today, there is still no other auditorium of comparable size where a large orchestra may play. Before the City Hall appeared, visiting pianists had to perform in the Loke Yew Hall at Hong Kong University in an atmosphere redolent of potted ferns and student graduation ceremonies, or in the hall of St John's Cathedral in the aura of incipient sanctity. And the redoubtable Jon Prescott, already mentioned lamenting the passing of the old architecture, used occasionally to organize local artists and others to show in a covered pier of the Star Ferry.

Once he built a temporary theatre to seat four hundred people just in front of the Star Ferry. 'It started with the idea of a matshed theatre [the traditional covering of temporary structures in China and Southeast Asia, of woven *rattan*] but the Fire Brigade soon put a stop to that. Finally I found a man making doors from hardboard. He gave me thousands of one-foot off-cuts and I made plaited walls for the theatre by weaving the hardboard like a giant basket.'

In those days there were two or three known local painters. Lui Shou-kwan, using traditional Chinese inks often in a very untraditional way, was one. Another was Douglas Bland, a successful businessman and a remarkable painter. The majority of Chinese who painted, then as now, were copyists. The death of Chinese painting as a really original and lively art came in part during the last dynasty (although it had roots in more distant times) with the skilful imitation by numerous more or less brilliant technicians of the works of former great painters. Great artists anywhere have often been followed by a 'school' whose works show their influence in one way and another. But with the Chinese, in the nineteenth century especially, originality disappeared in favour of technique. You might say with something near the truth that painting itself disappeared beneath technique's perfection; just as did the essence of Chinese ceramic genius of the past disappear beneath the new-found range of brilliant colours, the astonishing control of glazes, and that triviality whose perfect exemplar was the emperor Ch'ien-lung.

In Hong Kong members of this artistically effete majority who wield a Chinese brush are still served by many 'teachers', each with his utterly derivative style which the pupils, with tremendous talent, perpetuate in their numerous scrolls exhibited now by the hundred—not least in the public spaces of the City Hall rented by the day.

The two theatres of the City Hall provided room, and incentive to come, for many a fine orchestra from the West, for a burgeoning local orchestra, for Chinese instrumental ensembles, and for performances of plays by local groups and companies from abroad. The establishment of the Museum and Art Gallery with a growing display of Chinese antiquities in ceramics, bronze, jade, lacquer, as well as in painting, together with increasingly numerous exhibitions of international status caught on the wing as they pass toward Australia and New Zealand, or en route for Japan, had what can only be termed an explosive effect on young people in the Colony.

Very soon it was possible to name six or seven original and gifted young Chinese painters and sculptors, some of whom have lasted the pace and after a decade or so are still leading artists with long lists of local and foreign showings. The older generation—Kwong Yeu-ting, Luis Chan, Lui Shou-kwan, Douglas Bland—continued to paint in their extremely different styles until the early death of the latter two in 1975; while the Colony has now no need to hang its head in shame for lack of a brilliant younger generation. Cheung Yee is a sculptor quite unlike any other, taking his inspiration basically from the bronze age of the Shang and Chou in ancient China, but transmuting the rich sensual essences of that remarkable and intensely Chinese age by his own kind of magic in three dimensions. Other sculptors, and painters as well, seem less influenced by the heritage of Chinese art than by the kaleidoscopic scene in the West. Yet even in the most Western-orientated such as Hon Chi-fun, with his abstracts in acryllic or in screen print form, there is an overtone of China hard to define. And in such painters as Wucius Wong, despite his brilliance as a teacher of modern two- and three-dimensional design, and despite his basically Western training, the Chinese element comes through with a kind of warm inevitability.

It is true to say that now, from the artists of Hong Kong, a large exhibition could be mounted in the West—in London, Paris, Rome, New York—that would have nothing to fear in terms of essential originality and technical quality of the works of the painters and sculptors shown. For a community of four million, a colony moreover, and one with such a brief history of encouragement in the arts, this is a remarkable fact.

Viewed in another light, perhaps it is not so surprising. In the story of later Chinese painting we are now beginning to realize that the schools of Kwangtung province, the home of the Cantonese people, were the most original and thoroughly alive in all 19th century China. Most Hong Kong artists today are Cantonese, a people looked down upon by northerners as businessman and near barbarians, speaking a language both incomprehensible and rough. While it is true that few if any of the greatest Chinese artists of the past have come from the south it would be more correct to regard southerners as representatives of a rather different tradition within the Chinese orbit. Their speech, is more sensuous, and in its way more melodious in the manner of country tunes of long ago, than that of the north. Their painting, during the Ming and the Ch'ing dynasties, was often highly original, sometimes including great eccentric painters who, like one or two Hong Kong contemporaries, need fear no comparison with better-known names. So maybe there is some actual heritage from the past underlying the dramatic upsurge of painting today in the Colony.

In 1977 the Arts Centre opened, built with money contributed by private and corporate, but not governmental funds, although the government gave the rather small site. For a city that in the past has shown little taste above the level of operetta and amateur dramatics on the Western side, and no inclination on the Chinese part to do more than attend the New Year performances of Cantonese opera and purchase examples of derivative Ch'ing art, this may be a sign either of affluence or of genuine and growing interest.

Oddly enough, in the former cultural desert there have existed for many years one or two little groups of people whose taste and whose enthusiasm have coincided. One such society occasionally puts on a choice private showing of paintings and ceramics owned by its members, in rooms rented permanently as a sort of club for those members. As a guest on one such occasion when a display of 'blanc de Chine' porcelain had been arranged, the visiting American curator in whose honour it was displayed remarked that not if you ransacked the museums and private collections of all America could you mount a show of equal quality in this department of later Chinese porcelain.

Chinese literature, alas, seems not to have a distinguished practitioner in Hong Kong. There is no young Chinese poet to carry on that long, dreamlike tradition, or to follow Mao Tse-tung. There is no Chinese essayist, no dreamer of dreams in prose to continue that largest of all the world's literatures of the past. Perhaps the shock occasioned by the death of a way of life that lasted in its essences for more than two thousand years, and of its exposure as being inadequate to the needs of the modern world, has proved too paralysing a stroke for the Chinese tongue to be unleashed in today's Hong Kong. Sadly, few Chinese children now know much of the greatness of their own past, and few write even passable calligraphy. As the strip-light, blue jeans, and the high-rise have ousted the lamp, the gown, and the cottage in Chinese life, so does the ballpoint eventually overcome the brush.

Perhaps it is inevitable in this city of undigested ideas, of unparalleled rapidity in social and physical change (and to a large extent of intellectual stagnation and confusion) that a lament seems in some ways the form most fitted to express its boundless activity at large.

Hong Kong is not a beginning, as China over the wire fence and the little steam at the border *is* a new beginning. It is, harshly put, despite the boisterous loveableness, immense energy, and deep human warmth of its Chinese, and despite all their, and some Western, achievement in this bizarre metropolis, more nearly the beginning of an end. Like the former Shanghai, only more singularly, Hong Kong is an eccentric paragraph of extreme interest, brief as the detonation of a Chinese cracker, in the span of Oriental history.

POSTSCRIPT

THUS FAR AND PERHAPS NO FURTHER

A NY consideration of the future of Hong Kong must be tentative and take account of several circumstances peculiar to the Colony—its expiring lease, its status as a colony in days when colonies are rarities and much-condemned anachronisms, its usefulness to China as source of most of her foreign exchange and also in other ways; and the changing situation in the world, in the Far East in particular. All these matters are central to any reasonable discussion of the years to come. But there are at least two others not often assessed. The first is the emergence of a still youthful majority in Hong Kong who have no special allegiance to some geographical point in China since they were all born in the Colony. The second is the question of what the Chinese authorities may be likely to think about taking over a population of probably around six million (by 1997), most of whom will be natives of Hong Kong and deeply imbued with an ideology and life-style in diametric opposition to those of the parent country.

Living in the great hive of Hong Kong it is inevitable that you wonder sometimes—crossing the road at lunchtime in Central where most of the dense throng of people appear to be under 25, fashionable, assured, very much of Hong Kong and quite different from a similar crowd in Singapore or Canton—what is to be said, to be done about the youth of the city. With them lies the future. But, more importantly, the future weighs upon their shoulders, for it is they who will be the fully adult population of the time when the lease expires, and also of the possibly tense years preceding that event. There are signs that they feel, or are beginning to feel, they belong to Hong Kong, and Hong Kong to them. Despite the limited outlook for them in terms of time available, and more immediately in terms of job-availability within the confining shores of a place whose possibilities of industrial and other expansion are limited, they are beginning to feel that this is *their* place. In a sense the situation is a little like that in, say, New Zealand as the emigrants stopped feeling that Britain was really home, and settled down to be New Zealanders. But New Zealand had terrain and a future: Hong Kong has neither. A nearer parallel might be Gibraltar, but it lacks developed industry.

By 1997, the population of Hong Kong will be nearly all indigenous. Few will have any and near family connections with people in China itself. They will be profoundly conditioned to Hong Kong ways of life, to a capitalist style of thought, to money as the driving force in working life, to money as the sanction and prop of society—for most probably there will still be no major movement towards a culture not wholly based on monetary value. Politically, if the word may be used at all, the populace will be, most likely, as they are today apathetic, far right of centre, with an extreme left cell whose influence may be expected to be small. (There is only one other possibility, and that is a popular revolt if the government fails to ensure that wages and prices keep fairly

The border village of Sha Tau Kok where the border with China runs down the middle of the main street (Chung-ying or China-England Street). People's Liberation Army men cross the road and villagers on both sides are not restricted in movement

260

reasonably in step.) Despite the fact that the people will still be intensely Chinese they will also be extremely at odds with their compatriots over the border, who may be expected to be even more firmly socialist than they are now.

The question we ought to ask at this point is: What will be the mainland Chinese reaction to the prospect of suddenly acquiring a round six million compatriots whose minds have been attuned (not to use impolitely the word so often used of Communist bids for the minds of the people) to a system that is anathema to them? Will it be worthwhile taking on those millions of recalcitrant capitalists conditioned from birth to an environment of, and to participation in, rampant *laissez-faire* capitalism with all its delights, brutalities, monetary incentives for everything, its individualist personal stance, its sexual inequality and permissiveness, and its ultra-Western outlook in many areas?

In Shanghai where the West put its hands most closely, and where the capitalist system spread most persuasively, on a Chinese society in times past, the effects went much less deep and affected a smaller number of people for a shorter time than will be the case in Hong Kong. Direct colonial rule has permitted a more intimate hold, has imposed a bastard form of Western morality and an outmoded form of Western capitalism. The combination of the two things at work on the Chinese is what makes Hong Kong unique. By now, and even more by the end of the lease, the rooted, ardent equation—money equals the best in life—can hardly anywhere else in the globe be so uniformly, deeply, and universally rooted in the people of a city as it is in the people of Hong Kong. One cannot entirely blame them. What the Colony has been made or has become, has been their context—one in which, as in any other, life has to be supported in whatever way society decrees it will be supported. The chance to think otherwise, either in China or in Hong Kong, is not permitted—in the former country on ideological grounds, and in the Colony by force of necessity. It takes a brave Chinese in Hong Kong to stand up and protest in any radical way. He would soon find himself out of the job market. There are no other accepted norms of worth in Hong Kong but self-interest, except for charity which is the conscience-salver of the affluent and the duty of the religious.

So what might China think at that point, some twenty years ahead, about the neon-lit fantasy of Hong Kong? What sort of solution could be found, what means of reconciliation? Possibly China will decide to take over despite the danger from millions of dissidents, of potential and actual and moral saboteurs, to the fabric of socialism. Or some politically ambivalent compromise maybe reached.[1] It will be easier to deal with Taiwan than with Hong Kong—at least the islanders there can be contained. The Colony, as was once said, being a pimple on the backside of China, cannot be so simply managed. The infection would certainly not be lethal, but the disease, confined though it would be, might prove a troublesome one to eradicate. All the powerful incentives of Chinese nationalism will make it impossible for China to leave Hong Kong alone, or to renew its lease as such. And in any case the British will not want to do so in that precise colonial form in the face of world opinion. By that time the island and the little bit of Kowloon up to Boundary Street will almost certainly be the world's last colony—shorn of its airport, water, electricity, industry, agricultural land, and totally boxed in by territories and islands legitimately belonging to China. The People's Republic in fact has never recognized the validity of the treaty by which even the island itself was ceded to Britain.

A British Foreign Secretary, returning to London after a visit to China in 1972,[2] said as he paused in Hong Kong that Britain and China were 'broadly satisfied' with the way their governments viewed Hong Kong, the inference being that no changes in the *status quo* were envisaged for the time being.

The Hong Kong answer to the question of what will happen in 1997, is simple, ostrich-like, and confined to those who have and make money in the Colony (the majority of the population would just return a blank stare, not having thought about it at all). The answer is: 'We'll see when the time comes'. Which really means that in the meanwhile something will work out, probably.

Hong Kong is, of course, and has been for some time, a great anachronism. It has survived, grown somewhat obscenely (if you think in world terms) and has thrived as a kind of financial whorehouse out of reach of the established authority of established countries and their administrations. It had the luck after World War II, when by rights it ought to have been returned to China, to survive because of the weakness of China, and the further luck to flourish because of the population overspill from China's then desperate situation. It prospered because the Chinese know how to work, and work, and work; and because speculative and other capital in a troubled and restrictive world found in the basically nineteenth-century capitalist climate of a still buccaneering colony the opportunity to exploit that labour—with the advantages of minimal government interference, an efficient port, a resilient banking and financial set-up, and expanding world markets (give and take a Korean war, a China trade embargo, and a few other problems such as textile export quotas).

The factors now appearing and growing stronger, that will probably exert some influence on the years between now and 1997, are in some senses the reverse of, and the outcome of, those that encouraged the resurgence of post-war Hong Kong. The internal social-political situation has already forced the government to 'liberalize'—to spend more on social services of a rudimentary type, and on a whole area touching on the appalling conditions in the Colony's old and new slum living and affecting the majority of the people. It is hard for those who have not seen the living conditions of ten years ago in Hong Kong to credit that in the mid-twentieth century such human horror could be allowed to exist cheek by jowl with super-luxury and all the signs of vast, blandly exhibited riches. It is also hard to understand that only the 1967 incidents were violent in any degree. Rising standards of housing and rising wages have already made Hong Kong less competitive in world markets. And they have made some impression on the human horror of life as it was ten years ago.

Hong Kong industry depends on the continuing willingness of other countries to supply it with raw materials (basic plastics are one example that looked like being withheld during the world fuel and energy 'crisis' of 1973–4). Industry also depends as acutely on the willingness of other countries to accept Hong Kong goods. No one can tell what tariffs and quotas may be imposed by major markets in the future, making the Colony less competitive, even if that miserable symptom of uncontrollable capitalism, inflation, does not take final strange hold. And for Hong Kong the international money climate, outside China, poses a grave question—for Hong Kong has only money and labour—no resources in material, no hinterland, no separate existence.

For reasons such as these, the future of Hong Kong is at best mere speculation. Gone are the old days when an economic lurch was to some extent cushioned by slow communication. Gone the days before the 'electric telegraph' when you might have been bankrupt, or a father, or ennobled, for several months before discovering the felicitous or disconcerting fact. The ultra-sophistication of Hong Kong's commercial intelligence is by now legendary—we may recall how even in 1843 Canton merchants knew the facts several days before Captain Elliot received the information of his dismissal from office by London. And the Colony's great banks and great *hongs*, even its little gold-dealers and its rice-wholesalers, know about the tiniest world trend the moment

263

Hong Kong moves onward to an uncertain future, its young people the inheritors of a brief and enigmatic past

it appears—and adjust their posture (if we may use a euphemism for an attitude so aggressive) accordingly, and immediately.

No one talks much in Hong Kong of 1997. To fathom what most people are thinking who ought to be thinking ahead, is hard. Vast new schemes such as the Mass Transit project now under construction, are authorized by the government. Private enterprise still invests astronomical sums in property and in industry, presumably because a return of capital and a handsome profit will accrue before the impending death sentence takes effect. Like a man whose physicians have told him he will die in a given term, a man who has the chance of 'living it up' or of continuing soberly on his way, Hong Kong, doomed perhaps to paralysis by a commercial coronary thrombosis in 1997, has entered, in the last decade or so, on a terminal phase of frenetic, bizarre activity. The Colony has become imbued with the hectic flush of this fever, its eyes terribly bright. Having destroyed most of the natural amenities, it now constructs artificial ones, and every basement is booming with stereo sound and flickering with psychedelic light, and each top floor restaurant is full of marionettes in fancy dress looking out of windows on the panorama of other marionettes in fancy dress in other top floor restaurants, looking out at . . . .

The portrait of a major city ruled by a commercial aristocracy, and untouched since its birth by the concensus of opinion of the majority of its inhabitants is perhaps a unique image in the eighth decade of the twentieth century. In a political and in an urban sense it is also unedifying. The only redeeming feature must be the strange sense of comfort to be had from living among the tight-packed millions and being more interested in their hopes and aspirations than in the scrummage of that traditional Hong Kong élite, the merchants of the oriental trade. Like the Colony itself, their days are numbered. For the others that is not so.

NOTES

PREFACE
1 香港
2 兩嶺
3 香江
4 紅江

INTRODUCTION
1 The more exotic names of Bangkok, Singapore, Malacca, Penang, Ceylon (Serendib—hence our newly-coined serendipity), Goa, and others, come to mind before Hong Kong.
2 When I was in Hong Kong more than a couple of decades ago I sent to a relative in Scotland some photographs of New Territories scenery. His immediate response was how like parts of Scotland it was.
3 I am informed by botanists and zoologists that in fact Hong Kong, lying in the sub-tropics, presents several interestingly rare examples of vegetable and animal life—but they are not obvious to the untutored eye.
4 Hong Kong is fast becoming one of the jewel capitals of the world, and has in the past few years been the venue of auctions of important Chinese porcelain also.

1 BEGINNINGS: CAPTAIN ELLIOT'S FANCY
1 A body known as the Independent Commission Against Corruption was set up in Hong Kong in February, 1974. Its investigative powers would hardly be tolerated in Britain, and certainly fall outside the normal purlieu of British law as generally conceived and excuted in the parent country.
2 Geographically speaking. In fact Hong Kong was comparatively lacking in vegetation until late in the 19th century when a conscious plan of afforestation was undertaken at the suggestion of Charles Ford, first Superintendent of the Botanic Gardens. Ford's scheme for afforestation was implemented by Governor Hennessy in 1879 when Ford was made head of a new Botanical and Forestry Department. See Herklots, p. 167.
3 The story is briefly set out in *The East India Company* by Brian Gardner (Rupert Hart-Davis, London, 1971).
4 This Chinese attitude to the rest of the world was not unlike that of Victorian England at the height of empire.
5 A 'chest' of opium weighed (depending on the period referred to and the place

267

of origin) between 130 lb and 150 lb.

6 One of the few sane documents written by anyone on either side on the subject of opium. See *Commissioner Lin and the Opium War*.

7 The record is to be found in Captain Belcher's book *Voyage Round the World*, published in 1843, on p. 157 of Vol. II. 'The only important point to which we became officially partners was the cession of the island of Hongkong, situated off the peninsula of Cow Loon within the Island of Lama.... We landed on Monday the 26th January at fifteen minutes past eight, and being "bona fide" possessors, her majesty's health was drank [sic] with three cheers on Possession Mount.' It is likely that Belcher was mistaken about the date which was probably the previous day, the 25th.

8 Neither the first nor the last instance of the incomprehension shown in London about Hong Kong. A letter in similar terms from the Chinese emperor dismissed Commissioner Lin a little later.

9 For the interesting tale of Dr Peter Parker, see the author's *Barbarians and Mandarins*, and the volume by Edward V. Gulick.

2 THE ILL-CONDUCTED ISLAND

1 Like the author's relative, Legge too saw the geographical ressemblances between the two countries.

2 'Godowns'. From the Malay *gadong*, a warehouse or store.

3 Mrs Elsie Elliott, Urban Councillor.

3 LIBEL AND ARSENIC

1 The interesting paper 'The Emergence of a Chinese Elite in Hong Kong', by Carl T. Smith is to be found in the *Journal of the Royal Asiatic Society*, Vol. 11, 1971.

2 The story is told from the Siamese point of view in Moffat's *Mongkut the King of Siam*.

3 Lei Yue Mun 鯉魚門, The Gateway of the Carp, or Carp Pass.

4 In April 1861, *The Friend of China*, published; 'A Public Declaration of the Shop Keepers of Hong Kong, stating that when Mr Caldwell managed the Proprietorship of the Chinese here, the people of Hong Kong were at rest, but he resigned his office. They now present their petition to the Governor asking him to retain Mr Caldwell.' To the petition were appended sixteen names of companies as chief petitioners.

4 LAPRAICK AND DUDDELL

1 *The South China Morning Post*, 10 April 1977.

2 Commenting on the *Keying's* Chinese crew, Dickens wrote: 'Of all the unlikely callings with which the imagination could connect the Chinese lounging on the deck, the most unlikely and the last would be the mariner's craft. Imagine a ship's crew ... in gauze pinafores and plaited hair; wearing stiff clogs, a quarter of a foot thick in the sole.'

3 The Hongkong Club at that time was at the junction of Wyndham Street and Queen's Road, in sight of the clocktower; a fact which perhaps impelled the writer of the letters to greater efforts and greater ire than others.

4 In his book, Albert Smith gives a lively and (for those times) unique description of a dinner party with the Chinese comprador of the Peninsular and Oriental company, at which he was entertained to a sumptuous repast of Chinese food accompanied by Chinese music played on 'harsh stringed instruments' by women, and by 'the men [on] the most screeching fiddles I ever imagined'. But Smith obviously enjoyed himself, even appending a plan of the room in which he was entertained.

5 A TRIO OF IRISHMEN

1 *Journal of Royal Asiatic Society*, Vol. 13, 1973.
2 For some description of the sack of the Summer Palaces and related matters, see the author's *Barbarians and Mandarins*, and *From Bondage to Liberation*.

6 MR HENNESSY'S PROCEEDINGS

1 *Journal of the Royal Asiatic Society*, Vol. IX.
2 Reprinted in *Journal of the Royal Asiatic Society*, Vol. VIII.
3 賣豬血粥 and 賣魚生粥 respectively.
4 Probably a translation of *pak choi* 白菜
5 食晏晝
6 賣爛鐵爛銅, nowadays more commonly 賣爛銅爛鐵
7 兵頭
8 兵頭花園

7 PLAGUE AND A REVOLUTIONARY

1 In England, imprisonment for debt, except in certain cases, was abolished by the Debtors Act of 1869.

8 A NEW CENTURY

1 Possibly 鮮花 , Fresh Flower, an allusion to the Colony's comparatively new status in the empire.
2 Events in Peking are described by Peter Fleming in his *The Siege at Peking*, and from a rather different angle in the author's *Barbarians and Mandarins*.
3 The repetition—re-enactment, it sometimes seems—of past scandals in contemporary days in Hong Kong is so striking that the process is worth underlining for the benefit of those who do not follow closely the modern history of the Colony.
4 She was author of several books about China which make interesting reading. A resumé of her campaign against foot-binding is to be found in the author's *Barbarians and Mandarins*. Mrs Little's own books are long out of print.
5 Over seventy years later, they have only just done so.

9 COLONY INTO FACTORY

1 Wang An-shih 王安石, *Lin-ch'uan hsien-sheng wen-chi* 臨川先生文集
2 Amateur jockeys continued to race at Happy Valley until well into the 1960s. The frequency of race meetings, originally only once or twice yearly, increased to once nearly every week between a date in October and the coming of the hot and rainy season in May. Night racing was introduced in the last two years.

10 HONG KONG TODAY: THE KALEIDOSCOPE

1 *South China Morning Post*, 30 April 1977.

2 It is hardly significant to consider the expatriate equivalent since they are small in numbers by comparison and mostly here for a relatively short time. The tendency seems to be for many of them to assimilate with the ideals and life-style of the more affluent upper class of their home lands.

3 But see pp. 259 ff. for other views.

4 *Dim sum*— 點心 ; *Siu mai*— 燒賣 ; *Ha gao*— 蝦餃 ; *Cha siu bao*— 叉燒飽 ; *Ngau yok*— 牛肉 ; *Wu go*—芋角 ; *Pai Kwat*—排骨 ; *Chun gün*— 春捲 ; *Fung chao*—鳳爪 ; *Ham siu kok*—鹹水角 ; *Lang cheung min*— 冷醬麵 ; *Lin yung bao*— 蓮蓉飽 ; *Chi ma gün*— 芝麻捲 ; *Ma tai go*—馬蹄糕 .

5 The time-lag between the invention of porcelain in China and its introduction to the West was of the order of 11–13 centuries.

6 The words '*tung lo*' 銅鑼 mean 'brass gong' and 'beater'—but the gong gave its name to a basket similarly shaped. '*Wan*' means 'bay.'

7 The '*famille rose*' enamels of Ch'ing porcelain, controlled and painted with infinite subtlety by a nation whose potting and glazing traditions go farther back than any other, are based on a material (gold chloride) introduced from the West by Jesuit missionaries. The Chinese did things with it that the West never could. But many feel that technique for its own sake denies the basic strength of the object to which it is applied.

8 Sir Ronald Holmes, Director of Commerce and Industry in Hong Kong more than a decade ago, said recently (*South China Morning Post*, 30 April 1977) that the government could have done better in regard to roads. 'Not urban or suburban roads, the record is good in this field, but arterial roads into the New Territories, which are the basis for bringing the New Territories in to redress the balance and relieve ... the problems of dense concentration.

'... We break all records with state housing, we develop the world's third largest container port without one dollar of taxpayer's money being spent, we reclaim land before anyone is ready to buy it, and yet if you try to travel to Taipo or Yuen Long you might be in the rush hour in London.... To this day, if you except roads built by the British Army, by the Japanese, and for the purpose of water supply projects, the system is much the same as when I first drove over it in 1938.'

9 爆竹 , but more usually nowadays 炮仗 '*p'ao cheung*'—literally 'cannon' plus 'weapon of war', the one word reinforcing the other as so often in Chinese.

10 水蜢

11 The slightly oval form is 金橘 'gum gut', and the round one is 四季桔 or 桔子 , 'sei gwei gut' (four seasons fruit) or 'gut chi' in written form, but 'gut chai' 桔仔 in pronunciation.

12 利是 , formerly 利市

13 紅錢

14 恭喜發財

15 蘿蔔糕 (蘿白糕)

16 龍眼

17 風水 , literally 'wind and water'.

POSTSCRIPT

1 Other views, well thought out and current, may lessen the confusion surrounding the question. Norman Macrae, Deputy Editor of *The Economist*, writing in early 1977 suggested: '[Hong Kong] has accomplished the first part of the next requirement (keeping small government out of big business' way) because its colonial officials realize that colonial government is an absurd anachronism, so had better not be obtrusive. The big half-question remains: can it keep big business involved?'

During the years until the lease expires, 'the worst course for China would be to wait while there is [a] rundown, and capital and skilled businessmen and workers gradually evacuate to Taiwan. So either China will take over Hong Kong by force in the 1980s (it need not be by great force, because with a threatening telephone call and a decent interval for evacuation Britain would scuttle). Or else China will announce some time in the 1980s that the post-1997 lease will be renewed, possibly at a high rental.'

The Deputy Editor thinks, however, this will not come about, but that the Chinese will still find the foreign currency it gets from and through Hong Kong, together with the fact that Hong Kong's presence 'allows China a centre for gathering commercial intelligence about Western technology and it painlessly and flexibly teaches China how next to fit itself into the mysterious world economy.'

The economist Dick Wilson, Writing in the *Far Eastern Economic Review* in December, 1976, thought: 'officially the British Government's position echoes Peking's: it is still too early to discuss the matter.' He too discusses the question of run-down, the progressive reluctance of big business to invest if the return period is ten years or less. The last time the question was raised in Parliament, the Minister of State for Defence replied that there was an 'unarticulated understanding' between London, Peking, and Hong Kong to the effect that 'the *status quo* should remain . . . because it is of mutual convenience'.

'The gap,' Dick Wilson remarks, 'in his quoted reply betrays the censorious hand of the Foreign and Commonwealth Office, whose requests for certain sensitive passages of these proceedings to be omitted are thus indicated.'

'On Monday 30 June 1977,' he continues a little later, 'the position might be as it is today. On Tuesday 1 July 1997, Britain might still be regarded by China as *de facto* temporarily administrating the same Chinese territory pending the Chinese Government's decision to take up the matter of resolving this legacy of history.'

This is a closely reasoned and evocative article taking up in a fine and highly intelligent manner, with deep knowledge of the Chinese and the geographical situation and the recent past, the whole spectrum of questions involved.

David Bonavia, writing in the same issue of the *Far Eastern Economic Review* comes to similar conclusions, calling Hong Kong a 'multi-purpose laboratory for Peking. It can be [and in fact is] used to study unobtrusively such complex aspects of the capitalist world as banking, finance, insurance, tourism, aviation, and so on.' He also points out that in the event of a Sino-Soviet war, 'the Soviet fleet could blockade every port in China except Hong Kong.' If it did blockade Hong Kong this would at once involve the NATO alliance.

2 A comment made by the late Chou En-lai to Sir Alec Douglas-Home.

BIBLIOGRAPHY

ARLINGTON, L.C., *Through the Dragon's Eyes* (Constable, London, 1931).

ATKINSON, R.L.P. and WILLIAMS, A.K., *Hong Kong Tramways* (Light Railway Transport League, Rustington, Sussex, 1970).

AUDEN, W.H. and ISHERWOOD, C., *Journey to a War* (Faber and Faber, London, 1939; Revised edition, 1973). (Extract on p. 167 reproduced by permission.)

BERNARD, W.D. and HALL, W.K., *Narrative of the Voyages and Services of the Nemesis*, 2 vols. (Henry Colburn, London, 1844).

BIRD, ISABELLA L. (BISHOP, I.L.), *The Golden Chersonese and the Way Thither* (Oxford University Press, Kuala Lumpur, 1967).

BRASSEY, Lady, *A Voyage in the 'Sunbeam'* (Longmans, Green, London, 1878).

CAMERON, NIGEL, *Barbarians and Mandarins* (Walker/Weatherhill, Tokyo/New York, 1970; Chicago University Press, 1976).
From Bondage to Liberation—East Asia 1860–1952 (Oxford University Press, Hong Kong, 1975).

CAREW, TIM, *Fall of Hong Kong* (Blond, London, 1960).

CARTWRIGHT, H.A., *Twentieth Century Impressions of Hong Kong and Other Treaty Ports of China* (Lloyds Greater Publishing Co., London, 1908).

CHIU, T.N., *The Port of Hong Kong* (Hong Kong University Press, 1973).

COLLINGWOOD, Dr.C., *Rambles of a Naturalist on the Shores and Waters of the China Sea* (Murray, London, 1868).

COLLIS, MAURICE, *Foreign Mud* (Faber and Faber, London, 1946).

'COLONIAL' (JARRETT, VINCENT H.), 'Old Hong Kong', *South China Morning Post*, 17 June 1933–13 April 1935).

DAVIS, Sir JOHN F., *The Chinese: a General Description of the Empire of China, and its Inhabitants* (Charles Knight, London, 1836).
Sketches of China (Charles Knight, London, 1841).

Des Voeux, Sir William, *My Colonial Service* 2 vols. (Murray, London, 1903).

Eitel, E.J., *Europe in China. The History of Hong Kong from the Beginning to the Year 1882* (London, 1895).

Ellis, Henry T., *Hong Kong to Manila and the Lakes of Luzon in the Philippines Isles in the Year 1856* (Elder, Smith, London, 1859).

Endacott, G.B., *A History of Hong Kong* (O.U.P., London, 1958; revised edition, O.U.P., Hong Kong, 1973).
A Biographical Sketchbook of Early Hong Kong (Eastern Universities Press, Singapore, 1962).

Forster, L., *Echoes of Hong Kong and Beyond* (Ye Olde Printerie, Hong Kong, 1933).

Gulick, Edward V., *Peter Parker and the Opening of China* (Harvard University Press, 1973).

Herklots, G.A.C., *The Hong Kong Countryside* (South China Morning Post, Hong Kong, 1933).

Hong Kong Government, *Hong Kong* (The Annual Report published each year, its contents summing up the activities of the previous year. The Report for the Year 1976 is contained in *Hong Kong 1977*.)

Hughes, Richard, *Hong Kong: Borrowed Place, Borrowed Time* (Deutsch, London, 1968).

Luff, John, *The Hidden Years* (South China Morning Post, Hong Kong, 1967).

Moffat, Abbot Low, *Mongkut: the King of Siam* (Cornell University Press, New York. 1972).

Norman, Henry, *The Peoples and Politics of the Far East. Travels and Studies in the British, French, Spanish, and Portuguese Colonies, etc.* (T. Fisher Unwin, London, 1895).

Oliphant, Laurence, *Narrative of the Earl of Elgin's Mission to China and Japan in the Years 1857–59.* 2 vols. (Blackwood, London, 1880).

Ommanney, F.D., *Fragrant Harbour. A Private View of Hong Kong* (Hutchison, London, 1962).

Orange, James, *The Chater Collection* (Butterworth, London, 1924).

Pope-Hennessy, James, *Half-Crown Colony. A Hong Kong Notebook* (Cape, London, 1969).

Proulx, Benjamin A., *Underground from Hong Kong* (Dutton, New York, 1943).

Sayer, Geoffrey R., *Hong Kong: Birth, Adolescence, and Coming of Age* O.U.P., London, 1937).
Hong Kong 1862–1919 Years of Discretion. (Hong Kong University Press, 1975).

Scidmore, E.R., *China, the Long-Lived Empire* (The Century Co., New York, 1900).

Smith, Albert, *To China and Back* (Privately published, London, 1859; new edition, with an introduction by H.J. Lethbridge, Hong Kong University Press, 1974).

273

Stoddart, Anna M., *The Life of Isabella Bird (Mrs Bishop)* (Murray, London, 1907).

Thorbecke, Ellen, *Hong Kong* (Kelly and Walsh, Shanghai, no date, but *c.* 1938).

Tregear, T.R., and Berry L., *The Development of Hong Kong and Kowloon as Told in Maps* (Hong Kong University Press, Hong Kong, 1959).

Waley, Arthur, *The Opium War Through Chinese Eyes* (Allen and Unwin, London, 1958).

Wright, Rev. G.N., *China in a Series of Views Displaying the Scenery, Architecture, and Social Habits of that Ancient Empire.* (Fisher, London, 1843).

INDEX